MASTER YOUR MICROWAVE
by Glenda James

1st printing — November 1986
Copyright 1986 by
Glenda James

ISBN No. - 0-9692721-0-3

Photography by **Patricia Holdsworth Photography,** Regina, Sask.
Food Stylist **Marilyn Little**, Regina, Sask.

Illustrations in Guide to Great Microwave Cooking by **Ron Blackwell**
Published & Distributed by **Mainly Microwave,**
Box 1073,
Moose Jaw, Sask.
S6H 4P8

Cover:
Microwave oven courtesy of **Blackwell's,** Moose Jaw, Sask.
Pottery by **Ken Guenter**, Caronport, Sask.

Pictured on the cover:

Colourful Vegetable Platter, page 157
Peanut Butter Squares, page 253
Pecan Pie, page 218
Corn Chowder, page 55
Long Grain Rice, page 130
Alace's Curried Chicken, page 104
Cabbage Patch Bread, page 196
Pepper Steak, page 78

DEDICATED WITH LOVE

To my family: My husband, Larry and our children, Jamaal, Chantelle and Chelsea who have "lived" this book with me during the past three years. They have patiently eaten all of my experiments and sacrificed time with me to allow me the solitude I needed to work on this book.

THANKS

A project like this book is quite the undertaking for a mother of three preschoolers (two of whom were born during the course of its writing) and without question, could not have been accomplished without A LOT of help from my friends:

The BIGGEST THANKS must go to my good friend, Marianne Weber, who meticulously tested each recipe and edited this manuscript. She took this project on as a "labour of love" and this is her book, too. Without her help and encouragement, I doubt this book would ever have come to be. Thanks also to her husband, Chris and daughter, Julianne who tolerated all of these tests and offered their evaluations.

Special thanks to my parents, Henry and Dolores Heinrichs, who supported this venture in ways too numerous to mention.

Thanks to Ron Blackwell, who has kept me teaching (and learning) in classes at his store. He has promoted me, pushed me to get this book written and provided facilities for my work.

My dear friend, Chinelo Mora, was always available at the right moment to run an errand, watch the kids or clean up a mess or whatever when I was "stuck". Her practical help has been invaluable.

Many students, friends and family members shared recipes, suggestions and encouragement and I appreciate each one of them. A few, however, deserve special mention: Alace Frost and Pam Awtrey contributed delicious recipes and artistic advice. My mother-in-law, Thelma James, my Aunt Eva and my Aunt Edna shared quite a few recipes and hints. My neighbour, Vi Olson, faithfully entertained my children and took them on outings to give me time to work and to rest. All of these people contributed to this book in their own unique way, and I am grateful to them.

TABLE OF CONTENTS

Note to the Cook _____ 4
Welcome to Microwave Cooking _____ 6
Guide to Great Microwave Cooking _____ 9
Trouble Shooting Chart _____ 31

Snacks & Sandwiches _____ 34
Soups & Stews _____ 48
Meat & Poultry _____ 63, 98
Fish & Seafood _____ 115
Rice, Pasta & Cereal _____ 129
Vegetables & Their Sauces _____ 142
Eggs & Cheese _____ 163
Breads _____ 175
Desserts _____ 200
Cakes & Frostings _____ 220
Cookies, Squares & Candy _____ 243, 251, 260
Sauces & Preserves _____ 267

General Hints _____ 278
Index _____ 282

NOTE TO THE COOK

This book is the result of five years of teaching microwave cooking classes, mostly for Coteau Range Community College and Blackwell's store in Moose Jaw, Saskatchewan. It has been great fun to teach and has taught me a lot, as well. Over these years I have received numerous requests from my students for good homestyle recipes that I've tried. Three years ago I began compiling them for a handout which has expanded into this book. The recipes included in this book are primarily family favourites which I have converted to microwave recipes. Since I began this book many of my students, friends and family have shared their favourite recipes.

The information included in this book has come from the successes and failures I have had in my own kitchen preparing family meals or testing for this book, and through teaching classes. I made note of the questions I was most commonly asked in class and surveyed my classes about their ideas for the "ideal" microwave cookbook. I have incorporated many of their questions and suggestions into this book and its format.

I have designed this book to be used as a handy reference to supplement the book the manufacturer included with your oven. The times given in this book are correct for the ovens in which we tested them, but every microwave oven cooks differently and I have left a space at the bottom of each recipe for YOUR TIME. Read the section on CHOOSING THE RIGHT TIME to remind you of the variables in cooking times. Each recipe provides a range of times. When trying one for the first time, use the minimum time first and add extra time, if needed, during the standing time. Then record your time in the space provided so you can enjoy it another time without such careful tending. While I have included time suggestions for various types of food, the charts given in the manual the manufacturer provided with your oven are the most accurate for your oven. Mine are general guidelines. Use the two together.

No instructions for TURNING or ROTATING are given in the recipes. Our test ovens had turntables which eliminated the need for this technique. Different ovens vary in their need for this rotation, so follow the instructions for your unit.

I would be pleased if you would read the entire book, especially the coloured reference pages — you'll be more pleased with your cooking if you take time to read them. But I have organized it so that you should be able to look up specific information in just a minute when you are too busy to read an entire section. The GUIDE TO GREAT MICROWAVE COOKING will provide you with valuable information about microwave cooking including 3 KEYS TO SUCCESS WITH YOUR MICROWAVE. The coloured pages before each chapter also provide you with the KEY TO SUCCESS for each type of food. Check these pages before you start for best cooking results.

Included in each chapter introduction are guidelines for cooking each category of food, enhancements or toppings, HINTS including MICROWAVE PLUS other appliances, SEASONINGS and SERVING SUGGESTIONS. Many of the recipes feature TIPS, SERVING SUGGESTIONS and VARIATIONS.

All the information is intended to help you adapt microwave cooking to your own personal taste and make the most of your microwave oven. So the next time you start to cook a meal on the stove, pick up this book and you may find you can make it quicker, better and easier with your microwave oven.

IMPORTANT

Recipes in this book were tested in 700 watt microwave ovens:

Panasonic NE 9930C
Panasonic NE 7960C

If the oven you are using has a different output wattage, a time adjustment may be necessary. See the chart on page 17.

Ingredients in recipes were used at their common temperatures ie: dairy products and meat at refrigerator temperature and canned or packaged goods at room temperature.

Flour used in recipes is all-purpose flour unless otherwise stated. Sugar is white granulated sugar.

Recipes in this book serve 4 to 6 people unless otherwise stated.

Failure to follow instructions carefully could result in unsatisfactory results. Measure all ingredients carefully and accurately. Use the utensils specified. Substitution of ingredients or alteration of quantities could change the quality of the recipe. When making alterations, consult the GUIDE TO GREAT MICROWAVE COOKING to be sure to consider variables in the timing.

WELCOME TO MICROWAVE COOKING

The purpose of my classes and this book is to help you to enjoy and appreciate the convenience of having a microwave oven in your kitchen. No longer do you need to feel you can't buy or prepare certain foods because you don't have time to prepare them — the microwave oven saves 75% of the conventional cooking time! This time saving will allow you to use more fresh produce and still prepare a complete meal in less than half an hour. The microwave oven gives busy cooks the option of being creative without having to spend a great deal of time at it. So say good-bye to quickie convenience compromise meals and WELCOME to the world of delicious, nutritious microwave cooking!

WHEN SHOULD YOU USE YOUR MICROWAVE OVEN?

Whenever you can! The microwave oven can do many things with an advantage. Below is a list of these advantages to help you answer the question you should always ask yourself when you begin to cook, "Can I do it better in the microwave oven?"

MICROWAVE COOKING IS FAST

This is the main attraction of microwave cooking. It can cook most foods in one quarter of the time that conventional methods use. Use this as a general rule of thumb when you want to try a favourite recipe in the microwave oven and wonder how long to cook it.

MICROWAVE COOKING SAVES ENERGY

Microwave cooking uses half of the energy your conventional stove uses. It plugs into a standard, grounded 110 volt plug, instead of the specially installed 220 volt plug your stove requires. The microwave energy is not wasted on heating up a large space; all of the microwave energy produced is used by the food. Microwave cooking uses 75% less time, which translates into energy savings. The Saskatchewan Power Corporation says that a microwave oven costs half as much to operate as the conventional stove*. So, use your microwave oven to save energy!

MICROWAVE COOKING IS NUTRITIOUS

The speed of microwave cooking allows foods to retain more of their nutritional value and flavour. Very little water, if any, needs to be added to fruits and vegetables so valuable water soluble vitamins and minerals are not discarded with the water. Salt can be omitted or reduced for microwave cooking; the retention of natural flavour lessens the need for this flavour enhancer. Fat intake decreases with microwave cooked food; the dishes do not need to be greased for cooking.

MICROWAVE COOKING ENHANCES THE QUALITY OF GOOD FOOD

The colours of fresh fruits and vegetables remain bright and clear when they are microwave cooked, appealing to the eyes as well as the palate. The original quality of the food is retained when cooked by microwaves. Vegetables and fruits are crisp and juicy. Quality meats are also tender and juicy. However, microwave cooking also accentuates the flavour of poor quality food so be sure to use fresh, properly stored food.

MICROWAVE COOKING IS CLEAN COOKING

Cleanup is a snap. Microwaves heat only the food, resulting in less baked-on mess. No more soaking and scrubbing; most dishes wipe clean. The oven needs to be cleaned with only a wet, soapy cloth — no harsh cleaners or abrasive cleaning pads.

Food can be cooked on serving dishes or tableware, saving on the number of dishes to be washed. Most dishes can go straight from the table to the dishwasher without presoaking.

MICROWAVE COOKING IS COOL COOKING

The heat is in the food, so the oven and dishes do not get hot. Nor does turning on the microwave oven heat up the kitchen on those hot summer days. You can allow your children to help you in the kitchen or even cook by themselves without fear of them burning themselves on hot utensils or the hot oven.

MICROWAVE COOKING IS CONVENIENT

Microwave speed allows you to defrost foods in minutes instead of setting them on the counter for hours. Microwave defrosting not only saves time, but also preserves the quality of frozen food because less moisture is lost in a quick defrost.

Microwave cooking also offers warm up convenience. Leftovers taste fresh, retaining their moisture and firm texture. With microwave convenience you can prepare "Planned-Overs" for busy days. Only the cook will know the difference.

FOODS THAT COOK BEST IN THE MICROWAVE OVEN

- Roasted meat comes out moist, tender and juicy. Roasts over 4 lbs. (2 kg) brown beautifully.
- Fish and seafood turn out moist and flavourful.
- Poultry cooks quickly and retains its natural moisture.
- Soups and stews are quick with bright colour and fresh flavour.
- Casseroles cook very well with excellent flavour.
- Vegetables and fruits excel in the microwave oven.
- Cakes and desserts are very quick and easy in the microwave oven.
- Cakes rise higher and stay moister, too.
- Candies, jams and jellies cook very quickly!
- Sauces are a pleasure to make in the microwave oven — no more scorching!

FOODS THAT DON'T WORK & WHY

Home canning	Aside from the fact that the metal lids of the jars cannot be used in the microwave oven, the food cannot be properly processed in the microwave oven. A **constant** high temperature is required to kill the yeasts, molds and enzymes which cause food spoilage. This can only be accomplished in a standard canner.
Deep fat frying	The fat becomes dangerously hot in the microwave oven. The spatters of the hot fat could cause serious burns to your hands.
Eggs in their shells	Steam and pressure build up inside the egg as it is heated by microwave energy. The pressure could cause the egg to burst.
Popcorn in a paper bag	The paper bag is flammable. Arcing could occur which would start the bag on fire or damage the oven. Popcorn CAN be popped in a specially designed microwave popcorn popper.
Broiled or fried foods	Foods cook so fast in the microwave that there is not sufficient time for caramelization (browning) to take place.
Crispy pastry	Crispness is caused by hot, dry air and hot pans. There is no hot, dry air in the microwave oven nor do the pans become hot. .
Soufles, Angel food or sponge cakes	These foods do not hold their shape when cooked in the microwave oven. They rise very high while cooking and then fall flat when the microwave oven shuts off. However specially formulated microwave recipes using stabilizing ingredients can be used.

A GUIDE TO GREAT MICROWAVE COOKING

When new owners bring their microwave ovens home, they often wonder, " What now?" They are often in awe of the newness of the machine. The precise touch timer seems intimidating. Often they've heard a lot of dos and don'ts from well meaning friends and relatives. Cooking may have been something they did almost without thinking, but now they are confronted with a new experience and some feel that they need to learn everything completely before they start.

There is no need for intimidation. Soon the new owner will come to realize that while microwave cooking is new and different it really is very much like conventional cooking. Just faster! and easier!

The first thing to do is to read and review the manufacturer's instructions and then try to cook something. The more foods you try, the more you will learn. Let your own common sense prevail — you know more than you think you do. When in doubt, read the instruction book again. Before you know it, you will have found new ways to enjoy your microwave and will have fit it into your lifestyle in a way that is satisfying to you.

This GUIDE TO GREAT MICROWAVE COOKING is meant to supplement the book the manufacturer provided with your microwave oven. Microwave cooking is explained in a way that relates to things you already understand in order to take the mystery out of it. The most important cooking techniques are presented in a way that makes them easy to remember. Once you have a grasp of HOW things work in the microwave and WHY to do particular things, you will no longer need to rely on a rote list of techniques, but will be able to reason for yourself.

I have also made an index of the topics covered in this section so that you can refer back to a paragraph easily if you need to.

Let's Talk About Microwaves

Let's Talk About Microwaves — 11

What are Microwaves? — 11
Are Microwaves Safe? — 11
Microwave Ovens are Safe — 11
Microwave Cooking is Safer Than Conventional Cooking — 12
Microwave Ovens are Safer for Children — 12
Safety is Up to You — 12
How Do Microwaves Cook Food? — 12
What Happens When You Turn On Your Microwave Oven? — 13
Three Important Characteristics of Microwaves — 13
Reflection — 13
Transmission — 14
Absorption — 14
How Microwave Energy Cooks Your Food — 14
Microwave Penetration — 15
Do Microwaves Stay in the Food? — 15

Three Keys to Success with your Microwave Oven — 16

Programming — 16
Choose the Correct Power Level — 16
Power Level Guide — 17
Choose the Correct Time — 17
Time Varies According To:
Power — 18
Conversion Chart — 18
Size or Quantity — 19
Composition — 19
Shape — 20
Starting Temperature — 20
Position — 20
Think Round — 20
Better Yet, Think Donut — 20
Placement — 21
Rearrange — 21
Patience! — 21
A Guide to Standing Time — 22
The Golden Rule of Microwave Cooking — 22
How To Know When Food is Done — 22
"Burned Food" — 23

Microwave "Tricks of the Trade" — 23

To Cover or Not to Cover — 23
Pierce Foods Enclosed in A Pouch or Skin — 23
Shield Areas of Food That Are Prone to Overcook — 24
The Appearance of Some Foods Needs to be Enhanced — 24
Seasoning — 24
Microwave Meal Planning — 25

Utensils You Can Use — 25

LET'S TALK ABOUT MICROWAVES

WHAT ARE MICROWAVES?

Microwaves are high frequency radio waves, similar to those used by AM/FM radios. Their frequency is assigned and regulated by Transport Canada just as are other radio frequencies. Your microwave oven is like a mini broadcasting system, except that the energy is used to cook food rather than to produce sound or pictures.*

Microwaves are shortwave radio waves — thus the name, *microwave.* They are about the size of a thin pen (1/4 inch (.5 cm) diameter, 6 inches (10 cm) in length). They lose their energy very quickly as they move away from their source, usually within about 4 feet (1.3 m).*

ARE MICROWAVES SAFE?

One of the most common questions I hear is, "Are microwaves safe?" Yes, they are. To help you understand why they are safe, it is necessary to understand a bit about the radiation spectrum. You probably learned this in your science classes in school, but to refresh your memory and bring it into the context of microwave cooking, I'll briefly explain it.

In the radiation spectrum, there are two classifications of rays: ionizing and nonionizing. Ionizing rays are the kind of radiation that is harmful. Some examples of this type of radiation are gamma rays and X rays. They are harmful to human cell tissue because they accumulate, undetected, through repeated exposure.*

Nonionizing rays ARE SAFE. Some examples of these rays are sun rays, electrical currents and microwaves. MICROWAVES DO NOT accumulate and cause damage to human cell tissue. They DO have a thermal effect, for instance, you can feel heat from sun rays and likewise from microwaves if you are exposed to them. You can feel the heat long before the danger point and move away from them.*

MICROWAVE OVENS ARE SAFE

Microwave safety is regulated by the Health Protection Branch of Health & Welfare Canada which has established standards for design, construction and operations of a microwave oven to prevent hazards. They require that microwave ovens have on/off switches and interlock switches with backups to prevent the microwave oven from operating when the door is not completely closed. Microwave oven manufacturers are required to have at least this many safety features and some manufacturers of better quality ovens have exceeded these standards to ensure safety.**

* Saskatchewan Power Corporation. Selection Use & Care of Microwave Ovens.

** All electrical appliances, including microwave ovens are regulated by the Canadian Standards Association which tests appliances for safety from electrical shock and fire hazards.

MICROWAVE COOKING IS SAFER THAN CONVENTIONAL COOKING

The risk of being burned or starting a fire with a microwave oven is considerably less than with conventional ovens. Only the food gets hot. Sometimes the dishes become hot as the heat of the food or steam transfers to the dish but they do not become as hot as pots do on the stove. The microwave oven itself remains cool. Microwave ovens cannot be left running indefinitely the way that stoves can and they would not pose the same fire and safety hazard in the event that they were left running for a period of time.

MICROWAVE OVENS ARE SAFER FOR CHILDREN

Microwave ovens are safer than conventional ovens in homes with small children. Hot pots of food cannot be accidently knocked off as they can from the stove (a very common cause of children's burns). The appliance does not become hot so they cannot burn themselves by touching it. Even if small children do manage to climb up and turn on the microwave oven, the damage will be to the microwave oven, not the child. (If you have small children, you may want to keep a glass of water in the oven when it is not in use so that if they do turn the microwave oven on, it will merely heat the water.)

Because both the dishes and the oven remain cool, your children can cook without burning themselves on the appliance or utensils. They need only to be cautious about handling hot food.

SAFETY IS UP TO YOU

Microwave safety is really up to you. If you operate the microwave oven according to the manufacturer's instructions you should have no problems.

DO NOT try to modify or repair the oven by yourself, it is a job for professionals.

DO keep the oven clean, especially the door, so that the seals will work properly.

DO NOT operate the oven with nothing in it - it can cause damage to the oven itself, which is very expensive to repair.

DO NOT use metal in the microwave oven, except as allowed in the manufacturer's instructions.

HOW DO MICROWAVES COOK FOOD?

Other methods of cooking begin with a source of heat, such as a fire or a burner which heats up the air around the food and gradually penetrates the food, heating and cooking it. In microwave cooking the source of the heat is the food itself. The microwave oven does not produce heat, it produces microwave energy which causes the food to cook itself. To help you to understand this process and therefore to understand how to produce the cooking results you desire we'll follow the path of microwave energy from its production.

WHAT HAPPENS WHEN YOU TURN ON YOUR MICROWAVE OVEN?

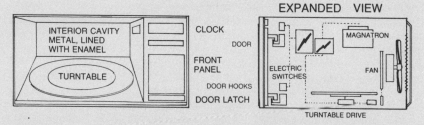

When you turn on your microwave oven, the magnetron tube converts electrical energy into electromagnetic energy in the form of microwaves. The microwaves are transmitted through a wave guide into your oven cavity. A stirring fan circulates the microwaves around the oven cavity. Microwaves travel in straight lines entering the food, or bouncing off the walls and bottom of the oven. If your microwave oven has a turntable, it rotates the food so that all parts are evenly exposed to the microwaves.

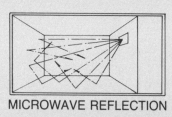

MICROWAVE REFLECTION

THREE IMPORTANT CHARACTERISTICS OF MICROWAVES

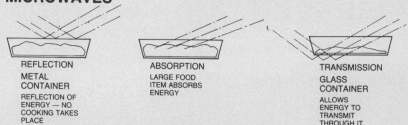

An understanding of how microwaves affect different substances can help the microwave cook to produce the desired cooking results.

1. REFLECTION

Microwave energy is reflected by metal. This is why metal pots and pans cannot be used to cook in the microwave oven. They would reflect the microwave energy away from the food, preventing it from cooking. Bands of metal such as twist ties and metallic trim around a plate can cause arcing, (a static discharge or blue spark between gaps in the metal or between the metal and the interior of the oven) which may cause damage to the oven walls.

This reflective property of microwaves is used to an advantage in the construction of the microwave oven. The interior walls of the oven are made of metal to reflect and contain the energy within its cavity. The glass door of the oven contains a perforated metal screen which reflects microwaves yet transmits light so that we can see into the oven.

I am often asked if the microwaves can escape through those little holes. The answer is no. Not only does the metal reflect the microwaves away from the door but the holes are too small for the microwaves (which are ¼ inch or 0.5 cm in diameter) to pass through.

The stirring fan is also made of metal, angled in such a way as to direct the microwaves around the food. Some manufacturers design the stirring fan in their ovens to reflect the microwaves in a more even pattern around the food, producing better cooking results than a random pattern.

Small bits of metal, such as aluminum foil, can be used purposely to prevent cooking of areas that are prone to overcooking. For example, strips of foil are often used to cover the wing tips and drumsticks of a turkey during defrosting and cooking. The foil prevents the microwaves from penetrating these areas.

2. TRANSMISSION

Substances such as paper, glass and plastic transmit microwave energy, that is, they allow the microwave energy to pass right through them just as sunlight passes through a window. Containers made of these products are ideal for cooking in the microwave oven. They do not become hot from microwave energy. They become hot only as heat is transferred from the food to the container itself, just as your coffee cup becomes hot when you fill it with hot coffee.

3. ABSORPTION

Microwaves are absorbed by food. They are particularly attracted to the water, sugar and fat molecules in the food. Substances which absorb microwave energy become hot.

HOW MICROWAVE ENERGY COOKS YOUR FOOD

Microwaves cause the molecules which have absorbed them, to vibrate very rapidly. They vibrate about 2 billion times per second, rubbing against each other. This movement causes friction which at that high rate of vibration generates intense heat. If you rub your hands together you can feel the heat caused by friction.

MOLECULE

AT REST

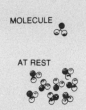

MICROWAVE ENERGY
APPLIED — THEY START
TO VIBRATE

AS THEY VIBRATE THEY HIT
EACH OTHER CAUSING
FRICTION (HEAT). IT IS
THIS HEAT THAT DOES
THE COOKING. WHEN
COOKING IS DONE THEY
NEED TIME TO SLOW DOWN
AND RELAX. THIS PERIOD
OF TIME IS CALLED
"STANDING TIME".

MICROWAVE PENETRATION

Microwaves lose their energy rapidly as they penetrate the food, most of it within approximately the first inch (2 cm) from the surface. This means that the production of friction heat takes place in that outer one inch (2 cm) of the food, therefore the outside edges of food tend to cook more and faster than the rest of the food. The centre of the food in large items is cooked by conduction as the heat from the outer edges of the food is conducted throughout.

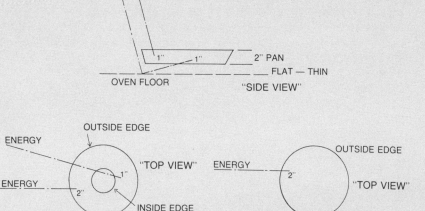

DO MICROWAVES STAY IN THE FOOD?

Microwaves do not remain in the food; they dissipate as they give off their energy. They cannot be stored in the food just as light cannot be stored in a box. Microwaves are similar to the light rays given off by the electric lights in your home. When the switch turns off the electricity, the light ceases to exist. Microwaves are the same. They exist only when the magnetron tube is on. When the switch turns it off they cease to exist.

Microwaves do not leave any residue. Microwaves are odourless and tasteless so nothing is added to or left in the food.

THREE KEYS TO SUCCESS WITH YOUR MICROWAVE

PROGRAMMING

The first key to success is to program your oven properly. Most ovens need to be programmed to cook at a particular power level for a specific time. Both of these functions determine the quality of your cooking results.

1. CHOOSE THE CORRECT POWER LEVEL

Just as your stove has various settings to cook food at different speeds, so do microwave ovens. In fact, microwave oven settings were named to correspond with those familiar settings on your stove because they are used in much the same way. On the stove the heat is most intense on the food surface closest to the burner. In the microwave oven, the heat is most intense in the outer 1 inch (2 cm) layer of food, that is, the part which has been penetrated by the microwaves. Just as the bottom of your food will burn on the stove if it gets too hot on the bottom, so the outside of the food will burn in the microwave oven if the heat becomes too intense on the food surface.

Power levels help to reduce the intensity of the heat on the surface of the food by reducing the amount of microwave energy available to be absorbed by the food in a given time. This not only prevents the outside from burning, it also produces more even cooking results because the heat has a chance to conduct through to the centre of the food.

To help you understand this process, think back to HOW MICROWAVE ENERGY COOKS YOUR FOOD. The magnetron produces microwaves which penetrate the outer 1-inch of the food and are absorbed by the water molecules. These molecules vibrate rapidly producing intense friction heat. On lower power levels, the magnetron stops sending out microwave energy for brief intervals, which allows the vibrations to slow down and therefore the intensity of the heat decreases and time is allowed for the heat to conduct to the centre. If you want to see a demonstration of this, sometime when you cook jelly, watch how it boils on MEDIUM power. You will see it boil up to the top of the dish and then come down for a few seconds before it boils back up.

Your conventional cooking experience has also taught you that many foods need to cook slower than others to tenderize, to improve flavour, to prevent curdling or to prevent boilovers. This experience also applies to microwave cooking. The power level guide below is to help you to choose the correct power level for a particular type of food, but you will notice it is very similar to what conventional cooking has taught you. You will notice that the HIGH setting is used less than the lower settings. There is a great improvement in the quality of the food when it is cooked at a slightly slower speed.

POWER LEVEL GUIDE

These are the settings for the PANASONIC microwave ovens used to test these recipes, but most microwave ovens have the same or similar settings:

HIGH — 100% — 700 watts — Level 10
- boil water or water based liquids
- cook fresh fruit & vegetables
- cook ground meat, bacon or sausage
- cook fish or poultry up to 3 lbs. (1.5 kg)
- Preheat browning dish

MEDIUM-HIGH — 90% — 650 watts — Level 9
- heat milk or milk beverages
- heat frozen foods
- reheat canned goods
- reheat leftovers
- make candy

MEDIUM — 70 % — 490 watts — Level 7
- bake cakes
- cook or roast meats and shellfish
- cook delicate foods such as those containing milk, eggs or cheese
- simmer stews, soups or sauces
- make candy containing milk
- cook puddings and custards

MEDIUM LOW — 50 % — 360 watts — Level 5
- simmer
- bake muffins
- melt chocolate
- cook custards

LOW — 27% — 200 watts — Level 3
- if you don't have this setting use the defrost setting on your oven (Defrost is 35% power or 245 watts)
- soften butter, cream cheese, ice cream
- "slow cook" stews, soups, ribs and other less tender cuts of meat

WARM — 10 % — 70 watts — Level 1
- keep foods at serving temperature for short periods of time
- rise yeast breads

2. CHOOSE THE CORRECT TIME:

The speed of microwave cooking makes accurate timing important. For best results, consult the timing charts that are included in your microwave oven manual. As with all things, "practice makes perfect." Experience will soon teach you the correct time. If you have an autocook feature on your microwave oven, by all means use it. It will make the timing decisions for you with amazing accuracy while you learn the correct times for foods without costly and annoying mistakes.

When trying a new recipe, compare it with a similar one in the manual and follow the instructions carefully. Not only are the times given in a recipe important, but all the other instructions are equally important because

TIME VARIES ACCORDING TO:

a. POWER

Most microwave ovens have between 500 and 700 watts of power. Of course, a 700 watt oven will cook faster than a 500 watt oven. When trying new recipes, check the wattage of the oven in which they were tested compared to the wattage of your oven and adjust the time accordingly.

It is important that your microwave oven be plugged into a circuit of its own. This does not mean that new wiring is necessary, just be sure that you do not have lights or other appliances wired into the outlet you use for your microwave oven. Other appliances on the same circuit will use power your microwave needs causing your microwave oven to cook more slowly than it would on a separate circuit. Remember, just because you have two different outlets does not mean you have two separate circuits.

Microwave owners in large cities may find that their microwave oven cooks more slowly at "peak power" times. This is because of the draw on the city's power supply and is not a problem with your microwave oven. Microwave oven owners in the country may have a similar situation, again because of the regional power supply.

I have also found through my cooking classes, that ovens of similar wattage vary in cooking time according to how efficiently the microwave energy is distributed and used in the oven. I often teach classes to which the students have brought their own ovens, which has given me the experience of cooking exactly the same thing in a variety of ovens. My experience is that microwave ovens with turntables cook the quickest and the most evenly. Microwave ovens with complex stirrer fans or dual wave cook quicker than simpler models. The reason you should know this, is so that you can adjust your time accordingly.

Below is a chart to help you compare times between ovens. Although wattage is the only difference listed, this chart can help with some of the other power variables I have listed above.

CONVERSION CHART:

To use this chart, set a 1-cup (250 mL) cup glass measure full of cold tap water into your microwave oven. Turn the power onto HIGH and the timer onto 3 minutes. Stay near the oven and watch for the water to begin to boil. Stop the oven when the water begins to boil. Note how long it took.

This took 2 minutes in our test ovens. If it also took 2 minutes in your microwave oven, the minimum cooking times in this book will be accurate for your oven. If your oven took 2 minutes and 30 seconds to bring the water to a boiling point, convert your times according to the 500 - 600 watt column, etc.

600 - 700 watts	500 - 600 watts	400 - 500 watts
15 seconds	18 seconds	20 seconds
30 seconds	35 seconds	45 seconds
45 seconds	55 seconds	1 minute
1 minute	1 minute, 15 seconds	1 minute, 30 seconds
2 minutes	**2 minutes, 30 seconds**	**2 minutes, 50 seconds**
3 minutes	3 minutes, 30 seconds	4 minutes, 15 seconds
4 minutes	4 minutes, 50 seconds	5 minutes, 45 seconds
5 minutes	6 minutes	7 minutes
6 minutes	7 minutes, 15 seconds	8 minutes, 30 seconds
7 minutes	8 minutes, 30 seconds	9 minutes, 50 seconds
8 minutes	9 minutes, 30 seconds	11 minutes, 15 seconds
9 minutes	10 minutes, 50 seconds	12 minutes, 30 seconds
10 minutes	12 minutes	14 minutes

Remember:
> More Power = Less Time
> Less Power = More Time

b. SIZE OR QUANTITY OF FOOD

In the microwave oven, the size or quantity of the food affects the cooking time. The more food you cook at once, the longer it takes to cook. To help you understand this principle, it is important to understand the difference between conventional and microwave cooking. In the conventional oven all food is equally surrounded by a mass of hot air, therefore, one or a dozen baked potatoes all take an hour at 350 F (180 C) because that is how long it takes for the hot air to conduct heat througout the potato. In the microwave oven, there is only so much microwave energy to be absorbed by the food. If there is only one potato it will take about 4 minutes, however, two potatoes would need almost twice as long because there is twice as much food to absorb the same amount of energy.

To help you to double or half recipes to suit your situation, I have included a little formula that works for most recipes:

"MICROWAVE MATH":
> ½ x Recipe = ⅔ Time
> 2 x Recipe = 1⅔ Time

c. COMPOSITION OF FOOD

Microwaves are attracted to water, sugar and fat molecules so foods containing large amounts of these substances tend to cook more quickly. Dense foods like meat cook more slowly than pourous foods like bread because the heat conducts more slowly through dense food.

d. SHAPE OF FOOD

The shape of foods affects the time they need to cook. Flat, thin foods cook more quickly than thick or deep foods. Remember, the microwave energy penetrates the food to a depth of 1 inch (2 cm) on all sides. If the food is less than 2 inches (4 cm) thick, the microwave energy penetrates it completely, therefore it cooks more quickly than the same food would if it were 4 inches deep. If it were 4 inches (8 cm) deep, the microwaves would penetrate the outside to a depth of 1 inch (2 cm) from all sides but there would still be approximately 2 inches (4 cm) in the centre to which the heat would need to conduct. This would increase the cooking time.

e. STARTING TEMPERATURE

The colder the food is, the longer it must cook. This is not a new principle of cooking, but it is one that is often overlooked by new microwave cooks. It is especially important to remember when warming leftovers. Heating food that became cool while sitting on the counter or table takes less time than heating food that was refrigerated.

Most foods need to be defrosted before being cooked in the microwave or they will not cook evenly. This is especially important for sauces and large, dense items like meat or casseroles. The exception to this rule is frozen fruits and vegetables which have a high water content.

O—ɪ POSITION YOUR FOOD PROPERLY

The position in which the food is placed in the microwave oven is important because of the way microwave energy cooks. Food cooks more quickly around the outside edges of the food because the microwave energy penetrates about 1 inch (2 cm) into the outside of the food. Cutting or placing your food in an even shape or dish helps food to cook more evenly.

How you place your food and how you rearrange it is important for even cooking results because COOKING CONCENTRATES ON OUTSIDE EDGES OF FOOD, therefore:

1. THINK ROUND

Place foods in a round dish rather than a square one so that microwave energy does not concentrate on the edges or the corners. Remember, microwaves will enter the food as they come into contact with it. In a square, the corners stick out so they tend to receive more microwaves. A round shape is even so all parts of the food cook at a consistent rate.

2. BETTER YET, THINK DONUT

A donut or ring shape cooks even better than round because it leaves the centre, where little cooking takes place, empty. This allows microwave energy to penetrate food from the centre as well as the outside edges resulting in quick, even cooking. When cooking several items like baked potatoes, place them in a ring shape on the oven floor, leaving the centre empty. Use a ring shaped pan or tube pan whenever possible.

3. PLACEMENT

Dense or slower cooking items towards the outside edges of the dish when cooking different types of food together. For instance, when cooking a cut-up chicken, the larger, meaty pieces like the thighs and breast should be placed around the outside of the dish while smaller pieces, like the wings, would be placed in the centre.

4. REARRANGE

If you rearrange the food during cooking time, it will equalize the cooking times of various parts of the food by exposing all parts of the food to the microwave energy.

a. STIR food to bring outside portions toward the centre and centre portions toward the outside edges. Stirring is the best method of rearranging. If it can be stirred, do so two or three times during cooking time for best results.

Stir with a fork or wire whip whenever possible. They distribute the smaller food particles better than a spoon. In the case of puddings and sauces, this is important to prevent lumps of thickener from forming.

Stirring is also a very helpful way to check food for doneness.

Stirring blends flavours. This is an important difference between conventional cooking and microwave cooking. Stirring is to microwave cooking what time is to conventional cooking.

b. MOVE pieces of food like chicken pieces, meatballs, etc. Bring the pieces that were placed on the outside of the dish to the centre of the dish and the pieces that were in the centre to the outside during the last third of cooking time.

c. TURN OVER large, dense items like potatoes and roasts. Foods tend to cook more slowly on the bottom because not as many microwaves circulate on the bottom of the microwave oven. If you turn them over about halfway through the cooking time, they cook more evenly.

d. ROTATE items which can't be stirred or rearranged in other ways. Eg: cakes, roasts, some casseroles. If your oven has a turntable, rotation is not necessary because the food is moved around at constant rate.

⚓ PATIENCE!

Yes, patience! with the fastest cooking method. It seems that despite the fact that the microwave oven can cook in minutes what conventional methods require hours to do, many novice microwave cooks still can't wait until it is cooked! The biggest mistake new *and* experienced microwave cooks make is checking their food before it is done. Microwaved food needs time to STAND in the oven or on the counter, AFTER THE OVEN STOPS, in order to COMPLETE cooking.

In fact, STANDING TIME IS COOKING TIME!

Standing time allows the temperature of the food to equalize throughout. To help you understand the importance of standing time, think back to HOW MICROWAVE ENERGY COOKS YOUR FOOD. The microwaves cause the food molecules to vibrate at a rate of more than 2 billion times per second. This movement produces friction heat which causes the food to cook itself. These moving molecules have built up momentum and they do not come to a standstill when the microwaves stop stimulating them.

This is similar to the momentum your car builds up when you are driving it on the highway at a speed of 100 km per hour. If you take your foot off of the gas pedal, your car does not stop, does it? In fact, this momentism would keep your car moving for quite awhile (although, never long enough if you've run out of gas!) if you do not apply the brakes. This is similar to what is happening inside your food. The microwave energy causes the molecules to move just like the gas makes the car move. The magnetron is like a gas pedal, it only provides energy for the movement. When the magnetron stops producing microwave energy, the buzzer sounds on your microwave oven. *But* the molecules need time to lose their momentum (there are no brakes on molecules). AS LONG AS THE MOLECULES ARE MOVING, THEY ARE PRODUCING FRICTION HEAT. AS LONG AS THERE IS FRICTION HEAT INSIDE YOUR FOOD, IT CONTINUES TO COOK!

A GUIDE TO STANDING TIME

Standing time varies for each food, according to the same variables as for cooking time but as a general rule, food should stand for about 1/4 to 1/3 of the time that it was cooked. The list below will give you a bit more specific information:

Vegetables, cakes, sauces — about 3 to 7 minutes

Casseroles, main dishes — about 7 to 10 minutes

Roasts, rice or large dishes — 10 to 15 minutes at least

THE GOLDEN RULE OF MICROWAVE COOKING:

IT IS BETTER TO OVERSTAND THAN TO O V E R C O O K ! ! !

If your food is not done after it has had its standing time, you can put it back into the microwave oven and cook it longer. You will be the only one who knows what happened. HOWEVER, if you cook it longer because it looks like it needs "just one more zap", it may overcook on its standing time. You cannot stop the cooking that takes place on standing time.

HOW TO KNOW WHEN FOOD IS DONE

When the microwave oven beeps, your food should look slightly underdone. You will have a temptation to give it that "one little zap". RESIST THAT

TEMPTATION! and let it stand. Baked goods will be set but somewhat moist, meat will be a bit pink, vegetables will be slightly crunchy and foods containing thickeners will be not quite thick enough. For specific information consult the chapter guidelines for each food type. This slightly underdone appearance will change to the one you desire during standing time.

"BURNED FOOD"

Microwave "burned" food doesn't usually look the same as conventionally burned foods, ie. black and smoking. It *does* become dry and hard, tough or rubbery. Often this "burned" texture will not be noticed until after the standing time. Foods high in fat or sugar may turn dark and have a scorched smell.

MICROWAVE "TRICKS OF THE TRADE"

TO COVER OR NOT TO COVER

Covers make microwave cooking efficient because they keep the heat inside the food. Covers also keep your oven cleaner because they contain spattering. However, not all foods need to be covered for cooking. Cover as directed in each recipe.

- If no cover is mentioned, it is assumed that the food is cooked uncovered.
- Do not cover foods that are starchy or sugary because the cover will often cause them to boil over.
- Do not cover foods like sauces, jams or candy which need to be stirred often.
- Covers of plastic wrap or glass keep in moisture and speed up cooking. Use them when you want to keep in moisture, as in the case of vegetables or rice.
- Wax paper keeps in some moisture. It also contains the spatters when cooking meat. Use wax paper to cover tender meats and cakes.
- Covers of paper towel or natural fibre cloth contain spatters and absorb moisture or grease. Cover bacon with paper towel. Cover or wrap baked potatoes and breads in paper towel or natural fibre towels to absorb excess moisture yet help maintain even heating.

PIERCE FOODS ENCLOSED IN A POUCH OR SKIN

Foods should not be cooked in sealed containers or tight skins. If they are in a sealed pouch or their own skin, like potatoes and squash, they need to be pierced to allow steam to escape. If the steam is sealed in the food or container, it often causes enough pressure to burst the food or the container open. This is also why you have been warned not to cook eggs in their shell. An egg shell cannot be pierced well enough to relieve the steam pressure, so it usually builds up to the point of a small "explosion".

SHIELD AREAS OF FOOD THAT ARE PRONE TO OVERCOOK

Shielding refers to the technique of covering unevenly shaped areas of food which are prone to overcook with small pieces of aluminum foil in order to reflect the microwaves away from these areas. Proper use of shielding does not harm most microwave ovens because while the metal does reflect the microwaves away from a particular area, they can still penetrate other areas of the food.

When cooking a whole chicken, the wing tips and drumstick bones are usually covered with a piece of foil. When cooking cake in a square or rectangular pan, the corners are covered with foil.

It may be helpful to use toothpicks to hold the foil in place to keep it from moving around. Be careful to keep the foil away from the oven walls or arcing may occur.

THE APPEARANCE OF SOME FOODS NEED TO BE ENHANCED

The appearance of some baked goods and small cuts of meat is somewhat different from what we are used to. However, it tastes no different. Often it doesn't matter because the foods are to be covered with a sauce or frosting. But when appearance is important, clever microwave cooks use browning agents, coating mixes or toppings to enhance the appearance of these foods to make them palatable. Sometimes these enhancements save time and effort as in the case of an upside down cake and often the enhancements cause the foods to be *more* attractive than their conventional counterparts. Wouldn't you rather eat a white cake dressed as a pineapple upside down cake than as a delicately browned plain cake?

Large pieces of meat, such as roasts, will brown themselves. Their natural fat content attracts microwaves so that the surface reaches a temperature high enough to cause browning. As a rule, meats that are microwave cooked longer than 10 minutes will brown. However, bacon, with its very high fat content, browns very nicely in only a minute per slice. Cooking meat on a lower power level will help it to brown better.

Each chapter of this book offers suggestions for enhancing the appearance of particular foods. Consult these sections for specific information.

SEASONING

Microwave cooking retains foods' natural flavour. Herbs and spices are full of flavour when cooked by microwaves. Some people find that they need to use less seasoning to achieve a desired piquance. The chapter introductions in this book suggest seasonings to add variety to foods and to take advantage of this palate pleasing feature of microwave cooking.

Salt is not usually necessary to enhance flavour as it is in conventional cooking methods which dry food and destroy its flavour. In fact, sprinkling salt on food is a microwave no. Salt toughens food and distorts the pattern of the microwaves when sprinkled on food. Many people won't notice if you eliminate salt in your cooking. For those who must have their salt, best results are achieved when salt is sprinkled onto food during its standing time or dissolved in the liquid or sauce in which the food is being cooked.

MICROWAVE MEAL PLANNING

Cooking is so fast in the microwave oven, that some organization is usually necessary when cooking a meal. Read through the recipe before beginning to cook. Assemble the ingredients. Some foods may need to be peeled or cut before you begin to cook.

Pot roast with vegetables or casseroles cook well as "all at once" meals but generally you will find that cooking foods separately in sequence with the microwave oven takes less time and produces better results.

When planning to cook a whole meal in the microwave oven, follow this sequence:

1. Cook foods that need to be served cool or foods that reheat well.
2. Cook large, dense foods that have a long standing time such as roasts, rice, and casseroles. Let stand covered, to keep warm.
3. Cook quick cooking dishes like vegetables and sauces or foods which do not reheat well such as eggs, fish and seafood.
4. Reheat precooked or canned foods, buns or bread.

Don't be a slave to your organization or to the speed of the oven. The quality of most food is unaffected when set aside and reheated just before serving. Only you will know.

Utensils

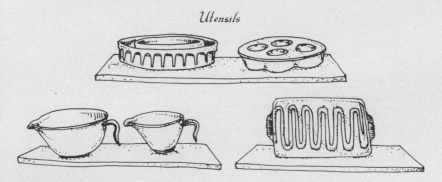

UTENSILS YOU CAN USE IN YOUR MICROWAVE OVEN

Although you cannot use your metal pots and pans in the microwave oven, you will find that microwave cooking offers the convenience of using many dishes you weren't able to cook in with conventional appliances. The best cooking utensils to use are made of glass and microwave safe plastic. You can also cook with paper. Wood and wicker may be used in the microwave oven for short periods of time.

Microwave energy passes through most materials except metal without affecting them. The concern in choosing microwave cooking utensils is not so much what the microwaves will do to them, as it is what the HEAT will do to them. While microwave energy passes through plastic margarine containers or styrofoam without affecting them, the heat from the steam or food melts them sometimes causing them to give off undesirable fumes.

Most glass and ceramic dishes are safe for microwave use but some dishes have metalic content in the greenware or the glaze. If you are wondering whether or not you should use a particular dish in the microwave oven do this simple utensil test:

UTENSIL TEST: Place a glass measuring cup of cold tap water in the microwave oven. Set the dish in question beside the cup of water. Turn the microwave on HIGH for 1 minute.

IF	THEN
The water is hot and the empty 'dish is cold.	The dish is safe for microwave
The empty dish is hot and the water is cold.	DO NOT use this dish in the microwave.
Both the water and the dish are warm.	The dish can be used for short periods of time in the microwave, such as warming leftovers.

UTENSILS YOU WILL FIND USEFUL FOR MICROWAVE COOKING:

Many of these dishes you may already have in your kitchen, others you may wish to buy. When you are shopping for dishes that you might want to use for microwave cooking follow these suggestions:

- Choose round or ring shaped containers with straight, not sloping sides.
- Food cooks quicker in broad, shallow dishes than in deep narrow dishes, however, sauces, jams and jellies cook best in deep, narrow containers like measuring cups.
- Dishes with handles and covers are convenient.
- Utensils made of oven safe (up to 400°F (204°C)) as well as microwave safe materials are versatile. I like the oven safe plastic because it is also lightweight and unbreakable.

A SET OF CASSEROLE DISHES

Most foods will cook very well in casserole dishes. Often casserole dishes can be used in place of special microwave dishes. The important thing to remember when using casserole dishes in place of the dish a recipe calls for, is that you keep the surface area and the volume the same as the recommended dish. For example, a round casserole dish with a diameter of 9 inches (24 cm) and a depth of more than 2 inches (4 cm) could be used in place of a 9 x 2½ inch (24 x 5 cm) cake pan. Or, a deep 2-qt. (2 L) casserole could be used in place of an 8-cup (2L) glass measure.

A SET OF LIQUID MEASURING CUPS

I use a set which includes a 1-cup, 2-cup, 4-cup and 8-cup (250 mL, 500 mL, 1 L, 2 L) and they are in constant use. Not only are they handy for measuring and mixing in the same dish, they are also very handy for cooking things that need to be poured such as sauces, candy and jam.

AN ASSORTMENT OF MICROWAVE SAFE BOWLS

Cereal or soup bowls can be used not only for making individual servings of cereal or soup, but also for warming up canned or frozen vegetables or individual casseroles. If you do not have a roasting rack, they can be inverted in a casserole dish to elevate a roast.

Custard cups can be used for custard, individual baked eggs or quiche. If you do not have a special microwave muffin pan, custard cups can be used to make big muffins or cupcakes. If you do not have a tube pan, a custard cup can be set in the centre of a round pan to act as a tube.

PIE PLATE

Pies, especially those with crumb crusts, are super simple and fast in the microwave oven. You will enjoy making them. If your pie plate is oven safe as well as microwave safe you can cook the crust in the microwave and brown the meringue under the broiler.

A 10 x 2-inch (25 x 4 cm) pie plate can also double as a cake pan for some single layer cakes.

CAKE PAN

Microwave cakes cook beautifully in the microwave oven in about 6 minutes per layer. They rise higher than conventional cakes, so the dish you use should be about 2½ inches (5 cm) deep to allow for this expansion. They cook better in round dishes than in square dishes because the corners of square cakes tend to burn. Special 9 x 2½ inch (24 x 5 cm) round microwave safe cake pans are available. I recommend one if you bake cakes often.

You may use an 8-inch (22 cm) round layer cake dish, but remember to fill it only half full. Use the leftover batter to make cupcakes.

TUBE PAN

Tube pans are used for more than just cakes in the microwave oven. They are a must for large cake recipes. I prefer to bake loaves in a tube pan rather than a loaf pan. I also use them for casseroles and meat loaves. Meat loaf in a ring has lots of potential for creative cooks. I turn it out on a larger serving platter, spoon sauce over it and fill the centre with rice pilaf! It makes a very elegant looking meatloaf.

MEAT RACK

It is important to keep meat elevated because if it sits down in its juices it will cook unevenly. There are a number of meat racks to choose from. I prefer racks that provide versatility. One meat rack is a large (13-inch or 33 cm) round, "bacon rack" with a groove around the edges to collect the juices. It works very well for any size of roast, bacon slices and several pieces of meat like pork chops. Turned over, it doubles as a baking sheet for cookies.

Another meat rack fits into an 8 x 12-inch (22 x 32 cm) baking dish. It has spaces between the grooves the meat rests on. It can be used for meat or to steam pudding. Without the baking dish, it can be used to elevate sandwiches or cakes during cooking to prevent them from becoming soggy on the bottom.

MUFFIN PAN

A microwave muffin pan can be very handy. A batch of six fresh, microwaved muffins takes the same time as a couple of slices of toast so you will want to make them often. Microwave muffin pans can also be used to poach eggs, make individual quiche or to hold baked potatoes or stuffed peppers.

BROWNING TRAY

A browning tray is a "microwave frying pan". It is coated with a microwave "absorbing" substance which causes the surface of the dish to become hot, like a frying pan. The food must lay flat on the hot surface in order to brown. Meat should be scored around the edges to prevent it from curling up and losing contact with the hot surface. Because its surface gets hot, browning trays which are not Teflon coated need to be greased with oil or butter to prevent food from sticking.

A browning tray's uses are the same as those of a frying pan. It can be used to sear food giving a "fried" flavour, crisp texture and browned appearance. Browning trays are a help for small cuts of meat and they make delicious grilled sandwiches. Microwave browning trays are particularly convenient for microwaving frozen convenience foods like breaded fish sticks or patties, frozen pizza, waffles and other foods which have a crisp surface. Microwave cooking without this browning tray often causes the crisp coating of these foods to become soggy. However, browning trays cannot be used to brown roasts or baked goods.

There are a variety of browning trays on the market. My preference is for Teflon coated trays. Some browners are shaped like casserole dishes which can saute or stir fry vegetables. A flat tray is more convenient for pizzas.

KITCHEN SCALE

A kitchen scale is helpful if your oven does not have an autocook feature. Most microwave time charts for foods are based on weight so it is a helpful device. You can also buy special microwave scales which not only tell you the weight of your food, but also suggest the cooking time.

GENERAL UTENSIL TIPS

- Follow the recipes' instructions as to the size of a utensil. Using a smaller dish than suggested could mean your food will boil over. Using a larger dish will shorten the cooking time slightly because you have enlarged the surface area of the food. If you do not have the size of dish the recipe recommends, use a size larger and watch the time.
- Sauces or foods that need frequent stirring should be cooked in a deep, round container in order to accomodate food expansion, boiling and stirring.
- Choose to cook in round or donut shaped dishes rather than in square or rectangular dishes. Round dishes cook more evenly.
- Single layers of food such as chicken pieces or corn on the cob can be cooked in a shallow rectangular or oval baking dish because the microwave energy can penetrate its entire depth (ie. 2 inches or 4 cm). Remember to rearrange and turn them over.
- Always be sure that there is food on a utensil. Except in the case of browning trays, NEVER operate the oven with *only* an empty dish inside it.
- The material the dish is made of makes a slight difference in the way foods cook. Most microwave recipes are tested in glass dishes. Food cooks quicker in plastic dishes and slower in ceramic dishes.
- Do not use chipped or cracked dishes for cooking in the microwave oven. The heat of the food could cause them to break.
- Beware of dishes with metal trim or decorations. Also watch for metal screws, or tacks on dishes.
- Melamine (Melmac dishes) is not microwave safe. It becomes hot and could crack.
- Do not use delicate glassware or lead crystal in the microwave. They will break.
- Be very careful when heating pancake syrup or other substances in narrow necked bottles. If the food becomes too hot, the pressure which builds up in the bottle becomes too great and could cause an explosion.
- When heating foods in jars or paper cartons, be sure to remove the metal lids or ends before placing them in the microwave oven.
- Styrofoam and most plastic products are safe for defrosting and warming foods. The food should not get HOT in non-microwave plastics.

- DO NOT cook very greasy foods (like sausage and bacon) or very sugary foods (like candy and jelly) in plastic containers unless labelled "safe for oven temperatures up to 400°F (204°C)". The heat of the FOOD will melt other plastics.

- Lift covers away from you or you could get a steam burn.

- Heavy plastic wrap or those labelled "microwave safe" are the best to use for covering foods. Thinner plastics will melt from the heat of the food.

- Covers of plastic wrap should be vented to allow some steam to escape. While some recommend that you pierce the plastic with a toothpick or knife, I find that unsatisfactory. The plastic tends to tear or "run" like pantyhose. It is best to fold back a corner of the wrap.

- Paper products can be used for cooking, but be sure the paper is sturdy enough to withstand the moisture. Thin paper will tear.

- Wax or plastic coated paper products work very well in the microwave oven.

- Use white paper products for best results. Sometimes the dyes of coloured or printed paper towels leaks onto the oven floor.

- Do not use recycled paper products in the microwave oven. Recycled paper products are usually labeled "recycled". They often contain metallic fibres and flammable chemicals.

- It is unlikely that you will have a fire in your microwave but it could happen so it's best to know what to do: DON'T panic! DO NOT open the oven door. Push the STOP button or turn off the power. Cover the top vent with a heavy towel. This should cut off the oxygen supply and extinguish the fire. Once the fire is out you can open the door and clean up the mess.

TROUBLE SHOOTING

Situation	Cause	Solution
GENERAL:		
Boilovers	Dish is too small.	Use a larger dish.
	Power level is too high.	Lower power level
Tough Food	Overcooked	Use less time.
	Food cooked too fast.	Use a lower power level.
DEFROST:		
Edges of meat are cooked but the center is not thawed.	Too long a defrost time	Use less time or let it stand for a few minutes halfway through defrost time and again at the end of defrost time.
Hamburger edges are cooked but centre is frozen.	Wrong technique	Remove ground meat as it thaws.
REHEATING:		
Some food hot and other parts are cold.	Technique	Flatten food such as mashed potatoes.
		Place larger, denser food like meat towards the edge of the plate and smaller moist pieces toward the centre.
Food is tough or rubbery	Wrong power level	Most foods reheat best on MEDIUM.
SNACKS & SANDWICHES:		
Rolls tough after heating.	Overcooked	Reduce time and/or power level.
Sandwich bread is soggy.	Wrong utensil	Place on paper towel to absorb moisture.
		Place on a plastic rack.
CASSEROLES:		
Center not cooked.	Technique	Stir, if possible or rotate.
		Increase standing time.
Outside is overcooked, the center is undercooked.	Power level too high	Lower the power level.
Flavour doesn't seem well blended.	Cooking too fast	Lower the power level to MEDIUM-LOW for a longer time.
	Technique	Stir more often.

MEAT:

Outside cooked but center not cooked.	Power level too high	Reduce power level.
	Standing time too short	Increase standing time.
Tough and chewy	Power level too high	Reduce power.
	Cooking time too long — overcooked	Reduce cooking time — allow longer stand time.
Roast done on top and ends but not evenly	Technique	Shield ends.
		Turn over halfway through cooking.
Outside is tough and inside is perfect	Power level too high	Reduce power level.
Roast not cooked although the temperature readout is correct.	Probe not inserted properly or it changed position during cooking.	Reposition the probe to go through centre of roast.

POULTRY:

Whole bird is not fully cooked but temperature readout is correct.	Probe is on bone or thin portion or probe has changed position.	Reposition the probe.
Meat is chewy and tough.	Power level too high	Reduce power level.
	Cooking time too long	Reduce time and allow more standing time.
Legs are overcooked.	Technique	Shield legs.

FISH & SEAFOOD:

Fish is tough.	Overcooked	Reduce time and allow it to finish cooking covered, on its standing time.
Fillets are done on the outer edges but centre is not done.	Technique	Rearrange fillets halfway through cooking time.

RICE:

Boils over	Wrong utensil	Use a larger dish.
Rice is too crunchy.	Technique	Let it stand, covered, to finish cooking.

EGGS & CHEESE:

Rubbery or tough	Overcooked	Reduce cooking time, let stand, covered, to finish cooking.
	Power Level too high	Reduce power level to MEDIUM.
Egg yolk pops	Steam build up inside egg.	Pierce yolk before cooking.

VEGETABLES & FRUITS:

Steaming but not hot throughout	Technique	Cover while cooking.
		Stir more often.
Dry or tough	Cooked too long	Reduce cooking time.
		Allow to finish cooking, covered on standing time.
Vegetables are soggy.	Too much water	Cook without water.
Vegetables are stringy or too crunchy.	Not enough water	Add about ¼ cup water to soften them.
When cooking several potatoes at once, some are done and others are not done.	Position	Arrange them in a circle with thick ends toward outside and thin ends toward centre, turn over halfway through.
Apples burst when baking	Expansion	Peel top of apple before baking.

BAKED GOODS:

Tough after heating	Overcooked	Reduce time.
	Power level too high	Heat on MEDIUM.
Bottoms soggy after heating	Technique	Place on paper towel or a plastic rack while heating.
Corners of cake or brownies are burnt, centre of cake is not done	Technique.	Shield corners.
	Wrong utensil	Use a round pan or use a tube pan.
Some areas of cake are too moist but most of it is done.	Technique	Cover cake with wax paper or a plate during cooking time.
Muffins are too moist.	Utensil	Use an extra paper liner to absorb excess moisture.

SAUCES, PUDDINGS OR GRAVY:

Not smooth	Technique	Stir more frequently.
Separates	Overcooked	Reduce time.

PIES:

Crusts is burned in spots	Technique	Rotate more often.
	Overcooked	Reduce time.
	Not blended well	Make sure butter in a crumb crust is completely melted and evenly blended.

CANDY, JAM & JELLY:

Boils over	Utensil too small	Use a larger utensil, fill only half full.
Boils over or burns before reaching a done stage	Power level too high	Reduce power level.

SNACKS & SANDWICHES

The Earl of Sandwich never dreamed of the hot and hearty lunch the microwave oven could make of his invention. Using your own imagination or the recipes given in this chapter, the variety of satisfying bread wrapped meals is endless. Included in this chapter are also recipes for other snacks, appetizers and hints for reheating pizza in the microwave oven.

UTENSILS TO USE WHEN MICROWAVING SANDWICHES

The convenience of the microwave sandwich meal extends from the heating operation to cleanup. Sandwiches are best heated by covering or wrapping them with a paper towel. This prevents the bread from losing moisture and becoming dry. Sandwiches with a runny filling are better prepared on a paper plate. You will find if you set bread on a glass plate or the glass tray in your oven, that the bottom of the sandwich becomes soggy. This happens because the steam is trapped by the glass. Paper will absorb the steam, leaving the bread drier. Setting the paper-wrapped sandwich on a plastic or ceramic rack further improves the product. It enables the air and the microwave energy to surround the sandwich, thus producing a more evenly heated sandwich. Cleanup is easy; you can just throw the paper towel or plate in the garbage.

⊶ THE KEY TO SUCCESS WHEN MICROWAVING SANDWICHES

The bread you choose and how you treat it can make the difference in the quality of your sandwich. Because the bread is on the outside and because of its moist, pourous composition, it tends to cook fastest and often becomes tough before the filling becomes hot. Don't judge the heat of the sandwich by touching the bread. The bread is often cool to the touch when the filling is hot. That is because its porous composition doesn't hold the heat. All baked goods, including bread, are better when heated on MEDIUM because the gluten in the flour tends to toughen when heated too fast. The advantage when microwaving sandwiches on MEDIUM, is that the heat of the sandwich will be more uniform throughout.

TRICKS WITH BREAD

- Frozen bread doesn't heat as fast as room temperature bread and so the time it takes to heat will correspond more with the time the filling takes to heat, giving you an evenly heated sandwich.
- Firm textured breads like whole wheat, rye or even day old white bread tend to stay firmer than fresh white bread when heated (also, day-old bread will "freshen" during the heating time).

34

- If you toast the bread before using it in the sandwich, it will be less likely to become soggy.
- If you like a crisper, grilled type outside to your bun or bread, heat your sandwich on a preheated, buttered, browning tray.

PREPARING SANDWICHES FOR MICROWAVE COOKING

While some sandwiches like hot dogs can be heated assembled because the filling heats very quickly, you will find that often it is better to heat the filling first. You can then assemble the sandwich and heat it in the microwave oven for 20 seconds, just to heat the bread. Or spread the filling on the bottom piece of bread and leave the top off while you heat the filling. Add the top for the last 10 to 20 seconds of heating. The filling determines the method of preparation and the heating time. If it is high in fat, like a hot dog, or high in sugar, like jam or jelly or if it is sliced or spread thinly, then the entire sandwich can be assembled before heating. If the filling is dense like roast beef or large, as in a submarine sandwich, you will be more satisfied if you heat it in two steps. You will also find if you spread the filling evenly, rather than mounding, it will heat better.

CHEESE FILLINGS

Cheese is a delicate food and needs careful handling to keep it from getting tough. When microwaving a sandwich with cheese in the filling, use MEDIUM power. Protect the cheese by placing it in the centre of layers of filling or by adding it for the last few seconds of heating time. Remember to microwave cheese only until it begins to soften. It will finish melting during standing time.

MICROWAVING PIZZA

Pizza made from scratch in the microwave is not very good because the crust tends to be limp and soggy. However, frozen pizza or leftover pizza reheats very well in the microwave with a little know how. If you set it on a layer or two of paper towel to absorb moisture, and also elevate it on a rack you will get satisfactory results when reheating pizza.

If a crisp crust is very important to you, then you will find that heating it on a preheated browning tray gives delicious results. You can buy a microwave accessory called a pizza crisper, but any browning tray on which your pizza fits will do just as well. Transfer the pizza to a board or plate for cutting and serving because knife cuts will ruin the surface of a browning tray.

MEXICAN MICROWAVE

Mexican food and the microwave seem to be made for each other. Tortillas and taco shells can be warmed in seconds. Wrap them in paper towel and set them on a rack. Microwave on HIGH for 10 seconds each. Soft shells can be set on wax paper for heating. The meat and bean fillings for most

Mexican dishes can be prepared easily in the microwave oven - with more intense spicy flavour.

Nachos are a natural in the microwave oven. You can even crisp up a bag of stale corn chips by microwaving them in the bag on HIGH for 10 seconds.

HINTS

- Be creative in making sandwich fillings; some leftover casseroles or salads make great fillings.
- Whenever possible, heat the sandwich filling before spreading it inside the bun. Then heat the entire sandwich, just until the bun is warmed. This will prevent moisture loss from the bun. Also, the less time a filling is inside a bun, the less chance there is for sogginess to occur.
- To heat a sandwich filling, place it on a plate, making a depression in the centre. Heat one minute. Microwaves are attracted to the edges of food rather than the centre.
- Sandwiches spread with a thin layer of filling will heat faster than sandwiches with thicker fillings. When making meat sandwiches, use thin, rather than thick, slices of meat.
- When preparing appetizers, keep the crackers crispy by spreading the mixture on the crackers just before microwaving.
- Help for stale crackers and potato chips: Microwave on HIGH for 10 to 20 seconds per cup (250 mL) to freshen them instantly.
- Popcorn should be popped only in a recommended popcorn popper according to its directions. Popping it in a paper bag is dangerous - the bag could set on fire. Popping corn without this special accessory could be harmful to your microwave oven.

PEPPY NUTS

These savory nuts toast beautifully in the microwave oven.

¼ cup	butter	50 mL
1 tbsp.	Worcestershire sauce	15 mL
½ tsp.	Tabasco sauce	2 mL
1 tbsp.	seasoned salt	15 mL
¼ tsp.	garlic salt	1 mL
1 lb.	whole, unsalted nuts: almonds, cashews, peanuts, filberts OR Brazil nuts	500 g

1. Place butter and seasonings in a 10-inch (25 cm) glass pie plate. Microwave on HIGH for 45 seconds or until butter is melted. Stir well.

2. Add nuts. Stir to coat. Microwave on MEDIUM-HIGH for 8 to 10 minutes, stirring several times during cooking.

3. Cool thoroughly on paper toweling. Store in tightly covered container.

Your Time: _____

SUGAR ALMONDS

These can be eaten as a snack or used as a garnish on salads and desserts.

⅓ cup	sugar	75 mL
¼ cup	water	50 mL
1 cup	whole unblanched almonds	250 mL

1. Combine sugar and water in a 10 inch (25 cm) glass pie plate. Microwave on HIGH for 1½ to 2 minutes, or until sugar is dissolved. Stir 2 or 3 times during cooking.

2. Stir almonds into sugar water. Microwave on HIGH for 1 minute at a time, stirring after each minute, until water is absorbed by the almonds. This will take 4 to 6 minutes.

Your Time: _____

POPPYCOCK

A snack of crunchy clusters that will please all ages.

8 cups	popcorn	2 L
2 cups	nuts: pecans, almonds OR peanuts	500 mL
1½ cups	white sugar	375 mL
1 cup	butter OR margarine	250 mL
½ cup	corn syrup	125 mL
½ tsp.	vanilla	2 mL

1. Combine popcorn and nuts in a large bowl. Set aside.

2. Place sugar, butter and syrup in a 4-cup (1 L) glass measure. Microwave on HIGH for 3 minutes. Stir and microwave on MEDIUM for 2 to 3 more minutes.

3. Stir vanilla into syrup mixture and pour over popcorn and nuts. Mix well and spread to cool on a greased cookie sheet. Store in a covered container.

Your Time: _____

SOMBREROS

A snack kids love to make as well as eat.

4	slices bologna	4
4	slices cheese	4
1 cup	mashed potatoes	250 mL

1. Place each slice of bologna on a microwave safe saucer.

2. Place a scoop of mashed potato in the centre of each slice of meat.

3. Top each "sombrero" with a slice of cheese.

4. Microwave each sombrero on MEDIUM-HIGH for 1 to 1½ minutes.

VARIATIONS: Use any luncheon meat that comes in a round shape instead of bologna. This would also work with a cooked hamburger or sausage patty.

Your Time: _____

MINI PIZZAS

When you are short on time, these are a quick-to-fix snack.

Melba toast rounds
Pizza sauce
Italian seasoning
Grated mozzarella cheese
Pepperoni sausage, sliced thin

1. Arrange melba toast rounds on a paper plate.
2. Spread 1 tbsp. (15 mL) pizza sauce on each. Sprinkle with Italian seasoning. Top with grated cheese and sausage slices.
3. Microwave 12 mini pizzas at a time on MEDIUM for 2½ to 3½ minutes.

VARIATIONS:

HAWAIIAN STYLE: Use ham or ham sausage instead of pepperoni sausage and sprinkle 1 tsp. (5 mL) of crushed pineapple on each "pizza".

MEXICAN STYLE: Substitute chili powder for Italian seasoning; cheddar cheese for mozzarella cheese and 1 tbsp. (15 mL) browned ground beef for sausage. If desired, garnish each with 1 tsp. (5 mL) finely chopped onion and green pepper.

The variations for this are as endless as those for pizza — use whatever you have in your fridge.

Your Time: _____

PAM'S NACHOS

This snack is hearty enough to serve as a light meal.

1 lb.	lean ground beef	500 g
1	medium onion, chopped	1
1-16 oz.	can refried beans	483 mL
1-4 oz.	can green chili peppers, drained, seeded and chopped OR 1 pkg. Taco seasoning	114 mL
1-8 oz.	pkg. tortilla chips	250 mL
1	medium avacado, sliced	1
1 cup	sour cream	250 mL
½ cup	sliced olives	125 mL
¾ cup	taco sauce (optional)	175 mL
1	tomato, cubed	1
1 cup	shredded Monteray Jack cheese	250 mL

1. In a 2-qt. (2 L) casserole dish, crumble ground beef. Microwave on HIGH for 4 to 5 minutes or until browned. Stir 2 or 3 times during cooking time. Drain. Stir in onion, beans, and peppers or Taco seasoning.

2. Spread chips on a large plate.

3. Spread burger mixture over chips. Layer remaining ingredients on top of the chips in the order they are listed.

4. Microwave on MEDIUM-HIGH for 4 to 6 minutes.

Your Time: _____

SKIFFLE SNACK

A calcium rich lunch.

1	can sardines, drained	1
1	egg, slightly beaten	1
1-10 oz.	can tomato soup	284 mL
	salt & pepper to taste	
4	slices of toast, buttered	4

1. Break up sardines and combine with egg and tomato soup. Microwave on MEDIUM-HIGH for 3½ minutes or until heated through.

2. Slice toast diagonally to form points. Place 2 points on each plate and top with sardine mixture.

Your Time: _____

BUN BASKETS

A fancy way to serve leftovers.

Kaiser bun OR large hard roll
Butter
Leftover meatballs in sauce or other meat
   mixture like Chili, Chicken a la King,
   Pepper Steak, etc.

1. Slice a thin slice off of the top of each roll. Hollow out the centre to form a basket.

2. Butter the inside of each roll and fill with meat mixture.

3. Place each basket on a plate and microwave on MEDIUM-HIGH for 1 to 2 minutes.

TIP: Use top and hollowed out portion of buns to make bread crumbs.

BUN BOATS: Garnish with a triangle of cheese on a toothpick to resemble a sail on the boat. Fill boat with Chicken Salad (page 112) or Egg Salad (page 44).

Your Time: _____

ROAST BEEF SUBMARINE SANDWICH

A sandwich with mouth watering flavour.

1	crusty submarine bun	1
1 tbsp.	butter	15 mL
1 tbsp.	prepared mustard	15 mL
¼ cup	mayonnaise	50 mL
¼ lb.	thinly sliced roast beef	125 g
4	slices mozzarella cheese	4
1	small onion, thinly sliced	1

1. Slice bun in half and spread each side with butter, mustard and mayonnaise.

2. Arrange beef, cheese and onion on bottom half of bun. Set on a napkin and microwave on MEDIUM for 3 to 4 minutes, until cheese is melted.

3. Set top half of bun on sandwich and microwave on HIGH for 20 seconds, just until warm.

Your Time: _____

BEEF SUB NAPOLITANA

A tasty "pizza in a bun".

1	crusty submarine bun	1
¼ cup	pizza sauce	50 mL
¼ lb.	thinly sliced roast beef	125 g
1	small tomato, sliced	1
1	small green pepper, sliced	1
1	small onion, thinly sliced	1
4	slices mozzarella cheese	4

1. Slice submarine bun in half. Spread each half with pizza sauce. On bottom half, arrange roast beef, tomato, onion, green pepper, and cheese.

2. Place on napkin and microwave on MEDIUM for 4 to 5 minutes, until cheese is melted.

3. Add top half and microwave on HIGH for 20 seconds, just until warm.

Your Time: _____

TUNA BURGERS

A tasty deviation from the traditional burger.

1-6½ oz.	can tuna	184	mL
¼ cup	chopped celery	50	mL
1/2 cup	finely diced cheddar cheese	125	mL
¼ cup	chopped pickles OR olives	50	mL
½ cup	mayonnaise	125	mL
1	green onion, chopped	1	
3	hamburger buns	3	
2 tbsp.	butter	25	mL
	Paprika		

1. Drain tuna and combine with celery, cheese, olives, mayonnaise and green onion.

2. Split hamburger buns. Spread each half with butter. Top with tuna mixture. Sprinkle with paprika.

3. Place each bun on a napkin and microwave on HIGH for 20 seconds or until warm.

Your Time: _____

BARBECUE BEEF DIP

Marianne and I both chose this as our favourite sandwich. You'll agree when you taste it.

1 lb.	thinly sliced roast beef	500	g
1	small onion, finely chopped	1	
1 cup	barbecue sauce	250	mL
1	loaf of French bread	1	
1 cup	beef broth, from bouillon OR a can	250	mL

1. In a 1-qt. (1 L) casserole dish, combine roast beef, onion and barbecue sauce. Cover and microwave on MEDIUM for 5 to 6 minutes. Stir once or twice during cooking time.

2. Pour beef broth into four custard cups. Microwave each for 30 seconds.

3. Slice French bread in half lengthwise. Spread meat mixture between halves. Wrap in a napkin or towel and microwave on HIGH for 1 minute.

4. Cut loaf into 4 sandwiches. Serve each on a plate with a custard cup of broth for dip.

* **Yield:** 4 sandwiches
Your Time: _____

MEAT & EGG SALAD BUNWICHES

In this recipe the microwave oven is used to cook the eggs as well as heat the sandwiches.

6	eggs	6
1	can luncheon meat	1
½ cup	mayonnaise	125 mL
¼ cup	sweet relish OR chopped pickle	60 mL
¼ cup	finely chopped celery	60 mL
2 tbsp.	finely chopped onion	30 mL
6	hamburger OR dinner buns	6

1. Break each egg into a section of a microwave muffin pan or a 4 oz. (125 mL) custard cup. Pierce each yolk with the tip of a sharp knife. Microwave the four eggs on MEDIUM for 4 to 6 minutes or until almost hard cooked. Let stand 2 minutes to finish cooking.

2. Grate luncheon meat. Mash eggs. Mix together with mayonnaise, relish, celery and onion.

3. Spread on halves of buns. Place each half on a napkin and microwave on MEDIUM-HIGH for 20 seconds, just until warm.

Your Time: _____

NACHOS

A tasty hunger-stopper.

2 cups	tortilla chips	500 mL
2 tbsp.	green chili peppers, seeded and chopped	30 mL
½ cup	sliced olives	125 mL
½ cup	sliced mushrooms	125 mL
½ cup	chopped, cooked bacon pieces or small canned shrimp	125 mL
1 cup	shredded cheese — your choice	250 mL

1. Spread tortilla chips in a single layer in a large glass plate or tray. (I use a 13 inch or 33 cm tray by Anchor Hocking, called VersaTray)

2. Sprinkle remaining ingredients over chips, in the order given.

3. Microwave on MEDIUM-HIGH for 2 to 4 minutes, until cheese is melted.

TIP: Lining the plate with paper towel will keep chips crisper.

Your Time: _____

OPEN-FACE REUBENS

This recipe makes four delectable sandwiches.

1 cup	sauerkraut, drained	250	mL
2	small carrots, shredded	2	
4	slices rye bread	4	
¼ lb.	sliced cooked corned beef	125	g
½ cup	creamy Russian salad dressing OR	125	mL
	Thousand Island dressing		
4	slices Swiss cheese 8 oz. or	250	g
2 tbsp.	butter OR margarine	25	mL

1. Preheat a 10-inch (25 cm) browning tray on HIGH for 5 minutes. (If you do not have a browning tray, toast the slices of rye bread in your toaster and then butter them.)

2. Combine sauerkraut and carrots in a small bowl.

3. On bread slices arrange corned beef, then salad dressing, Swiss cheese and sauerkraut mixture.

4. Coat surface of browning tray with butter and arrange sandwiches on tray. Microwave on MEDIUM-HIGH for 2 to 3 minutes, just until cheese is melted. (If you do not have a browning tray, set sandwiches on a napkin on top of a plastic rack and microwave on MEDIUM-HIGH for 3 to 4 minutes.)

VARIATION: This recipe can also be served as an appetizer: Use party size rye bread or crackers instead of rye bread slices (about 3 dozen). Arrange as directed above and place 12 appetizers on a paper plate. Microwave on MEDIUM for 2 to 3 minutes, or until cheese is melted. Repeat with remaining ingredients.

Your Time: _____

PIZZA BUNS

A make ahead and freeze recipe — so handy!

1 lb.	bacon, chopped	500	g
1 lb.	lean ground beef, crumbled	500	g
1	large onion, chopped	1	
1 lb.	cheddar cheese	500	g
1 lb.	mozzarella cheese	500	g
1-14 oz.	can tomato sauce	398	mL
1 tsp.	oregano	5	mL
1 tsp.	Italian seasoning	5	mL

1. In a 3-qt. (3 L) casserole dish combine chopped bacon, ground beef and onion. Cover and microwave on HIGH for 10 to 12 minutes or until meat is browned and onion is tender. Stir 2 or 3 times during cooking time. Drain well.

2. Meanwhile, grate cheddar cheese and mozzarella cheese into a large mixing bowl. Stir in meat mixture and remaining ingredients. Mix well.

3. Divide into 4 to 6 portions in plastic freezer containers. Freeze until ready to use.

4. Defrost each container of pizza topping for 8 minutes. Stir and allow it to stand for a few minutes to finish thawing.

5. Spread on bun halves and microwave each on HIGH for 30 to 40 seconds, just until cheese melts.

VARIATION: Substitute 1 can of luncheon meat for ground beef but do not cook it with the bacon. Grate it with the cheese.

Your Time: _____

SLOPPY JOES

This is a favourite of my children — I wonder if it's because it lives up to its name!

1 lb.	lean ground beef	500	g
1	small onion, chopped	1	
1	green pepper, chopped	1	
1	clove garlic, minced OR ¼ tsp. (1 mL) garlic powder	1	
1 tsp.	oregano	5	mL
1 tsp.	parsley	5	mL
	salt & pepper to taste		
1-14 oz.	can tomatoes	400	mL

1. Crumble ground beef into a 2-qt. (2 L) casserole dish. Add onion. Cover and microwave on HIGH for 5 minutes or until browned. Stir twice during cooking time. Drain fat.

2. Stir in remaining ingredients. Microwave, covered, on HIGH for 5 to 8 minutes. Stir twice during cooking.

3. Spoon over open buns. If desired, warm each bun on MEDIUM-HIGH for 15 seconds before spooning mixture over them.

TIP: Break up pieces of ground beef while browning by stirring with a wire whisk or potato masher.

Your Time: _____

Homemade soups and stews may have been crowded out of your busy schedule but microwave convenience offers a chance for a comeback with hearty homemade soups and stews, some of which you could make on your lunchbreak! In just minutes you can make a hearty soup with flavour and aroma as tantalizing as those of a soup that simmers for hours with the added microwave bonus of brightly coloured, fresh tasting vegetables.

○━┓ THE KEY TO SUCCESS WITH SOUPS

The key to full flavour in microwave soups and stews is stirring. Stirring helps to blend the flavours in the same way that time does conventionally. Cream soups, however, do not need the constant stirring that they do conventionally. They are quick and easy to prepare with very little tending.

UTENSILS

For added cleanup convenience, cook soup right in your soup tureen or casserole dish and take it straight from your microwave oven to the table. Soups and stews can also be reheated in their serving bowls.

COOKING SOUPS

Clear soups can be microwaved on HIGH power while those containing milk or cheese should be cooked on MEDIUM. If your microwave oven has a temperature probe, it can be used to simmer by setting the power level and a temperature of 150° to 160°F (65°-71°C).

REHEATING SOUPS:

Soups can be heated in individual serving dishes (one at a time for best results) or in a casserole dish, soup tureen or glass measuring cup. Don't fill the container to the brim — allow space for boil overs, especially when heating milk based soups. Covers speed up heating and aid in even heating. They are also important in helping the rehydration process of dry mixes. Stirring at least once during heating time also improves heat distribution.

DRY SOUP MIXES

In a 4-cup (1L) glass measure, prepare according to package directions. Microwave, covered, on HIGH for 3 to 4 minutes. Allow 5 minutes standing time.

CUP A SOUP

Combine mix with water in a mug or bowl. Microwave on HIGH 1 to 2 minutes. Stir halfway through.

CANNED SOUP

In a 4-cup (1L) glass measure, prepare according to label directions. Microwave on HIGH for 4 to 6 minutes. Or divide into equal parts and prepare in soup bowls. Microwave on HIGH for 1 to 2 minutes per bowl.

ADAPTING SOUPS & STEWS

- Clear soups made with chicken or prepared stock can be microwaved on HIGH for approximately ¼ of the conventional time. Most other soups and stews should be microwaved on MEDIUM power for ¼ to ½ the conventional time.
- Most soups and stews require a reduction of ¼ in the amount of water and salt. The exception is in those containing dry ingredients like peas or beans which need no reduction in water.
- For uniform cooking, cut vegetables and meat into small pieces.
- In the microwave, milk boils up higher than conventionally so make allowance by filling container only half full.

HINTS

- Reheating improves flavour.
- Standing time is important to complete cooking — especially of vegetables.
- Freeze leftover soup in ice cube trays and store in plastic bags. Thaw and heat in a mug or bowl — 3 cubes make a cup. Microwave each cup on HIGH for 2 to 3 minutes.
- Freeze soup stock in an ice cube tray. It makes adding to soups, stews, sauces, or gravy much easier.

FRENCH ONION SOUP

Gourmet, yet simple.

¼ cup	butter	60 mL
3	large onions, sliced	3
2-10 oz.	cans beef broth	284 mL
2½ cups	water	625 mL
4	slices toasted French bread	4
¼ cup	grated Parmesan cheese	60 mL
1 cup	grated Gruyere cheese	250 mL

1. Place butter and onion in a 3-qt. (3 L) casserole dish. Microwave, covered, on HIGH for 8 to 10 minutes or until onion is tender.

2. Add beef broth and water. Microwave, covered, on HIGH for 5 to 7 minutes or until mixture boils.

3. Butter French bread. Sprinkle with Parmesan cheese. Place on paper towels or plastic rack and microwave on HIGH 1 minute. Cube.

4. Place a small handful of cubed French bread into each individual serving bowl. Pour soup over bread. Top with a handful of grated Gruyere cheese. Microwave each bowl of soup for 1 minute, or until cheese is melted.

Your Time: _____

FRESH TOMATO SOUP FOR ONE

This has the most wonderful garden-fresh flavour.

2	large fresh tomatoes	2
1 tbsp.	butter	15 mL
	salt & pepper to taste	
⅛ tsp.	baking soda	.5 mL
2 tbsp.	cream or milk	25 mL

1. Cut tomatoes into quarters and place in a 10-oz. (284 mL) soup bowl. Cover and microwave on HIGH for 2½ to 3 minutes.

2. Remove tomato skins and chop up cooked tomatoes. Stir in butter, salt and pepper and baking soda.

3. When baking soda has finished bubbling, stir in milk or cream. If necessary, reheat on MEDIUM-HIGH for 1 minute before serving.

Your Time: _____

TOMATO CONSOMME

This soup is nice for company — easy on the hostess, too.

2 cups	fresh tomatoes, peeled and chopped OR tomato juice	500 mL
2 cups	beef consomme	500 mL
1 tsp.	Worchestershire sauce	5 mL
	salt & pepper to taste	
1 tbsp.	lemon juice	15 mL

1. Combine all ingredients in a 1½-qt. (1.5 L) casserole dish. Cover and microwave on HIGH for 10 minutes.

2. Garnish each serving with a lemon slice and a sprig of fresh dill or basil.

Your Time: _____

HAMBURGER SOUP

A complete meal in a bowl.

1 lb.	lean ground beef	500 g
1	envelope dry onion soup mix	1
¼ tsp.	pepper	1 mL
¼ tsp.	oregano leaves	1 mL
¼ tsp.	basil leaves	1 mL
¼ tsp.	seasoned salt	1 mL
1 tbsp.	soy sauce	15 mL
1½ cups	boiling water	375 mL
1 cup	sliced celery	250 mL
1 cup	sliced carrots	250 mL
1-19 oz.	can tomatoes	540 mL

1. Crumble beef into a 3-qt. (3 L) casserole dish. Microwave on HIGH for 5 minutes, or until beef is no longer pink. Stir once or twice during cooking time. Drain.

2. Add seasonings and water. Cover and microwave on HIGH for 10 minutes.

3. Add vegetables and microwave, covered, on HIGH for 15 minutes or until vegetables are tender. Let stand 10 minutes.

VARIATION: Add 1 cup (250 mL) cooked macaroni after step 3 and sprinkle each serving with Parmesan cheese.

Your Time: _____

CREAM OF MUSHROOM SOUP

This silken soup is so easy and so-o-o good — you'll throw away the canned soup.

1 lb.	fresh mushrooms, sliced	500	g
½ cup	butter	125	mL
1 tsp.	lemon juice	5	mL
1	small onion, chopped	1	
⅓ cup	flour	75	mL
3 cups	chicken broth	750	mL
1 tsp.	salt	5	mL
¼ tsp.	pepper	1	mL
1 cup	whipping cream	250	mL

1. Sprinkle mushrooms with lemon juice. Place butter in a 3-qt. (3 L) casserole dish and microwave on HIGH for 1 minute. Add mushrooms and microwave on HIGH for 8 to 10 minutes. Remove mushrooms and set aside.

2. Add onions to butter and microwave on HIGH for 5 minutes, or until tender. Stir in flour. Gradually add chicken broth, stirring with a wire whisk.

3. Microwave on HIGH for 8 to 10 minutes, or until thickened, stirring after each minute.

4. Stir in cream. Add salt, pepper and mushrooms. Microwave on MEDIUM-HIGH for 2 minutes, just until heated through. Do not boil.

VARIATIONS:

CAULIFLOWER SOUP: Prepare as above making the following substitutions:

1	head of cauliflower, cut into flowerets instead of 1 lb. (500 g) mushrooms	1
2 cups	milk plus 1 cup (250 mL) chicken broth instead of 3 cups (750 mL) chicken broth	500 mL
½ lb.	grated old cheddar cheese OR 1 cup (250 mL) process cheese spread in place of whipping cream	250 g

BROCCOLI SOUP: Prepare the same as cauliflower soup using broccoli in place of cauliflower. For either cauliflower or broccoli soup you may like to run the soup through the blender before serving.

HAM & CAULIFLOWER CHOWDER: Prepare as for cauliflower soup, substituting 2 cups (500 mL) chopped ham for cheese.

CHEDDAR CHEESE SOUP: Prepare as for Cream of Mushroom Soup making the following changes:

	Omit mushrooms and lemon juice		
2 cups	**milk plus**	500	mL
1 cup	**chicken broth instead of 3 cups (750 mL) chicken broth**	250	mL
1 lb.	**grated old cheddar cheese instead of 1 cup (250 mL) whipping cream**	500	g

The variations for a good cream soup like this one are virtually endless. I've given you my favourites here but you might like to experiment with anything else you have in your fridge, such as celery or cooked chicken.

Your Time: _____

CHICKEN VEGETABLE SOUP

Old country flavour, but quick and easy to prepare.

2-2½ lbs.	chicken parts	1-1.5	kg
3	ribs celery, cut into ½-inch (1 cm) pieces	3	
1 tbsp.	poultry seasoning	15	mL
1 tsp.	peppercorns or pepper to taste	5	mL
1	onion, chopped	1	
8 cups	hot water	1	L
3	carrots, thinly sliced	3	
1	turnip, cubed	1	
1	large potato, cubed	1	
1½ cups	frozen mixed vegetables	375	mL

1. In a 5-qt. (5 L) casserole, combine chicken, celery, poultry seasoning, peppercorns, onion and water. Cover and microwave on HIGH for 10 minutes and then on MEDIUM-LOW for 35 to 37 minutes, or until chicken is tender.

2. Strain broth and return to casserole dish. Remove chicken meat from bones and add to broth.

3. Add carrots, turnip and potato (and salt, if desired) to broth. Cover and microwave on HIGH for 10 to 12 minutes.

4. Add frozen vegetables. Cover and microwave on HIGH for 12 to 14 minutes or until vegetables are tender.

Your Time: _____

BUTTER SOUP

This very simple soup is made without meat — butter or cream are used instead. Do not use margarine.

8 cups	water	2 L
1	large onion, chopped	1
4	medium potatoes, cubed	4
	salt & pepper to taste	
1	parsley root	1
1	bay leaf	1
¼	star aniseed	
	butter or cream	

1. Combine all ingredients except butter or cream in a 3-qt. (3 L) casserole dish. Cover and microwave on HIGH for 20 to 25 minutes, or until potatoes are tender.

2. Add a spoonful of butter or cream to each serving.

Your Time: _____

POTATO SOUP

A satisfying meal for a cold winter day.

4 cups	potatoes, cubed	1 L
½ cup	water	125 mL
1	bay leaf	1
1	medium onion, chopped	1
	salt & pepper to taste	
2⅓ cups	milk	575 mL
¼ cup	butter	50 mL
1 tsp.	dried parsley leaves	5 mL

1. Combine potatoes, water, bay leaf, onion, salt and pepper in a 3-qt. (3 L) casserole dish. Cover and microwave on HIGH for 10 minutes.

2. Mash potatoes. Stir in remaining ingredients and microwave on MEDIUM-HIGH for 5 to 6 minutes, just until it comes to a boil. Stir halfway through cooking time.

Your Time: _____

54

CORN CHOWDER

A favourite of everyone who tastes it, (pictured on the cover).

3 cups	potatoes, peeled and cubed	750 mL
¼ cup	water	60 mL
½ lb.	bacon	250 g
1	small onion, chopped	1
2 tbsp.	flour	25 mL
1 tsp.	salt	5 mL
¼ tsp.	pepper	1 mL
3 cups	milk	750 mL
1-14 oz.	can cream style corn	398 mL

1. Place potatoes and water in a 1½-qt. (1.5 L) casserole dish. Microwave, covered, on HIGH for 8 to 10 minutes or until potatoes are tender. Set aside.

2. Arrange bacon slices in a 3-qt. (3 L) casserole dish. Microwave on HIGH for 10 to 12 minutes or until bacon is crisp. Remove bacon from drippings and set aside.

3. Stir onion into bacon drippings. Microwave on HIGH for 2 minutes, until tender. Stir in flour, salt and pepper. Gradually add milk, beating with a wire whisk to prevent lumps. Add corn and potatoes.

4. Microwave on MEDIUM-HIGH for 8 minutes, or until hot but not boiling, and slightly thickened. Stir 1 or 2 times during cooking.

5. Crumble bacon and add to soup. Serve.

Your Time: _____

AUNT EDNA'S NEW ENGLAND CLAM CHOWDER

When I told my mother I was writing this book she said that I HAD to have this recipe.

6	strips bacon, cut into 1-inch (3 cm) pieces	6
1	onion, chopped	1
5	medium potatoes	5
2	large carrots	2
2	stalks celery	2
2 tbsp.	cornstarch	25 mL
½ cup	cream	125 mL
1½ cups	milk	375 mL
2-10 oz.	cans clams	284 mL

1. Place bacon and onion on a glass plate. Microwave on HIGH for 6 minutes. Drain and set aside.

2. Meanwhile, cut potatoes into ½ inch (1 cm) cubes; slice carrots and celery into ½ inch (1 cm) pieces. Place vegetables in a 3-qt. (3 L) casserole dish. Cover and microwave on HIGH for 15 to 18 minutes, or until vegetables are tender. Stir several times during cooking.

3. Mix cornstarch into cream. Add cream mixture and milk to vegetables. Microwave on MEDIUM-HIGH for 5 minutes, or until thickened. Stir 1 or 2 times during cooking time.

4. Add bacon, onion and clams. Microwave on MEDIUM-HIGH for 3 to 5 minutes, just until heated through.

Your Time: _____

BEET BORSCHT

You'll love this colourful, pungent borscht.

1	ham bone	1
1	large onion, sliced	1
1	stalk celery, sliced	1
2 tbsp.	lemon juice	25 mL
1 tsp.	dill	5 mL
	salt & pepper to taste	
8 cups	hot water	2 L
1 cup	tomato juice	250 mL
2	carrots, sliced	2
1	large potato, cubed	1
2 cups	chopped cabbage	500 mL
1 cup	cooked beans	250 mL
4	beets, cooked and cubed	4
	leaves from the beets	
	sour cream	

1. In a 5-qt. (5 L) casserole combine ham bone, onion, celery, lemon juice, dill, salt and pepper, water and tomato juice. Cover and microwave on HIGH for 10 to 12 minutes. Stir and microwave on MEDIUM-LOW for 35 to 40 minutes.

2. Add carrots, potato and cabbage. Cover and microwave on HIGH for 8 to 10 minutes.

3. Add beans, beets and beet leaves. Cover and microwave on HIGH for 5 to 7 minutes or until beet leaves are tender. Serve with a dollop of sour cream in each bowl.

NOTE: Depending on what is available in my kitchen, I sometimes use fresh green beans and sometimes dried white beans. To prepare white beans for this recipe: In a 2-qt. (2 L) casserole cover ½ cup (125 mL) white beans with 4 cups (1 L) hot water. Cover and microwave on HIGH for 16 to 18 minutes. Let stand covered for one or two hours. Drain and add to soup as instructed above.

Your Time: _____

CHILI

Cook this while your family is coming to the table.

1 lb.	lean ground beef	500	g
1	medium onion, chopped	1	
½ cup	chopped green pepper	125	mL
	salt & pepper to taste		
1-14 oz.	can red kidney beans	398	mL
1-14 oz.	can tomato sauce	398	mL
2 tbsp.	chili powder (or to taste)	25	mL

1. Crumble ground beef into a 2-qt. (2 L) casserole dish. Mix in onion and green pepper. Microwave on HIGH for 8 to 10 minutes, or until beef is no longer pink. Stir ingredients 3 times during cooking time. Drain.

2. Mix in remaining ingredients. Microwave on HIGH for 10 minutes or until heated through.

VARIATIONS: Add any or all of the following: 1 tsp. (5 mL) oregano leaves, ½ tsp. (2 mL) garlic powder or a clove of minced garlic, ½ cup (125 mL) chopped ripe olives, 1-10 oz. (284 mL) can sliced mushrooms. My mother used to add almost anything out of her fridge to chili, including leftover macaroni which tasted surprisingly good.

SERVING SUGGESTION: Serve leftover chili on hot dogs, topped with a slice of cheese.

Your Time: _____

SUMMER GROUND BEEF STEW

This became a favourite stew the first time I made it — such bright colour and fresh flavour.

1 lb.	lean ground beef	500	g
2	medium onions, quartered	2	
4	cloves garlic, minced OR ½ tsp. (2 mL) garlic powder	2	
1 tsp.	basil leaves	5	mL
1 tsp.	salt	5	mL
¼ tsp.	pepper	1	mL
½ cup	hot water	125	mL
8-12	small (1½-inch or 4 cm diameter) new potatoes	8-12	
1½ tbsp.	cornstarch	23	mL
4	medium tomatoes, quartered OR	4	
1-19 oz.	can tomatoes	540	mL
2	medium green peppers, cut into strips	2	

1. Crumble ground beef into a 3-qt. (3 L) casserole dish. Microwave on HIGH for 6 to 8 minutes. Stir 2 or 3 times during cooking.

2. Add onions. Cover and microwave on HIGH for 3 minutes.

3. Add seasonings, water and potatoes. Cover and microwave on HIGH for 10 to 12 minutes, or until potatoes are tender.

4. Mix cornstarch with juice from tomatoes or an equal amount of stew liquid and stir into stew. Add tomatoes and green peppers. Microwave, covered, on HIGH for 4 to 5 minutes or until vegetables are tender.

Your Time: _____

BEEF RAGOUT

A robust, full-flavoured stew.

1 tbsp.	butter	15	mL
2 lbs.	beef stew meat	1	kg
1	large onion, chopped	1	
2	cloves garlic, minced	2	
1-10 oz.	can beef broth	284	mL
1 cup	hot water	250	mL
1-7½ oz.	can tomato sauce	213	mL
1 tbsp.	parsley	15	mL
½ tsp.	thyme	2	mL
1	small bay leaf, crumbled	1	
½ tsp.	salt	2	mL
¼ tsp.	pepper	1	mL
4	medium carrots	4	
2	stalks celery	2	
¼ cup	cornstarch mixed with 1/4 cup (60 mL) cold water	60	mL

1. Place butter in 3-qt. (3 L) casserole dish. Microwave on HIGH for 30 seconds. Stir in meat, onion and garlic. Cover and microwave on HIGH for 5 minutes.

2. Add broth, water, tomato sauce and seasonings. Cover and microwave on MEDIUM for 15 minutes. Stir once or twice during cooking time.

3. Add vegetables and cornstarch mixture. Cover and microwave on MEDIUM for 20 to 25 minutes. Stir 3 times during cooking time.

Your Time: _____

QUICK BEEF STEW

A quick, nutritious meal.

3 cups	leftover beef roast, cubed	750 mL
¼ cup	onion, chopped	60 mL
1 cup	carrots, sliced	250 mL
1 cup	celery, chopped	250 mL
½ cup	peas (optional)	125 mL
2 cups	beef broth (made with either roast drippings OR bouillon cubes)	500 mL
1 tsp.	salt	5 mL
2 tbsp.	cornstarch	30 mL
2 tbsp.	cold water	30 mL

1. Combine all ingredients except cornstarch and water in a 3-qt. (3 L) casserole dish. Microwave, covered, on HIGH for 20 to 25 minutes.

2. Mix together cornstarch and cold water. Stir into stew. Microwave, on HIGH for 5 more minutes or until thickened. Stir every 2 minutes.

Your Time: _____

COUNTRY STYLE TURKEY STEW

An old-fashioned delight.

3 lbs.	turkey pieces	1.4 kg
1	large onion	1
6	small potatoes	6
8	small carrots	8
3	stalks celery	3
4	chicken bouillon cubes	4
2½ cups	hot water	625 mL
1½ tsp.	poultry seasoning	7 mL
¼ tsp.	pepper	1 mL
1 tsp.	salt	5 mL
1½ cups	peas, fresh OR frozen	375 mL
¼ cup	cornstarch	60 mL
¼ cup	cold water	60 mL

1. Place turkey pieces in a 4-qt. (4 L) casserole dish. Microwave on ME-DIUM-HIGH for 30 to 40 minutes, or until meat comes off bone easily. Remove bones.

2. Meanwhile, chop onion, dice potatoes and slice carrots and celery into ½ -inch (1 cm) pieces.

3. Dissolve bouillon cubes in hot water. Stir in poultry seasoning, salt, and pepper. Pour liquid over turkey meat. Add vegetables and mix. Micro-wave, covered, on HIGH for 15 to 20 minutes.

4. Add peas. Combine cornstarch and cold water. Stir into stew. Microwave on HIGH for 5 minutes or until thickened. Stir every 2 minutes.

Your Time: _____

MEAT

Most meats cook quickly in the microwave with results that equal or excel conventional recipes. Cooking meat in the microwave oven takes one half to one third of the conventional cooking time. Microwave cooking brings out the full flavour of quality fresh meats. The meat turns out tender and juicy, whether it is a tender roast or a less tender cut of meat. Large cuts weighing more than three pounds, like a roast, come out nice and brown. Smaller cuts such as chops and steaks cook too quickly to brown so microwave cooks use sauces, browning agents, coating mixes and browning trays to enhance their appearance. Meats in this chapter are classified according to cut because similar cuts of most meats cook the same way.

⊙━⊱ THE KEY TO SUCCESS WITH MEAT

The secret to success with microwaved meats is to use the variable power settings on your oven. You will always get good results if you remember to cook meat on MEDIUM or a lower power level. Meats shrink less and turn out more tender and juicy if you use these power levels. Prolonged exposure to HIGH power, as with high heat in conventional cooking, toughens meat fibres.

Cooking less tender meats in a liquid or sauce on a MEDIUM or LOW power level will further tenderize the meat, and will still be quicker than conventional simmering.

REMEMBER:

Meat is not a cheap dish to experiment with, but if you follow the guidelines given in this chapter, use the lower power levels and a little more time, you will end up with a far better product, a complimentary family and a hungry dog.

CHOOSING MEAT FOR MICROWAVE COOKING

- Look for evenly shaped cuts of meat that have good marbling and an even fat covering. They will cook better than other cuts of meat in the microwave.
- Quality meat is juicier and more flavourful when cooked in the microwave oven; however, if the meat has deteriorated through poor storage, microwaving will intensify the "off" flavour of rancid fat.
- Choose cuts of meat that have a firm, fine grained meat with bright colour. Bones should look pourous and red. Fat should be very firm and creamy white. Avoid meats with a soft or coarse grained texture. Beware of a watery surface or signs of oozing and fat that appears yellow and soft or oily looking.
- Roasts should weigh 3 or more pounds (1.5 kg) and smaller cuts should be 1½ inches (3 cm) thick.
- Boneless cuts are usually best because meat around the bone tends to overcook. However, centre bones that are surrounded by more than 1

inch (2 cm) of meat make very little difference. Boneless meats may also be more economical because they yield more servings per pound.

- Choose thick chops and steaks rather than thin, "fast fry" cuts. Lean cuts of meats with little marbling such as pork chops should be cooked covered, coated with crumbs or cooked in sauce so that they don't dry out.
- Choose recipes for casseroles and meat dishes that use small pieces of meat.
- Any recipe for meat cooked in a sauce will be much nicer when cooked in the microwave oven. Meat should be partially cooked before adding the sauce.

FOODS THAT DON'T WORK & WHY

Don't attempt to deep fry meats in the microwave oven. The fat gets dangerously hot very quickly in the microwave oven. It could seriously burn you or start on fire.

Pizza, meat pies or any other recipes cooking meat in a crust don't turn out well. The crust doesn't brown or crisp; sometimes it becomes very soggy. However, DO use your microwave oven to reheat these items. Remember to place them on a paper towel.

FLAVOUR AND COLOUR ENHANCEMENTS

- To achieve a "roasted brown" look on small cuts of meat, use a browning sauce (Kitchen Bouquet) alone or in combination with flavourings such as honey, paprika, soy sauce, or teriyaki sauce.
- Before cooking, brush meat with BROWNED BUTTER: Place ½ cup (125 mL) of butter or margarine in a microwave safe dish, it should be able to withstand an oven temperature of 400°F (204°C). Microwave on HIGH for 5 to 6 minutes or until deep golden brown. Stir several times during cooking. Skim off the foam and if desired, stir in 1 tsp. (5 mL) fresh snipped herbs or lemon juice.
- Cook meat in a sauce or cover with a glaze or jelly. Meat should be partly cooked before adding any glaze or sauce.
- Use a coating mix like Shake 'N' Bake to coat chops and ribs.
- Add variety to beef roasts and casseroles with caraway, whole peppers, ginger, bay leaf, tarragon, savory, parsley rubbed into roasts or sprinkled on meat dishes.
- Pork can be topped with applesauce, pineapple or orange glaze. It is tasty when rubbed with garlic or herbs such as rosemary, thyme, parsley, sage, caraway, cumin, fennel, bay leaf. Stud ham or pork roasts with whole cloves.
- Veal can be cooked covered with orange marmalade or currant jelly and/ or seasoned with rosemary, paprika, basil, sage, parsley or bay leaf. Break apart star aniseed and press into veal roast for decoration as well as flavour.

1. Beef Sub Napolitana, page 42.
2. Cheddar Cheese Soup, page 53.
3. Apple Crisp, page 205.

- All lamb is tender but a marinade of lemon juice or tomato can add delicious flavour. It can be rubbed with garlic or herbs such as rosemary, thyme, basil, coriander, marjoram (this is the herb that gives that distinct flavour to Greek lamb dishes) or tarragon.

UTENSILS & COVERS

Meat should be cooked in glass or microwave safe dishes that can withstand conventional oven temperatures up to 400°F (204°C). You may already have glass baking dishes or casserole dishes that will work very well. Pieces of meat, such as chops and patties, should be arranged in a circle or in a round dish. Place thicker, meatier portions of meat towards the outside of the dish and thinner, bony portions towards the centre. Casseroles cook best in round or oval shaped shallow baking dishes that have straight sides. A microwave safe tube pan works very well for meat loaves and casseroles that cannot be stirred.

MEAT RACK

For best results, elevate meat on a microwave safe rack so that it does not sit in its juices during cooking time. This will help achieve uniform cooking results on roasts and it also allows the meat to brown and crisp more than it would if it sat in the drippings. There are a variety of meat or bacon racks on the market but there are two styles I find are particularly versatile. A small rectangular roasting rack fits inside an 8 x 12-inch (20 x 33-cm) baking dish which allows you to use dishes you already own. Anchor Hocking makes a round shaped bacon rack with a groove around the outside to catch meat drippings; when flipped over this dish can also double as a baking sheet. Both of these styles of meat rack provide maximum versatility for a small price and take up very little storage space. Of course, if you do not own a meat rack, you can set a roast on an overturned saucer in a casserole dish.

COVERS

Meat is usually cooked covered to keep in the spatters. The cover you use is determined by the meat dish you are cooking and the results you desire. Tender meats that are well marbled can be cooked covered by wax paper or paper towel which retard spatters without keeping in moisture. This allows the meat to form a crisper exterior. Less tender meats, meats with little marbling or meats cooked in sauce should be covered with plastic wrap or a glass lid. Pork should be cooked covered with plastic wrap or a glass lid. Pot roasts and picnic shoulder roasts or hams also cook very well in roasting bags. Remember to pierce the bag and use a rubber band in place of the metal twist tie.

SHIELDING

Pieces of aluminum foil can be used to cover parts of a large cut of meat that would be prone to overcooking. This is not always necessary because people differ in their preferences, therefore, an unevenly cooked roast, with very well done, almost burnt parts as well as an almost rare centre may satisfy everyone's tastes in a particular group.

The two ends of a large rolled type of roast, can be shielded for the first half of cooking time which would allow the centre to cook. An uneven shaped roast with one thick end and one thin end will cook evenly if the thin end is shielded with foil for the first ⅔ of cooking time. If a roast has a large bone or thick layer of fat on the outside, the meat close to it will cook faster than the rest of the roast. If this is undesirable, the bone or fat can be covered with foil for two-thirds of the cooking time.

BROWNING TRAYS

Small cuts of meat can be cooked on a browning tray. Browning trays are "microwave frying pans". When preheated in the microwave oven they become hot and sear the food. You may cook the meat completely on the browning tray or sear it on the browning tray before adding to a casserole or sauce. They are particularly useful for heating precooked convenience foods like frozen pizza or breaded cutlets.

TEMPERATURE PROBLEM

A temperature probe can be helpful in cooking roasts to a desired temperature. If your microwave oven comes equipped with a temperature probe, insert it as close to the centre of the meat as possible. It works best when inserted at least 3 inches (6 cm) into the food so it may be necessary to insert it from the side of the meat rather than the top. The tip of the probe should not be touching a bone or a large piece of fat. Bone and fat become hot faster than the meat does and having the probe against either of these will cause the oven to shut off before the meat is cooked. Once the probe is properly positioned in the meat, set the microwave oven to cook by temperature according to the manufacturer's instructions.

MEAT THERMOMETER

Microwave safe meat thermometers are available, however, they are not necessary. A standard meat thermometer can be inserted into the meat *after* it is removed from the microwave oven to check the temperature. Allow 15 to 20 minutes of standing time before checking the temperature. If the meat is not done, remove the meat thermometer before returning the meat to the microwave oven.

HOW TO KNOW WHEN MEAT IS DONE

The best way to judge whether or not a large piece of meat, like a roast, is done is to check its internal temperature. It should be removed from the microwave oven when it is 10 to 20 degrees lower than the desired finished temperature because the temperature will rise by that much during standing time. Meat should be covered with a "tent" of aluminum foil, shiny side in, to keep the heat in the roast during standing time. The following guide will help you to take the meat out of the microwave oven at the right time according to the desired doneness:

RARE: Remove roast at 120°F (49°C). Internal temperature will rise to 140°F (60°C).

MEDIUM: Remove roast at 125°F to 135°F (52-57°C). Internal temperature will rise to 145°F to 150°F (63-65°C) during standing time.

WELL: Remove roast at 150°F to 165°F (65-73°C). Internal temperature rises to 160°F to 170°F (71-76°C) during standing time. The leaner the meat, the less the temperature rises during standing time.

Note: The temperatures above apply to beef, veal, lamb and pork. Veal and pork are both normally served well done. Research has shown that cooking pork to these temperatures is safe.

Large cuts of meat are brown on the outside when done. Small cuts of meat look greyish on the outside. Allow 5 minutes of standing time for small cuts of meat and 15 to 20 minutes for large meat dishes before checking for doneness. Well done, tender meats are firm, not yielding to pressure when touched with a finger. Less tender meats will be fork tender, splitting at the fibres when pierced.

After standing time, you can cut into the meat with a knife. Well done meat will feel tender but firm as you cut it. Well done meat runs clear or slightly pink juices when you cut into the centre. If the meat appears dry or does not run any juice, you may have overcooked it.

OVERCOOKED MEAT

It is very easy to overcook meat in the microwave oven if you don't remember the importance of STANDING TIME to microwave cooked foods. For well done meats, especially roast pork or meatloaf, the standing time is especially important, since it is actually part of the cooking process. The meat finishes cooking while standing. Meat is a dense, slow cooking food and so it takes extra time for the heat to conduct to the centre of the meat. Always use the minimum time specified in the recipe and allow 10 to 20 minutes of standing time before judging a meat dish not done. If it still isn't done after standing time, it will be improved by adding more time and reheating. If you check it too soon and give it more time in the microwave, it may overcook during its standing time.

Overcooked meat is dry and tough. It is usually rather crumbly but it could get rock hard if it is a fatty meat. If it turns black or starts to smoke, you have really overdone it! There is no way to rescue it, so be careful!

REHEATING

● Most meat should be reheated on MEDIUM. Casseroles, meats in sauce, ground or processed meats can be reheated on MEDIUM HIGH or HIGH. If you are in doubt, use a lower power level. It is better to sacrifice speed than quality.

● Sliced cooked meat can be reheated in minutes. Microwave on MEDIUM for 30 seconds per ¼ inch (.5 cm) thick slice. If you reheat meat on HIGH it will become tough.

- Spread thin slices evenly over the plate.
- Cover the meat with plastic wrap or wax paper to ensure even heating. If there seems to be more moisture that you like, put a layer of paper towels under the plastic film. The paper will absorb some of the moisture giving the meat a more crisp, dry texture.
- Heat meat just to serving temperature or it will become tough and dry.
- Reheating will not tenderize tough or overdone meat.

MICROWAVE PLUS
COMBINATION MICROWAVE/CONVECTION OVENS

Meats excel on the combination cooking mode of these ovens. Since these ovens vary significantly in their operations, consult the manual that came with your oven for instructions as to how to cook meats with combination cooking, but DO use this feature. Combination meats come out full of flavour, tender and juicy with beautiful crisp brown exteriors.

If you have a combination microwave/convection oven, you could also cook a casserole or meat dish by microwave until it is almost done and then for the last 10 minutes on the convection or broil mode to brown the top.

CONVENTIONAL OVEN

Prepare your favorite casserole recipe in the microwave oven. During the last 10 minutes, preheat your conventional oven to 400°F (204°C). Then sprinkle crumbs or cheese topping on your microwaved casserole and pop it in the oven for 10 to 15 minutes.

THE BROILER

If you like well done meat, you may prefer to partially cook steaks and chops, covered, on MEDIUM in the microwave oven, just until they are slightly pink. Meanwhile preheat the broiler to its highest setting and quickly brown the meat.

THE GRILL OR FRYING PAN

Well done meat often becomes tough and dry when fried to a well done state. Precook steaks and chops, covered, in the microwave on MEDIUM for 3 minutes each and then finish them in the frying pan or on a hot grill for tender, juicy well done meat.

THE BARBECUE

The microwave oven and the barbecue were made for each other. The microwave oven does not heat up the house on hot summer days, and precooking food in the microwave shortens the time you have to stand over a hot barbecue grill.

- Barbecued meat often burns before it is completely cooked, but if you precook it in the microwave oven, the results can be moist, tender and juicy with the barbecued flavour and appearance you love. This combination works especially well for chops and thick steaks you want to cook to well done.

- When barbecuing kebobs, precook the meat cubes in the microwave oven before assembling on skewers with vegetables. This way the meat and the vegetables will be done at the same time.

DEFROSTING MEAT

As meat defrosts, it begins to lose its juices, which can result in tough dry meat when cooked. The microwave oven enables you to defrost meat quickly, immediately before cooking, and retain maximum moisture.

Remove wrapping as soon as possible, it contributes to cooking on the outside.

CONVERTING MEAT RECIPES

- Reduce or eliminate the fat called for in meat recipes. Meat does not stick to the cooking dish so the fat is unnecessary.

- Do not sprinkle salt on meat. Salt dries out and toughens the meat.

- Reduce liquid in most recipes by ¼ to ⅓. Do not reduce the liquid in recipes that call for ingredients like rice, pasta, dried beans or peas. They need all of the liquid to rehydrate.

- Use MEDIUM or LOW power levels to cook most meat recipes. Meats covered with a sturdy sauce such as a tomato based sauce can sometimes be cooked on HIGH. Ground or processed meats can be cooked on HIGH.

CASSEROLES

- If your casserole contains raw vegetables, cut each vegetable into the same size pieces so they will cook evenly.

- Don't top casseroles with cheese. Cheese turns rubbery when cooked for long periods of time.

- Adding crushed tortilla chips, crackers, or dry seasoned bread crumbs, to the top of a casserole is a nice treat.

- Start by cooking those foods that take longest to cook; then add the other ingredients, including leftovers.

- Casserole toppings such as bread crumbs will become soggy if you put them on when assembling the casserole. They are best added after the casserole is done and just heated.

- Best toppings for casseroles are crushed potato or corn chips, croutons, crushed canned onion rings or grated cheese.

FROZEN CASSEROLES

Line your favorite dish with plastic wrap before adding the casserole. Place in the freezer. When the casserole has frozen, lift it out of the dish and put it into a freezer bag. This frees the dish for other uses. When you want to serve it, put the casserole back into the dish to defrost and reheat.

A 4-cup (1 L) casserole with a noodle or cooked rice and meat base will defrost in 6 to 8 minutes. Allow the casserole to stand for 5 to 10 minutes, then heat in the microwave oven for 3 to 4 minutes, rotating the container after 2 minutes. The casserole will be ready from the freezer to table in just 14 to 16 minutes.

ROASTS

CHOOSING ROASTS FOR MICROWAVE COOKING

- Choose boneless roasts with an even shape for easiest even cooking. Bone in roasts and unevenly shaped roasts can be used, but may need a bit more attention. Long thin roasts cook faster than short thick ones.
- Choose roasts that are well marbled with an even fat covering for maximum colour, flavour and tenderness.
- Choose roasts that are at least 3 to 4 lbs. (1.4 to 1.8 kg.). In my opinion, larger roasts develop better colour and flavour when microwave cooked. Larger roasts have more time to brown, and tend to be nicer than conventionally cooked roasts because they do not dry out on the outside during the long cooking time as they do when conventionally roasted.

DEFROSTING ROASTS

Allow 10 to 12 minutes per pound (22 to 25 minutes per kg.) of defrost time for large cuts of meat. Defrosting requires standing time just as cooking does. Allow a roast 15 to 20 minutes of standing time before cooking. Meat is defrosted when a skewer can be smoothly inserted into the centre of the roast.

Leave the roast in its wrapper for the first quarter of defrost time. Then remove wrapper and place the roast on a roast rack. Feel the roast for warm spots and cover these with a small piece of foil. Defrost for second quarter of time or until surface is soft when pressed. Turn the roast over. Let it stand 10 minutes if it is more than 6 lbs. (2.5 kg) or if you have an older microwave oven that does not have cyclic defrost. Defrost for third quarter of time. Shield warm areas with foil. Turn over and drain off any liquid. Let stand for 10 to 20 minutes to complete thawing.

Make sure that the temperature is even throughout the meat before starting to cook it. Remember that microwave energy loses strength every ¾ inch of food penetration so meat that is cold in the center will not cook as rapidly as the outside.

STARTING TEMPERATURE IS IMPORTANT ·

You must allow time for roasts and other large pieces of meat to defrost completely and to equalize the temperature throughout the meat. Remember, the microwave energy decreases rapidly every ¾-inch of food it penetrates, so partially frozen meat or food that is room temperature on the outside and extremely cold on the inside will not cook evenly.

Starting temperatures assumed for all meats are refrigerator temperature because beef shouldn't be allowed to come to room temperature.

ROASTING TIMES FOR MEATS

To seal in juices and get meat hot before roasting, microwave all roasts on HIGH for 3 minutes per pound (1½ min. per kg). Turn them over and continue cooking for times given in the following chart:

MEAT		POWER	MINUTES PER POUND	MINUTES PER KILOGRAM
BEEF — tender cuts like rib and loin roasts	RARE	MEDIUM	7 TO 8	15 TO 18
	MEDIUM	MEDIUM	8½ TO 10	19 TO 22
	WELL	MEDIUM	10 TO 12	22 TO 26
BEEF — chuck rump, flank, brisket		LOW	20 TO 27	40 TO 60
PORK LEG & UNCOOKED HAMS	BONELESS	MEDIUM	10 TO 13	22 TO 30
	BONE-IN	MEDIUM	11 TO 14	30 TO 35
PORK LOIN		MEDIUM	11 TO 13	23 TO 29
PORK SHOULDER		MEDIUM	14 TO 18	35 TO 45
FULLY COOKED HAM	BONELESS	MEDIUM	12 TO 16	26 to 35
	BONE-IN	MEDIUM	10 TO 13	23 TO 32
LAMB	MEDIUM WELL	MEDIUM MEDIUM	8 TO 10 10 TO 13	18 TO 22 22 TO 29

PREPARING TENDER ROASTS FOR MICROWAVE COOKING

Do not sprinkle roasts with salt. It dehydrates and toughens meat fibres. Do sprinkle with other seasonings such as pepper, garlic, herbs or sauces. Roasts can be sprinkled with salt immediately upon removal from the microwave oven. During the standing time the flavour will cook into the meat.

Roasts over 3 lbs. (1.5 kg) brown well without help, but if you like, you can enhance their colour by spreading with Kitchen Bouquet, Worcestershire sauce, powdered gravy mix, bouillon or onion soup mix.

POSITION

You will have a more evenly cooked roast if you elevate the roast on a rack to keep it out of the juices. If you let your meat sit in the juices, the bottom of it "boils" taking a longer time, while the top of your meat roasts.

A thick layer of fat on a roast will cook faster than the rest of the meat, so remember to place the fatty side of your meat either to the bottom of your dish or to the side.

COVERS FOR ROASTS

Cover tender beef and lamb roasts with wax paper to keep it from spattering all over your oven. Plastic wrap and glass lids keep in moisture which is desirable for veal and pork roasts. Veal can also be covered with strips of fat or marmalade.

Small lean roasts with little marbling can be covered with strips of bacon to aid browning, keep in moisture and add flavour.

Shield fatty portions and bones with aluminum foil if you do not wish them to overcook. Shielding both ends of a large rolled roast can also reduce shrinkage.

REARRANGE THE ROAST

Rotate roasts two to three times (depending on its size) during cooking time if your microwave oven does not have a turntable.

It is important to turn the roast over halfway through the cooking time because it cooks more slowly on the bottom than on the top.

The roast will cook more quickly if you drain the juices from beneath it during cooking time. I like to make gravy with the drippings so I leave them under the roast to brown.

STANDING TIME

All roasts require at least 15 to 20 minutes of standing time to complete cooking. Cover the roast with a "tent" of foil, shiny side in, during standing time.

Standing time not only completes cooking, but also allows juices to settle and meat to become firm for better carving.

PREPARING ROASTED MEAT FOR SERVING

Remember to carve roasts across the grain for maximum tenderness.

If roast slices are too rare, microwave slices right on the dinner plate at MEDIUM power until they reach desired doneness. This also works if you need to serve the meat before the roast is done.

LESS TENDER CUTS

Any rapid cooking tends to toughen meat fibres. There are several ways, however, to use your microwave oven with less tender meats and still obtain quick cooking and tenderness. These methods are especially good for round or rump roasts which don't tenderize well in a short cooking time because they have little marbling of fat to break up the long fibres. Other less tender cuts such as chuck, flank and brisket need slow, moist cooking in order to develop rich, homemade flavour and fork tender texture.

HOW TO PREPARE LESS TENDER CUTS FOR MICROWAVE COOKING:

- Use your favorite marinade or commercial tenderizer for at least an hour and preferably longer.
- Pierce meat deeply with a long pronged fork to allow moisture to penetrate to the interior and tenderize the meat throughout.
- Dredge meat in flour if you like, but don't brown it before cooking.
- Don't sprinkle the meat with salt, add salt to the liquid instead.
- Add a tenderizer, such as tomatoes, oil and spices when cooking less tender meats.
- Add only as much water as needed for gravy — about ½ cup (125 mL). Less added liquid is needed than conventional cooking because less evaporation takes place.

UTENSILS & COVERS TO USE WHEN ROASTING LESS TENDER MEATS

Less tender meats should be cooked in liquid and covered with plastic wrap or a glass lid to keep in the moisture. Cooking bags work well — remember to fasten with string or rubber band rather than the metal twist tie included in the package.

COOK LESS TENDER MEATS SLOWLY

The slower you cook it the better the finished product. For best results cook less tender roasts at MEDIUM LOW or LOW if you have time. If you are in a hurry, to save a little time, you could bring the liquid to boiling on HIGH and then continue cooking at the lower temperature until the meat is done. If your microwave oven does not have these lower settings, DEFROST can be used instead.

ROASTS NEED TO BE REARRANGED FOR EVEN COOKING

If your microwave oven does not have a turntable, the roast should be rotated two or three times during cooking time.

Halfway through cooking time, turn roast over and add vegetables. Vegetables add an extra 5 to 10 minutes per pound (.5 kg) of cooking time. Vegetables should be cut in small uniform pieces — aproximately 1 inch (2 cm) lengths.

STANDING TIME IS ESSENTIAL

Standing time completes the cooking and tenderizing, allows flavours to blend and gives the juices time to settle which makes carving easier. Allow 15 to 20 minutes of standing time for roasts.

STEAKS & CHOPS
DEFROSTING STEAK & CHOPS

Defrosting time for steaks and chops depends on the thickness of the pieces as well as how many pounds of meat you are defrosting at once.

Allow 8 to 10 minutes per pound (.5 kg) for thin steaks and chops and 12 to 14 min per pound (.5 kg) for thick ones.

Separate if possible. Defrost a package of steaks or chops for half the time then turn over and defrost for remaining time. Let stand 10 minutes or until meat can be pierced with a fork.

Barbecue extra steak and chops to freeze for later. Slightly undercook them. Wrap and freeze to serve during winter. DEFROST them for 5 to 7 minutes per lb. (11 - 15 min/kg). Reheat on MEDIUM for 5 to 7 minutes per pound (11 - 15 min/kg). Let them stand to finish. Cook them on a meat rack to keep them out of the juices so it won't lose the crisp outside. Turn over halfway through.

COOKING STEAKS & CHOPS IN THE MICROWAVE OVEN

Tender cuts don't have the same flavour and colour of grilled steaks because they cook too fast to brown. However, they can be brushed with sauce or seasonings which not only add colour, but also flavour.

Less tender cuts, such as round steaks need to be cooked slowly with moisture and turn out very similar to conventionally cooked meat in much less time. Their flavour is usually much better.

To prevent steaks and chops from curling, slash fat at one inch intervals around edges before cooking.

SMALL CUTS — CUBES, STRIPS AND LIVER

- **DEFROSTING:** Allow 10 to 12 minutes per pound (.5 kg) defrost time. Defrost for half time, separate pieces and spread out on a plate or casserole and defrost for remaining time or until surface is soft. Let stand 5 to 10 minutes or until they can be pierced with a fork.

- Choose chuck for stew meat — it is better marbled than the round that is usually sold as stew meat and hence more tender — it is often less expensive too.

- Pork and lamb are tender so no extra cooking needed however, beef needs extra simmer time.

- Use bamboo skewers instead of metal skewers for Kebobs. Meat should be precooked before assembling on skewers with vegetables.

GROUND MEAT
DEFROSTING GROUND MEAT

- Ground meat defrosts quickly, usually 5 to 6 minutes per pound (.5 kg). To avoid cooked spots while defrosting, turn meat over and around after 3 ½ minutes and remove any defrosted portion.

- Super quick method (but you have to stay with it): Microwave on HIGH for a minute at a time. Scrape off any thawed portions into a bowl after each minute. Total defrost time is 2 to 3 minutes per pound (.5 kg).

HINTS FOR GROUND MEAT

- Ground meat can be microwaved on HIGH.

- Brown ground beef in a dishwasher safe or microwave safe colander set in a bowl. The juices drip into the bowl. It is important to stir while browning to break up pieces and distribute heat.

- To dress up a meat loaf try some of these simple suggestions: Spread chili sauce, barbecue sauce, pizza sauce, a can of tomato or cream of mushroom soup over the top of the meat after removing from the microwave oven. Or, sprinkle with Parmesan cheese or arrange cheese wedges over the top of the hot meat loaf and let the cheese melt.

- Increase meatloaf filler by ¼ cup (50 mL) for 1½ lbs. (.8 kg) of raw meat and reduce liquid by half because microwave cooking renders more fat from meatloaf.

- Cook meatloaf in a tube pan rather than a loaf pan.

- Meatballs, meatloaves and patties need at least 1 egg to hold them together.

- Microwave meatballs on MEDIUM in sauce to give meatballs time to absorb the sauce's flavour.

PORK AND HAM ROASTS

Check pork in several places with meat thermometer to make sure that it has reached an internal temperature of 170°F (36°C) before serving

Standing time is important — wrap roast in foil during this time to be sure it maintains its internal temperature.

If you are concerned about ensuring very well done pork, allow it to stand on the WARM or hold setting for 30 minutes.

COOKING HAM IN THE MICROWAVE

Ham is a natural choice when serving a crowd. It provides plenty of food with no waste. You can make several meals with the leftovers, and soup with the bone.

Choose a ham weighing less than 5 lbs. (2 kg). Large hams are best cut in half to allow better heat penetration although they can still be cooked together. Muscle in large hams may separate, while the outside will dry before the interior cooks.

Ready to eat hams need only to be heated through to serving temperature — (130°F or 55°C — the temperature will rise during standing time) while cured and smoked hams should be fully cooked (165°F or 73°C which will rise during standing time).

Cover the cut surface of hams with plastic wrap.

The narrow end should be shielded with aluminum foil for half of the cooking time.

Turn ham over halfway through cooking time to ensure even cooking.

Fat layer and skin should be removed near or at the end of cooking time.

Sauce or glaze should be added near end of cooking time — after the skin and fat have been removed.

HAM SLICES & STEAKS

- ¾-inch (2 cm) thick slices cook for 10 to 12 minutes per pound (22 to 30 minutes per kg) for fully cooked, ready to eat ham; or 12 - 13 min. per pound (30 to 33 minutes per kg) for cured and smoked ham.
- ¼ inch (.5 cm) slice will take 7 to 10 minutes per pound (18 to 26 per kg) if fully cooked or 11 to 13 per pound (23 - 30 per kg) for cured and smoked slices.
- Slash around edges at one inch intervals to prevent curling.
- Save time when microwaving a casserole like scalloped potatoes or rice to serve with ham slices by placing ham on top of casserole food during cooking time.

SAUSAGE, WIENERS & BACON

Sausage, wieners and bacon are quick, tender with no mess when cooked in the microwave oven.

They cook best when set on a rack to keep them out of drippings. They should be cooked covered with paper towel to absorb spatters. They can also be cooked on a paper towel lined glass plate.

Bacon slices can be microwaved on HIGH for 1 minute per slice - 45 seconds each when doing six or more at a time.

To separate stuck-together bacon slices, just heat the refrigerated package on HIGH for 15 to 30 seconds. This softens the bacon enough so you can slide a spatula between the slices.

Remember to poke sausages and wieners with a fork in several places before cooking.

For even cooking rearrange and turn over sausages and wieners halfway through cooking time.

Sausage Links:
2-4 links on HIGH for 1½-3 minutes.
6-8 links on HIGH for 3-6 minutes.

Wieners:
on HIGH for 20-30 seconds each.

4 take 1½ to 2 minutes.

6 take 2½-3 minutes

A wiener in a bun, wrapped in paper towel takes 45 seconds to 1 minute.

PEPPER STEAK

A treat for the eyes as well as the palate, pictured on the cover.

1 lb.	round steak, ½-inch (1 cm) thick	500 g
1 tbsp.	paprika	15 mL
2 tbsp.	butter	30 mL
1 cup	sliced green onion, tops included	250 mL
2	green peppers	2
2	large tomatoes	2
2	cloves garlic, minced	2
1 cup	beef broth	250 mL
2 tbsp.	cornstarch	30 mL
¼ cup	soy sauce	60 mL

1. Pound steak to ¼-inch (.5 cm) thickness. Cut into ¼-inch (.5 cm) wide strips. Sprinkle meat with paprika and allow to stand while preparing vegetables: slice green onions and tops, cut green peppers in strips and tomatoes into eighths.

2. Place butter in a shallow 2-qt. (2 L) casserole dish. Microwave on HIGH for 30 seconds. Add meat and microwave on HIGH for 5 to 6 minutes or until no longer pink. Stir twice during cooking time.

3. Add garlic and broth. Cover and microwave on MEDIUM for 8 to 10 minutes.

4. Add onion and green pepper. Microwave on HIGH for 2½ minutes.

5. Mix together soy sauce and cornstarch. Stir into meat mixture and microwave on HIGH for 3 to 4 minutes, until thickened.

6. Add tomatoes and microwave on HIGH for 1 minute. Serve over rice.

Your Time: _____

BEEF STROGANOFF

Marvelous flavour achieved with very little time and effort.

1 lb.	sirloin OR round steak, ½-inch (1 cm) thick	500	g
2 tbsp.	flour	30	mL
1 tsp.	salt	5	mL
¼ tsp.	pepper	1	mL
2 tbsp.	butter OR margarine	30	mL
¼ cup	finely chopped onion	60	mL
1	clove garlic, minced	1	
1-10 oz.	can mushroom soup	284	mL
1 cup	sliced fresh mushrooms OR 1-10 oz. (284 mL) can sliced mushrooms	250	mL
1 cup	sour cream	250	mL

1. Trim excess fat from meat. Combine flour, salt and pepper. Pound into both sides of meat. Cut beef into thin strips.

2. Place butter in 2-qt. (2 L) casserole dish. Microwave on HIGH for 30 seconds. Add meat. Microwave on HIGH for 5 to 6 minutes, or until meat is no longer pink.

3. Stir in onion, garlic and mushrooms (If you are using canned mushrooms, add them with the soup in step 4). Microwave on HIGH for 2 to 3 minutes or until tender.

4. Stir in soup. Microwave on MEDIUM for 10 to 15 minutes or until meat is tender.

5. Stir in sour cream. Microwave on MEDIUM for 1 minute.

Your Time: _____

SWISS STEAK

A family favourite made in half the time with half the effort.

1½ lbs.	round steak	750	g
3	carrots, sliced diagonally	3	
3	stalks celery, sliced diagonally	3	
1	medium onion, sliced	1	
1-19 oz.	can tomatoes	540	mL
1 tbsp.	Worcestershire sauce	15	mL
½ tsp.	oregano	2	mL
¼ tsp.	garlic powder	1	mL
1½ tbsp.	cornstarch	25	mL
1½ tbsp.	cold water	25	mL

1. Cut round steak into aproximately 6 pieces. Pound each to ¼-inch (.5 cm) thickness. Place in a shallow 2½-qt. (2.5 L) casserole dish. Microwave, covered, on HIGH for 6 to 8 minutes. Turn over halfway through cooking time.

2. Layer carrots, celery and onion over meat.

3. Break up tomatoes. Mix Worcestershire sauce, oregano, garlic powder into tomatoes and pour over steak.

4. Microwave, covered, on HIGH for 4 to 5 minutes. Stir. Microwave, covered, on MEDIUM for 20 to 25 minutes.

5. Combine cornstarch and water. Stir into sauce. Microwave on HIGH for 3 to 4 minutes, or until thickened. Stir 2 or 3 times during cooking time.

Your Time: _____

AUNT EVA'S CORDON BLEU ROLLS

Elegance with ease.

1 lb.	minute steaks OR veal cutlets	500 g
¼ lb.	thinly sliced ham	125 g
¼ lb.	Swiss cheese	125 g
¼ cup	milk	60 mL
1	egg	1
	salt & pepper to taste	
1-10 oz.	can mushroom soup	284 mL
¼ cup	beef broth	60 mL
1 cup	dry bread crumbs OR cornflake crumbs	250 mL

1. Cut each steak or cutlet into 2-inch (4 cm) wide strips. Cut ham slices and cheese into 2-inch (4 cm) wide strips. On each strip of steak place a strip of ham and a strip of cheese. Roll up. Secure with wooden toothpicks.

2. Combine milk, egg, salt and pepper in a small bowl. Dip each roll in egg mixture and then coat with crumbs. Place in a shallow 2-qt. (2 L) casserole dish.

3. Combine mushroom soup and broth or wine. Pour over rolls. Microwave on MEDIUM for 15 to 20 minutes.

* **Yield:** 6 rolls

Your Time: _____

GRAVY

2 tbsp.	cornstarch	30 mL
½ cup	water	125 mL
½ cup	roast drippings	125 mL
	salt & pepper to taste	

1. Combine cornstarch and water.

2. Microwave drippings on HIGH for 30 seconds or until hot. Slowly stir in the cornstarch and water.

3. Microwave on HIGH for 30 seconds at a time until thickened. Stir well after each 30 seconds. It should take 1 to 2 minutes depending on how hot your drippings were when you started.

4. Stir in salt and pepper.

Your Time: _____

VEAL PARMIGIANA

Subtle flavours blend together to make a memorable dish.

2	eggs, beaten	2	
¼ cup	milk	60	mL
	salt & pepper to taste		
½ cup	bread crumbs	125	mL
2 tbsp.	grated Parmesan cheese	30	mL
4	veal cutlets, pounded thin	4	
1 tbsp.	oil	15	mL
1 cup	shredded mozzarella cheese	250	mL
1 tsp.	oregano	5	mL
2 cups	tomato sauce	500	mL
¼ cup	grated Parmesan cheese	60	mL

1. Preheat browning tray on HIGH for 5 minutes.

2. Meanwhile, in a small bowl, mix together eggs, milk, salt and pepper. On a plate, combine bread crumbs and 2 tbsp. (30 mL) Parmesan cheese. Dip veal cutlets in egg mixture and then coat with crumbs.

3. Grease browning tray with oil and place veal cutlets on tray. Microwave on HIGH for 5 minutes. Turn cutlets over and microwave on HIGH for another 5 minutes.

4. Place cutlets in a shallow 2-qt. (2 L) casserole dish. Cover with mozzarella cheese. Mix oregano into tomato sauce and pour over cutlets and cheese. Sprinkle with ¼ cup (60 mL) Parmesan cheese. Cover and microwave on MEDIUM for 15 to 25 minutes, until veal is tender.

TIP: If you don't have a browning tray for steps 1 and 3; you can brown the cutlets in a frying pan on the stove.

Your Time: _____

SMOTHERED LIVER

So tender and flavourful you'll be smothered with compliments - even from dedicated "liver haters".

4	bacon slices	4
1 lb.	beef liver, sliced	500 g
1 tbsp.	flour	15 mL
1	medium onion, sliced	1
1-7½ oz.	can tomato sauce OR 1-10 oz. (284 mL) can tomato soup	213 mL

1. Lay bacon strips in shallow 2-qt. (2 L) casserole dish. Cover with paper towel and microwave on HIGH for 5 to 6 minutes.

2. Crumble bacon and set aside. Coat liver with flour. Set liver in bacon drippings, turn liver pieces over so both sides are coated with drippings. Microwave on HIGH for 2 to 3 minutes. Turn liver over.

3. Add sliced onion and bacon. Pour tomato sauce over top. Cover and microwave on MEDIUM for 10 to 12 minutes or until liver is no longer pink.

SERVING SUGGESTION: This tastes good served over rice.

TIP: My mother, a "liver hater", says that if you soak the liver in milk (just enough to cover it) it will take away that "liver" taste.

Your Time: _____

MEATLOAF

A meatloaf like no other - moist and full of flavour.

1 lb.	lean ground beef	500 g
1 cup	bread crumbs	250 mL
1	egg	1
1	medium onion, chopped	1
1-8 oz.	can tomato sauce	213 mL
1-5 oz.	can evaporated milk	160 mL
	salt & pepper to taste	

1. Mix together all ingredients. Pat into an eight-cup (2 L) tube pan.

2. Microwave on HIGH for 15 to 17 minutes.

SERVING SUGGESTION: If you want to dress this meatloaf up, unmold it on a serving platter and fill the centre with Rice Pilaf (page 134).

VARIATION:

MEATLOAF SURPRISE: Spoon half of the mixture into the tube pan. Top with cheese or bacon slices, sausages or vegetables (use your imagination or clean out your fridge). Add remaining meatloaf mixture. This addition may add 1 to 2 minutes of cooking time to the meatloaf.

Your Time: _____

MEATBALLS

These flavourful meatballs disappear fast.

1 lb.	ground beef OR pork	500	g
1	small onion, finely chopped	1	
⅓ cup	dry bread crumbs	75	mL
1	egg	1	
1 tsp.	salt	5	mL
⅛ tsp.	pepper	.5	mL

1. Combine all ingredients in a large mixing bowl. Mix well. Form into balls, about 1½ inches (3 cm) in diameter. Arrange in a 9 X 2-inch (22 x 4 cm) round dish or on a meat rack.

2. Cover with wax paper. Microwave on HIGH for 4 to 6 minutes, or until meat is cooked. Drain.

3. Serve with sauce of your choice. Some recipes are given on pages 86, 93, 96.

TIP: If you make bread crumbs using the crusts of whole wheat bread, it will give a browner appearance to the meatballs.

Your Time: _____

CHINELO'S SPAGHETTI SAUCE

A tangy sauce

1 lb.	lean ground beef	500 g
1	medium onion, chopped	1
1 cup	sliced mushrooms	250 mL
3	stalks celery, chopped	3
1-19 oz.	can tomatoes	540 mL
1 7½ oz.	can tomato sauce	213 mL
3 tbsp.	vinegar	45 mL
½ tsp.	paprika	2 mL
1 tsp.	Italian seasoning	5 mL
1 tsp.	dry oregano leaves	5 mL
	salt & pepper to taste	

1. Crumble beef into a 3-qt. (3 L) casserole dish. Microwave on HIGH for 4 to 6 minutes. Stir 2 or 3 times during cooking. Drain.

2. Add onion, mushrooms and celery. Cover and microwave on HIGH for 5 minutes. Stir once or twice during cooking.

3. Add remaining ingredients. Cover and microwave on HIGH for 15 minutes. Stir several times during cooking time.

Your Time: _____

SPAGHETTI SAUCE

Fast preparation with excellent results.

1-14 oz.	can tomato sauce OR 1-19 oz. (540 mL) can tomatoes	398 mL
1	small onion, chopped	1
1	clove garlic, minced OR ¼ tsp. (1 mL) garlic powder	1
	salt & pepper to taste	
¼ tsp.	dry basil leaves	1 mL
¼ tsp.	dry oregano leaves	1 mL
1 tsp.	Italian seasoning	5 mL

1. In a 1½-qt. (1.5 L) casserole dish combine above ingredients and microwave, covered, on HIGH for 5 minutes. Stir.

2. Microwave, covered on MEDIUM-LOW for 10 to 15 minutes. Stir occasionally during cooking. Serve over spaghetti or with meatballs.

MEATSAUCE: Microwave 1 lb. (500 g) of ground beef, crumbled, on HIGH for 4 to 6 minutes. Drain. Continue with step 1.

Your Time: _____

STUFFED PEPPERS

An even more attractive dish when microwaved - peppers retain their bright green colour.

1 lb.	lean ground beef	500	g
1	medium onion, chopped	1	
6	green peppers	6	
2	stalks celery, chopped	2	
1-7½ oz.	can tomato sauce OR 1-10 oz. (284 mL)	213	mL
	can tomato soup		
1 cup	cooked rice	250	mL
	salt & pepper to taste		

1. Combine ground beef and onion in a 2-qt. (2 L) casserole dish. Microwave on HIGH for 6 to 8 minutes, or until beef is no longer pink. Stir halfway through cooking time. Drain.

2. Meanwhile, cut off tops of each green pepper and hollow out the shells.

3. Combine ground beef with remaining ingredients and fill peppers. Place peppers in a 2-qt. (2 L) casserole dish. Cover and microwave on MEDIUM-HIGH for 12 to 15 minutes, or until filling is heated through.

SIMMERED GREEN PEPPERS: Place filled peppers in a 2 qt. (2 L) casserole dish. Pour a 14-oz. (398 mL) tin of tomato sauce over all. Cover and microwave on MEDIUM-LOW for 30 minutes.

Your Time: _____

MOM'S CABBAGE ROLLS

The secret to the unique flavour of these cabbage rolls is the creamy tomato sauce they are cooked in.

1	small head cabbage	1
½ cup	water	125 mL
1 lb.	ground beef	500 g
1	egg	1
	Salt & pepper to taste	
1 cup	cooked rice	250 mL
1-7½ oz.	can tomato sauce	213 mL
1-10 oz.	can tomato soup	284 mL
1-5 oz.	can evaporated milk	160 mL
1	large onion	1

1. Core the cabbage. Place, core side up, in a casserole dish. Add water and cover with plastic wrap, leaving a small vent to allow steam to escape. Microwave on HIGH for approximately 10 minutes, until cabbage leaves are soft enough to roll. If it is not soft all the way through, let it stand, covered with the plastic for another 5 to 10 minutes. Drain and allow to cool slightly. I usually peel back as many of the outer leaves as possible to speed up the cooling.

2. Combine ground beef, egg, salt & pepper and cooked rice.

3. Peel leaves from cabbage head one at a time. On each leaf place a heaping tablespoon of the meat mixture. Fold the sides of each leaf over the meat. Starting at the stem end, roll up each leaf. Set each cabbage roll in a shallow 4-qt. (4 L) casserole dish.

4. Combine, tomato sauce, tomato soup and evaporated milk. Pour over cabbage rolls. Slice onion on top. Microwave on MEDIUM-HIGH for 25 to 30 minutes.

TIP: To speed the cooling of the cooked cabbage head, put ice cubes in the hollow left by the core and between some of the cabbage leaves.

To speed this recipe up a bit, you may cook and drain the ground beef for 4 to 6 minutes before mixing it with the rice etc. in step 2.

Your Time: _____

AUNT EDNA'S PORCUPINES

So tasty your family will ask for more.

1 lb.	lean ground beef	500	g
½ cup	uncooked rice	125	mL
1	small onion, chopped	1	
1	egg	1	
	salt, pepper and paprika to taste		
1½ cups	chopped cabbage OR sauerkraut	375	mL
2½ cups	tomato juice	625	mL
½ cup	ketchup	125	mL

1. Mix together beef, rice, onion, egg, salt, pepper and paprika. Form into meatballs.

2. Place cabbage or sauerkraut in the bottom of a 3-qt. (3 L) casserole dish. Place meatballs on top.

3. Mix together tomato juice and ketchup. Pour over meatballs and cabbage. Cover and microwave on HIGH for 10 minutes. Let stand for 10 minutes.

4. Microwave on HIGH for 15 to 20 minutes.

TIP: Save time by using 1 cup (250 mL) of cooked rice and eliminating the 10 minutes of cooking time and the 10 minutes of standing time in step 3.

Save time by microwaving tomato juice and ketchup in a glass measuring cup on HIGH for 3 minutes before adding it in step 3. This reduces the time in step 4 to 10 to 12 minutes.

Your Time: _____

GLAZED BAKED HAM

Something special for the holidays.

3 lb.	**ready to eat ham**	**2 kg**
1-14 oz.	**can pineapple slices (save the juice)**	**398 mL**
	whole cloves	
½ cup	**brown sugar**	**125 mL**
	Dash of nutmeg	
1 tbsp.	**cornstarch**	**15 mL**

1. Place ham fat side down on a roasting rack set in a glass baking dish.

2. Microwave on MEDIUM-HIGH for 12 minutes.

3. Turn ham over. Slash through fatty part of ham at 1-inch (2 cm) intervals, so as to make a diamond checkered pattern on the ham. Arrange pineapple slices over ham using cloves and wooden toothpicks to hold slices in place.

4. In a 2-cup (500 mL) glass measure, mix juice from pineapple with brown sugar, nutmeg and cornstarch. Microwave on HIGH for 1 to 2 minutes, until clear. Spoon over ham.

5. Microwave, uncovered, on MEDIUM for 6 to 7 minutes or until heated through.

VARIATION: *ORANGE GLAZED HAM:* Prepare as above, substituting 1 sliced orange for pineapple rings; 1 cup (250 mL) orange juice for pineapple juice and ginger for nutmeg.

TIP: If your oven has a temperature probe, heat to an internal temperature of 170°F (76°C).

Your Time: _____

HAM STEAK & PINEAPPLE

An easy dressup for a ham steak.

1½-inch	thick ham steak	3	cm
2 tbsp.	brown sugar	30	mL
1 tbsp.	pineapple juice	15	mL
1	pineapple slice	1	

1. Place ham steak on a glass plate.

2. Mix together brown sugar and pineapple juice. Spoon over ham. Set pineapple slice on top of ham.

3. Microwave on MEDIUM-HIGH for 4 to 6 minutes.

Your Time: _____

PORK CHOPS IN MUSHROOM SAUCE

Quick preparation with tasty results.

5 to 6	pork chops	5 to 6	
	salt & pepper to taste		
1-10 oz.	can mushroom soup	284	mL

1. Trim fat from pork chops. Sprinkle with salt and pepper. Arrange pork chops in 8 x 12-inch (1.5 L) glass baking dish. Cover with mushroom soup.

2. Cover with wax paper. Microwave on MEDIUM-HIGH for 20 to 25 minutes or until chops are tender. Turn over and rearrange pork chops halfway through cooking time.

Your Time: _____

BARBECUE PORK STEAKS

Delicious steaks in a peppery sauce.

4	½-inch (1 cm) thick pork shoulder steaks	4
1	large onion, sliced	1
1	large green pepper, sliced	1
2	tomatoes, sliced	2
1	recipe Barbecue Sauce, page 96	1
	dash of Tabasco sauce (optional)	

1. Trim fat from steaks. If desired, brown them on a preheated browning tray: Preheat empty browning tray on HIGH for 5 minutes. Spray with Pam. Place steaks on hot tray. Microwave on HIGH for 3 minutes. Turn over steaks and microwave on HIGH for another 3 minutes.

2. Place pork steaks in a shallow 2-qt. (2 L) casserole dish. Slice vegetables over steaks. Stir Tabasco sauce into Barbecue Sauce and pour sauce over steaks.

3. Cover and microwave on MEDIUM-LOW for 30 minutes or until steaks are tender.

TIP: The browning in step 1 is simply to add a "browned flavour" to the dish. If you do not have a browning tray or do not miss the "browned flavour", you can omit step 1 and add an extra 10 minutes cooking time to step 3.

Your Time: _____

PORK RIBS

It takes just 1 hour in the microwave to get tender, slow-cooked ribs that would take several hours of conventional cooking.

2 lbs.	**pork ribs**	
3 cups	**water**	**750 mL**
1	**recipe of Sweet and Sour Sauce below OR Barbecue Sauce (p 96)**	

1. Place ribs in a glass 8 x 12-inch (1.5 L) baking dish. Cover with water. Microwave on HIGH for 7 minutes and then on MEDIUM for 20 minutes. Rearrange ribs halfway through cooking time.

2. Drain water from ribs. Pour sauce over ribs and microwave on MEDIUM for 20 to 25 minutes.

Your Time: _____

SWEET & SOUR SAUCE

A versatile sauce recipe. I make it with or without the tomato sauce depending on the meal and my mood.

1-14 oz.	**can pineapple chunks**	**398 mL**
1 cup	**water**	**250 mL**
1-7 oz.	**can tomato sauce (optional)**	**213 mL**
2 tbsp.	**soy sauce**	**30 mL**
¼ cup	**brown sugar**	**60 mL**
1 tbsp.	**cornstarch mixed with 1 tbsp. water**	**15 mL**

1. Drain juice from pineapple chunks into a 4-cup (1 L) glass measure. Set chunks aside. Mix water, tomato sauce, soy sauce and brown sugar together with pineapple juice. Microwave on HIGH for 2 to 3 minutes, until boiling.

2. Stir in cornstarch mixture. Microwave on HIGH for 1 to 2 minutes, or until thickened. Stir 2 or 3 times to prevent lumps.

3. Add pineapple chunks and serve over meat - ribs, meatballs.

Your Time: _____

MOUSSAKA

Adapted from a traditional Greek recipe.

Meat Sauce:

1½ lbs.	ground lamb or beef	750 g
1	medium onion, choppped	1
1	clove garlic, minced	1
½ cup	tomato paste	125 mL
⅛ tsp.	allspice	.5 mL
⅛ tsp.	cinnamon	.5 mL
⅛ tsp.	thyme	.5 mL
⅛ tsp.	sage	.5 mL
¼ tsp.	oregano	1 mL
1½ tbsp.	parsley	25 mL
	salt and pepper to taste	

1. In a 2-qt. (2 L) casserole dish, microwave meat on HIGH for 5 to 7 minutes, uncovered. Stir twice during cooking time. Drain.

2. Add onion and garlic; microwave on HIGH for 2 minutes, covered.

3. Add tomato paste, and spices. Blend well. Set aside.

Vegetables:

1	eggplant, peeled and thinly sliced (or 2 medium zucchini)	1
4	medium potatoes, peeled and thinly sliced	4
2	medium tomatoes, sliced	2

1. To prevent discolouring, place eggplant and potatoes in salt water in a large bowl as they are being sliced. Drain and rinse.

2. In a covered 3-qt. (3 L) casserole dish, microwave eggplant and potato slices on HIGH for 5 minutes. Rearrange and microwave on HIGH for another 5 minutes. Set aside.

Cheese sauce:

¼ cup	butter	60 mL
¼ cup	flour	60 mL
2 cups	milk	500 mL
½ cup	grated Parmesan cheese	125 mL
1½ cup	grated cheddar cheese	325 mL
¼ cup	fine, dry bread crumbs	60 mL
2	eggs (beat well)	2

1. Melt better on HIGH for 45 to 60 seconds. Add flour, blend well.

2. Mix in milk a little at a time. Microwave on MEDIUM-HIGH for 4 minutes. Stir every 30 seconds until it thickens.

3. Mix in cheese and bread crumbs. Microwave on MEDIUM-HIGH for 30 seconds to melt the cheese. Stir.

4. Let cool 5 minutes. Add eggs, blend into mixture well; do not cook again. Sauce should be quite thick.

5. Arrange all ingredients in layers, dividing them equally between two 2-qt. (2 l) casserole dishes. Begin with layer of eggplant and potatoes, then add a layer of meat sauce and tomato slices. Put a small amount of cheese sauce on each layer and repeat, ending with a topping of cheese sauce.

6. Microwave each casserole on MEDIUM-HIGH for 15-20 minutes.

Your Time: _____

MARIANNE'S TANGY LAMB CHOPS

Lamb chops cook smothered in a flavourful vegetable mixture.

2 lbs.	lamb chops	1	kg
⅓ cup	apple juice	75	mL
1	small onion, chopped	1	
½ tsp.	oregano	2	mL
1	clove garlic, minced	1	
½	green pepper, sliced	½	
2	stalks celery, julienne sliced	2	
2	carrots, julienne sliced	2	
1 cup	sliced mushrooms	250	mL
1 tbsp.	lemon juice	15	mL
2	tomatoes, sliced	2	

1. Trim the fat from the lamb chops and place in a shallow 2-qt. (2 L) casserole dish. Cover with wax paper and microwave on HIGH for 10 to 12 minutes. Drain.

2. Add remaining ingredients, except lemon juice and tomatoes. Cover with plastic wrap or glass lid and microwave on HIGH for 12 minutes.

3. Add tomatoes and lemon juice. Cover and microwave on HIGH 2 minutes. Serve over rice.

TIP: You could cook the rice in this casserole. Add 1 cup (250 mL) rice and 2 cups (500 mL) of water between steps 1 and 2. Cover rice and lamb chops with plastic wrap or a glass lid and microwave on HIGH for 10 minutes and let stand for 10 minutes. Then proceed with step 2 but increase the cooking time on HIGH in step 2 from 7 minutes to 15 minutes.

Your Time: _____

LARRY'S BARBECUE SAUCE

This spicy sauce is good with any meat.

1 cup	ketchup	250 mL
1	medium onion, finely chopped	
2	cloves garlic, minced OR 1 tsp. (5 mL) garlic powder	2
1 tsp.	hickory smoke	5 mL
1 tsp.	salt	5 mL
2 tbsp.	Worcestershire sauce	30 mL
½ cup	boiling water	125 mL
¼ cup	brown sugar	60 mL
2 tsp.	dry mustard	10 mL
½ cup	vinegar	125 mL

1. Mix all ingredients together in a 4-cup (1 L) glass measure. Microwave on HIGH for 2 minutes or until boiling.

2. Pour over browned meat (ribs, chops, chicken, meatballs or beef strips). Meat should be spread in a single layer in a shallow 2-qt. (2 L) casserole dish. Microwave on MEDIUM for 20 to 30 minutes or until meat is tender.

VARIATION: This recipe is almost like Larry's Southern mother's sauce except that she adds a hot sauce (like Tabasco Sauce) to hers. Try that if you enjoy the extra spice.

Your Time: _____

MARIANNE'S BARBECUE SAUCE

This sauce adds tangy flavour to meats.

1 cup	ketchup OR tomato paste	250 mL
½ cup	brown sugar	125 mL
1 cup	celery, finely chopped	250 mL
	salt and pepper (to taste)	
1	small onion, finely chopped	1
¼ cup	water	60 mL
¼ cup	vinegar	60 mL

1. Combine ingredients in a 4-cup (1 L) glass measure. Cover with plastic wrap. Microwave on HIGH for 5 minutes. Stir.

2. Microwave on MEDIUM-LOW for 8 to 10 minutes. Stir occasionally during cooking time.

Your Time: _____

1. Curried Rice, page 133.
2. Marianne's Tangy Lamb Chops, page 95.
3. Parsley Buttered Carrots, page 151.
4. Southern Banana Pudding, page 210.

SWEET & SOUR SMOKED SAUSAGE

An attractive, inexpensive dish that's fit for company.

1 lb.	smoked farmer sausage	500	g
1-14 oz.	can pineapple chunks	398	mL
2 tbsp.	cornstarch	30	mL
1	green pepper, cut into 1-inch (2 cm) pieces	1	
1	medium onion, sliced	1	
1 cup	diagonally sliced celery	250	mL
1-19 oz.	can tomatoes	540	mL
1	clove garlic, minced OR ¼ tsp. garlic powder	1	mL
1 tbsp.	brown sugar	15	mL
¼ tsp.	black pepper	1	mL
3 cups	cooked rice	750	mL

1. Slice sausage into ½-inch (1 cm) pieces. Place in a 2-qt. (2 L) casserole dish. Microwave on HIGH for 5 minutes, or until sausage is no longer pink.

2. Drain pineapple chunks. Set fruit aside. Mix liquid from pineapple with cornstarch. Pour over sausage and add remaining ingredients - except pineapple chunks and rice. Microwave on HIGH for 12 to 14 minutes. Stir 2 or 3 times during cooking time.

3. Add pineapple chunks. Microwave on HIGH for 2 minutes or until heated through.

4. Serve over cooked rice.

Your Time: _____

POULTRY

The natural tenderness of poultry makes it an ideal food for the fast cooking of the microwave oven. Chicken illustrates all the advantages of microwave cooking. It is more tender, flavourful and juicy than conventionally roasted poultry. Microwave energy cooks poultry rapidly and it requires very little attention while cooking. Plain microwaved chicken is perfect for salads and casseroles. It remains firm which makes it easy to slice or dice.

⊙━┱ THE KEY TO SUCCESS WITH POULTRY

The shape of poultry is awkward for uniform microwave cooking. The legs and wings stick out from the body of a whole bird, causing them to overcook. Cut-up pieces vary in size, density, and fat content. As a result they all cook at different speeds. The key to even cooking is the way poultry is positioned in the microwave oven.

Chicken pieces should be arranged with large, meaty pieces toward the outside edges of the dish and smaller, bony parts toward the centre. Arrange drumsticks in a round pan like spokes in a wheel, with bone end to centre and meaty portion toward the outside. Chicken pieces should be set skin side down for the first half of cooking and then turned over for the last half. The bony wings and drumsticks on a whole bird should be tied close to the body to keep them from sticking out. They should also be shielded with pieces of aluminum foil.

Poultry should be elevated on a meat rack or an inverted saucer so that it stays out of the juices while cooking. Any parts that sit in the juices will cook slower than the rest. Elevation will also keep the skin crisper.

POULTRY SHOULD BE COVERED DURING COOKING

A cover promotes even cooking of poultry. It also helps retain its natural moisture. Wax paper is the best covering. It helps to hold in the heat and spatters, yet allows the poultry to brown and the skin to crisp. Roasting bags work well, but remember to remove the metal twist tie. Close it with a rubber band or plastic tie. Make several slits in the top of the bag to vent steam.

ENHANCING THE COLOUR & FLAVOUR OF CHICKEN

- Because they cook so quickly, chicken pieces do not get brown and crisp. Unless they are cooked in a sauce, they will be more attractive if brushed with a browning agent or coated with crumbs. Following is a list of the coatings that work best:
- Brush a whole bird with melted butter (not margarine, because margarine does not brown as well as butter) and sprinkle with paprika — ½ tsp. (2 mL) paprika to 2 tbsp. (30 mL) butter.
- Brush pieces or a whole bird with soya sauce. This not only gives brown colour, but also adds salty flavour.

- Brush with a commercial browning sauce like Kitchen Bouquet. If the colour and flavour of this sauce is too strong for your taste, dilute it with melted butter. Commercially prepared Teriyaki sauce also works well; it has a golden colour.
- Coat chicken pieces with Shake & Bake coating mix. If you like it in the conventional oven, you will love Shake & Bake in the microwave. Be sure pieces are set on a meat rack or the coating will become soggy.
- Cook cut up chicken in a sauce. The liquid will help pieces to cook more uniformly. Microwave cooking renders more fat from the chicken so drain before adding the sauce.

BONUS FOR WEIGHT WATCHERS

If you are concerned about calories or cholesterol, skin chicken before cooking, since most of the fat is located directly below the skin. If cooked in a sauce, the flavour will be absorbed by the meat instead of the skin. Skinned chicken pieces may also be brushed with a browning agent or coated with crumbs.

DON'T

Don't deep fry poultry in the microwave oven. The fat becomes dangerously hot.

Don't dredge poultry in flour before cooking. It becomes pasty rather than crusty. For best results add flour to the sauce in which you are cooking the poultry.

Don't sprinkle with salt; it toughens the skin and meat. Soy sauce gives same flavour and colour as well.

Don't microwave extremely large turkeys (over 15 lbs. or 7 kg). They are awkward to handle. Cooking them in the microwave oven saves very little time.

HOW TO KNOW WHEN POULTRY IS DONE

Chicken and turkey are judged done when the leg moves easily in its socket or when the juices are clear and no longer pink. Microwaved poultry meat retains its shape and has a firm texture, so don't overcook it by trying to cook it until it falls apart as does a well-done conventionally cooked bird.

DEFROSTING POULTRY

Chicken pieces and small birds should be defrosted for 10 minutes per pound (500 g). Large whole birds take closer to 15 minutes per pound (500 g). Turn chicken over every 15 minutes during defrosting time. Whole birds will remain icy inside. To finish defrosting, soak or rinse in cold water. If you continue to microwave it, the chicken will begin to cook on the outside. These defrosting steps also apply to other poultry, such as ducks or cornish game hens. Two cornish hens take about the same amount of time as one chicken.

MICROWAVE PLUS

THE BROILER: Cook chicken pieces in the microwave until almost done. Brush with sauce and cook under the broiler until bubbly and browned.

THE BARBECUE: Precooking your chicken in the microwave can keep it from being burned on the barbecue. Instead of black, tough, dry barbecued meat you can have tender, moist chicken with that crisp browned skin and delicious charcoal flavour. Microwave a 3 lb. (1.5 kg) cut up fryer on HIGH for 10 to 12 minutes or a 5 to 6 lb. (3 kg) cut up fryer on HIGH for about 20 minutes. Brush with sauce and place on the barbecue until browned.

THE CONVENTIONAL OVEN: Microwave a whole chicken until almost done. Then set it in a preheated hot oven (375 - 400°F 190 - 200°C) while you cook the rest of the meal in the microwave. During this time (about 20 minutes) the skin will turn brown and you will have all parts of the meal ready at the same time.

THE CONVECTION OVEN: If you have a combination microwave/convection oven, roast whole poultry on the combination mode (follow the manufacturer's instructions because different models of ovens operate quite differently). It will produce the most perfectly browned, tender, juicy poultry imaginable.

THE CROCKPOT: I often precook chicken in the microwave before putting it in the crockpot. This is because many of my favourite slowcook dishes take 12 hours of cooking and I decide to make them 4 to 6 hours before supper. If you have this need, try it. You'll get fall-apart chicken with the same unique slow cooked flavour, but in half the time.

GENERAL HINTS FOR COOKING POULTRY IN THE MICROWAVE

- Pierce the skin of poultry to prevent the fat from popping.
- Line the cavity of a bird with cheesecloth to hold the stuffing. This makes it much easier to remove the stuffing.
- Dice leftover meat into bite-sized pieces. Freeze it for sandwiches, casseroles, salads, or quiche. Save broth in the freezer for soups and sauces.
- Cook up a quick pate with chicken livers. Pierce skins of 1 lb. (500 g) of chicken livers. Place in a covered dish and microwave on MEDIUM for 7 to 8 minutes, or until no longer pink.

WHOLE CHICKEN OR TURKEY

- When cooking whole poultry, small birds are placed breast side up, while turkey is placed breast side down and then turned over halfway through the cooking time.
- If stuffing the bird, weigh it with the stuffing to determine cooking time however, you will find that stuffing does not alter time significantly.
- Poultry cooks on HIGH for 5 to 7 minutes per lb. (500 g) for small birds or cut up pieces and on MEDIUM 9 to 12 minutes per lb. (500 g) for large, whole birds.

- With whole birds like turkey, best results are obtained by reducing the power to a lower setting. Since the bird finishes cooking more slowly, a shorter standing time before carving can be used. Remove the juices from a large bird as they gather beneath it.

CUT UP CHICKEN

With frozen packages of one-of-a-kind pieces, you will need to use your judgement. Bony pieces, such as wings, will take less time than meaty pieces, such as thighs.

STEWING HEN

Microwave in a covered casserole with vegetables and spices. Cover with hot water and microwave on HIGH for 10 to 15 minutes. Turn over pieces, bringing bottom pieces to the top. Cover and microwave on MEDIUM-LOW for 2 to 2 ¼ hours. Rearrange again after 1 hour. Test for doneness with a fork — it should be fork tender. Let it cool in juices, so meat will remove easily from bones.

COOKED POULTRY

- Casseroles need to be microwaved just until heated through.
- Don't wait for leftovers — just microwave parts of the chicken to make the amount of cooked meat the recipe requires — 1 large breast yields 2 cups (500 mL) diced cooked meat.

STUFFED WHOLE ROAST CHICKEN

So moist, even the white meat runs juices.

1. Wash and prepare bird. Fill cavity with your favourite dressing or mine (recipe on next page). Do not use metal skewers to close the cavity, try round wooden toothpicks or bamboo skewers. Use kitchen string to tie legs together.

2. Brush outside of chicken with melted butter. Sprinkle with paprika or a commercial browning agent like Kitchen Bouquet or Microshake.

3. Place chicken, breast up, on a roasting rack in a large casserole dish or 8 x 12-inch (1.5 L) glass baking dish. Cover with wax paper.

4. Microwave on MEDIUM-HIGH for 6 to 8 minutes per pound (13 to 15 minutes per kg) including weight of stuffing. Let stand 10 to 15 minutes to complete cooking. Covering with foil as soon as you remove it from the oven helps to keep it hot.

5. Poultry is judged to be done if the leg moves easily in its socket or when the juices are no longer pink.

TIP: For salt lovers: If you sprinkle the bird with salt, it will get tough so brush it with Soy Sauce instead — you'll get salt flavour and a brown colour!

VARIATION: I often cook my roast chicken for the minimum time per pound in the microwave and finish it off in the conventional oven at 375°F (190°C) for 20 to 25 minutes. If you have a combination microwave/convection oven you will love roast meat done on the combination mode — it gives the same results without the work.

Your Time: _____

POULTRY DRESSING

This mild-flavoured stuffing recipe comes from my mother. When I serve it for company, they often ask for the recipe.

½ cup	melted butter	125 mL
1	medium onion, chopped	1
3 cups	bread cubes	750 mL
¼ tsp.	salt	1 mL
¼ tsp.	pepper	1 mL
1 tsp.	poultry seasoning	5 mL
1 cup	warm water or chicken broth	250 mL

1. Place butter in 3-qt. (3 L) casserole dish. Microwave on HIGH for 1 minute or until melted.

2. Add onion and microwave on HIGH for 2 minutes or until tender.

3. Stir in bread cubes and seasonings. Pour water or broth all over and toss to moisten. Stuff bird.

TIP: This can be cooked separately in a casserole dish if desired. Cover and microwave on HIGH for 5 minutes or until heated through.

Your Time: _____

ALACE'S CURRIED CHICKEN

Alace brought the original recipe back from Africa. It is pictured on the cover.

3	carrots, sliced	3
3	stalks celery, sliced	3
3	potatoes, sliced	3
3 lb.	fryer, cut up	1.4 kg
1-19 oz.	can tomatoes	540 mL
1½-3 tbsp.	curry powder	25-35 mL
1 tsp.	salt	5 mL

1. Place sliced vegetables in bottom of a 3-qt. (3 L) casserole dish. Arrange chicken pieces on top, placing larger pieces toward corners and smaller pieces toward the centre. Sprinkle lightly with curry powder. Cover and microwave on MEDIUM-HIGH for 14 to 16 minutes. Turn chicken pieces over.

2. Break up tomatoes. Stir curry powder and salt into tomatoes. Pour tomatoes over chicken and vegetables.

3. Cover and microwave on MEDIUM-HIGH for 15 to 20 minutes, or until chicken is tender.

SERVING SUGGESTION: Serve this with African style fried rice: Fry rice and peanuts together in butter.

Your Time: _____

BARBECUE CHICKEN

Popular demand will have you serving this often.

3-lb.	fryer, cut up	1.4 kg
2 cups	Barbecue Sauce, page 96	500 mL

1. Arrange chicken pieces in an 8 x 12-inch (1.5 L) glass baking dish, with larger pieces at corners and small pieces towards centre. Pour sauce over chicken.

2. Cover and microwave on HIGH for 15 to 20 minutes, or until chicken is tender. Turn chicken pieces over halfway through cooking time. Baste with sauce.

Your Time: _____

ORIENTAL CHICKEN

Several of my friends gave me similar recipes for this and I blended them to create this one. Any way you do it, it is delicious.

¼ cup	soy sauce	60 mL
2 tbsp.	honey	30 mL
2 tbsp.	molasses	30 mL
1 tbsp.	dry mustard	15 mL
3	cloves garlic, minced, OR 1 tsp. (5 mL) garlic salt	3
½ tbsp.	cornstarch	25 mL
3 lb.	fryer, cut up	1.4 kg

1. Combine all ingredients except chicken in 2-cup (500 mL) glass measure. Blend well.

2. Arrange chicken pieces in 2-qt. (2 L) shallow casserole dish with larger pieces, such as thighs and breasts, at corners. Place small pieces, such as legs and wings toward center. Pour sauce over chicken. Microwave on HIGH for 20 to 25 minutes, or until chicken is tender. Turn chicken pieces over halfway through cooking time and baste with sauce.

VARIATION: Add ¼ cup (50 mL) apricot jam or plum sauce for extra flavour.

TIP: If you use a deep casserole dish that causes you to layer the chicken pieces on top of each other rather than spreading them out, you will increase the time by at least 10 minutes.

Your Time: _____

LEMON CHICKEN

A very light-flavoured oriental chicken dish.

3 lb.	fryer, cut up	1.4 kg
2 tbsp.	soy sauce	30 mL
1/3 cup	lemon juice	75 mL
2 tbsp.	sugar	30 mL
1/8 tsp.	ginger	.5 mL
1/8 tsp.	garlic powder	.5 mL
	lemon slices	

1. Brush soy sauce over chicken pieces. Arrange pieces in a shallow 2-qt. (2 L) casserole dish, placing meaty parts towards the outside and thin, bony pieces like wings, towards the centre.

2. Mix together lemon juice, sugar, ginger and garlic powder and pour over chicken. Cover and microwave on MEDIUM-HIGH for 15 to 20 minutes. Halfway through cooking time chicken should be turned over and basted with lemon sauce. During the last 5 minutes, pieces should be rearranged. Bring centre pieces toward outside and outside ones to centre.

3. Garnish with lemon slices before serving.

Your Time: _____

SHAKE 'N' BAKE CHICKEN

If you like this cooked in the conventional oven, you'll love it cooked in the microwave oven.

| 3-lb. | fryer, cut up | 1.4 kg |
| 1 pkg. | Shake 'N' Bake coating mix | 1 |

1. Wash the chicken pieces. Place them in the plastic bag of coating mix and shake them to coat. Place pieces on a roasting rack or microwave meat tray, arranging them so that the larger, meatier pieces are towards the outside and the smaller pieces toward the centre.

2. Microwave, covered loosely with wax paper, on MEDIUM-HIGH for 20 to 25 minutes. Turn the pieces over halfway through cooking time.

3. Allow them to stand, uncovered, for 5 to 10 minutes to finish cooking.

Your Time: _____

COUNTRY STYLE CHICKEN

The smell of this cooking makes your mouth water. It's so good that I save the broth to make into soup the next day.

½ cup	flour	125	mL
½ tsp.	salt	2	mL
¼ tsp.	pepper	1	mL
¼ tsp.	paprika	1	mL
3 lb.	fryer, cut up	1.4	kg
¼ cup	butter	60	mL
2	onions, quartered	2	
2	carrots, sliced diagonally	2	
½ tsp.	rosemary	2	mL
2 tbsp.	chopped parsley	30	mL
½ tsp.	thyme	2	mL
1½ cups	chicken stock	375	mL

1. Mix together flour, salt, pepper and paprika. Roll chicken pieces in flour mixture to coat.

2. Place butter in a 3-qt. (3 L) casserole dish and microwave on HIGH for 45 seconds or until melted. Roll chicken pieces in butter to coat. Arrange chicken pieces in casserole dish with large meaty pieces toward outside of dish and smaller, bony parts towards the centre. Cover and microwave on HIGH for 5 minutes. Turn pieces over and microwave on HIGH, covered, for another 10 minutes.

3. Add remaining ingredients. Cover and microwave on MEDIUM for 15 to 20 minutes, or until chicken pieces are tender. If desired, thicken broth with remaining seasoned flour mixture or leave as is and make soup with it.

TIME SAVING TIP: Preheat chicken stock on HIGH for 2 to 3 minutes before adding to casserole dish.

Your Time: _____

CHICKEN VELVET

The most rich, elegant, wonderful company dish! I like to serve it with noodles.

2 tbsp.	butter	30	mL
½ lb.	fresh mushrooms, sliced	250	g
¼ cup	onion, chopped	60	mL
2	whole large chicken breasts, halved and skinned	2	
2 tbsp.	flour	30	mL
1 cup	whipping cream	250	mL
1 tsp.	salt	5	mL
⅛ tsp.	pepper	.5	mL

1. In a 3-qt. (3 L) casserole dish, combine butter, mushrooms and onions. Cover and microwave on HIGH for 3 to 5 minutes, or until tender.

2. Add chicken breasts and cover. Microwave on MEDIUM-HIGH for 5 to 7 minutes.

3. In 2-cup (500 mL) glass measure, combine flour, cream, salt, pepper. Remove chicken from dish. Stir cream mixture into vegetables. Return chicken to dish and spoon cream sauce over chicken.

4. Cover and microwave on MEDIUM for 12 to 14 minutes, or until chicken is tender and no longer pink. Rearrange chicken and cover with sauce halfway through cooking time.

CHICKEN PARISIAN: Prepare as above making the following changes: Sprinkle chicken with paprika before cooking. Make the sauce with 1 cup (250 mL) sour cream instead of whipping cream.

Your Time: _____

CREAMED CHICKEN & BROCCOLI

An easy meal with many possibilities.

1	**small head of broccoli OR 1-10 oz. (300 g) pkg. frozen broccoli**	1
3 tbsp.	**butter**	**35 mL**
¼ cup	**flour**	**60 mL**
¼ tsp.	**celery salt**	**1 mL**
½ tsp.	**paprika**	**2 mL**
2 cups	**milk**	**500 mL**
1 cup	**chicken broth**	**250 mL**
2 cups	**chicken meat, diced**	**500 mL**
¼ cup	**grated Parmesan cheese**	**60 mL**

1. Place broccoli in 1-qt. (1 L) casserole dish. Cover and microwave on HIGH for 5 to 7 minutes. Set aside.

2. Place butter in 2-qt. (2 L) casserole dish. Microwave on HIGH for 45 seconds or until melted. Stir in flour, celery salt and paprika. Using a wire whisk, gradually stir in milk.

3. Microwave on MEDIUM-HIGH for 4 minutes, stirring and checking thickness of sauce after each minute.

4. Stir in chicken broth, chicken meat and broccoli. Sprinkle with Parmesan cheese. Microwave on MEDIUM-HIGH for 3 to 5 minutes, just until heated. Do not boil. Serve over hot noodles, rice or baked patty shells.

TIP: For a milder flavour, omit the celery salt

VARIATION: If broccoli is not available, use green peas or celery. Sometimes I add mushrooms to this.

Your Time: _____

CHICKEN A LA KING

Turn leftovers into a company casserole with this recipe.

¼ cup	butter	50 mL
¼ cup	flour	50 mL
	salt & pepper to taste	
1 cup	chicken broth	250 mL
1½ cups	dairy half & half	375 mL
1 tbsp.	butter	15 mL
1	medium onion, chopped	1
¼ cup	chopped green pepper	60 mL
¼ cup	chopped red pepper	60 mL
½ lb.	fresh mushrooms, sliced	250 g
2 cups	chicken, cooked and cubed	500 mL

1. Place ¼ cup (60 mL) butter in 4 cup (1 L) glass measure. Microwave on HIGH for 45 to 60 seconds or until melted.

2. Stir in flour, salt and pepper. With wire whisk, gradually stir in chicken broth and half & half. Microwave on MEDIUM for 5 to 6 minutes, stirring after each minute, until thickened. Set sauce aside.

3. Place 1 tbsp. (15 mL) butter in 2-qt. (2 L) casserole dish. Microwave 30 seconds or until melted. Add onion, green and red peppers, and mushrooms. Microwave on HIGH for 3 to 5 minutes or until tender crisp. Stir once or twice.

4. Add chicken and thickened sauce to vegetables. Cover and microwave on MEDIUM for 7 to 10 minutes. Serve over baked patty shells.

Your Time: _____

MOO GOO GAI PAN

Once you get past the name, the rest is easy!

2	whole large chicken breasts	2
2 tbsp.	soy sauce	30 mL
1 tsp.	cornstarch	5 mL
¼ tsp.	ground ginger	1 mL
¼ tsp.	sugar	1 mL
1	clove garlic, minced OR ⅛ tsp. (.5 mL) garlic powder	1
1 tbsp.	vegetable oil	15 mL
4	green onions	4
1 lb.	fresh mushrooms	500 g
1 cup	peas, fresh OR frozen	250 mL
2 cups	long grain rice, cooked	500 mL

1. Cut each chicken breast in half lengthwise; remove skin and bones. Then with knife held in slanted position, almost parallel to the cutting surface, slice across width of each half into ¼-inch (.5 cm) thick slices.

2. In a small mixing bowl, combine chicken, soy sauce, cornstarch, ginger, sugar and garlic. Set aside.

3. Preheat 10-inch (25 cm) browning pan on HIGH for 5 minutes. Meanwhile, slice mushrooms and onions.

4. Spread vegetable oil on surface of preheated browning pan. Add chicken. Microwave on HIGH for 3 to 5 minutes, stirring once or twice. (If you don't have a browning pan, omit the oil and the preheating step. Microwave for 5 minutes in a 2-qt. (2 L) casserole dish.)

5. Add onions and mushrooms. Microwave on HIGH for 3 minutes. Stir.

6. Add peas and cover. Microwave on HIGH for 2 minutes. Serve over rice.

Your Time: _____

SPEEDY CHICKEN SALAD

Fast for the family on the run.

1	large chicken breast	1
½ cup	finely diced celery	125 mL
¼ cup	chopped green onion	60 mL
¼ cup	mayonnaise	60 mL
	salt and pepper to taste	

1. Place chicken breast on a glass plate. Cover with plastic wrap. Microwave on MEDIUM-HIGH for 6 to 8 minutes, or until juices run clear when sliced. Let stand, covered, for 5 minutes to complete cooking. Remove cover and cut into chunks.

2. Mix remaining ingredients together. Add cooled, chopped chicken meat. Chill. Use to fill tomato cups or sandwiches.

TIP: Use the instructions in step 1 to prepare chicken meat for any recipe that calls for cooked chicken.

SERVING SUGGESTION: Use this to fill "Bun Boats" for a child's party: Hollow a hard bun (like a Kaiser) and fill with chicken salad. Garnish with a cheese triangle "sail" on a toothpick.

Your Time: _____

TURKEY & HAM BAKE

A delectable way to use holiday leftovers.

¼ cup	butter	60	mL
¼ cup	flour	60	mL
	salt & pepper to taste		
1 cup	turkey OR chicken broth	250	mL
1 cup	dairy half & half	250	mL
1 cup	sliced mushrooms	250	mL
½ cup	chopped onion	125	mL
2 cups	diced cooked ham	500	mL
2 cups	diced cooked turkey	500	mL

1. In a 4-cup (1 L) glass measure, microwave butter on HIGH for 45 seconds, or until melted. Stir in flour and seasonings. Using a wire whisk, gradually stir in broth and the half & half. Microwave on MEDIUM for 4 to 5 minutes, or until thickened. Stir every half minute.

2. Add mushrooms and onion and set aside.

3. Spread ham and turkey in a 3-qt. (3 L) casserole dish. Pour sauce over top. Microwave on MEDIUM for 7 to 9 minutes, or until heated through.

VARIATIONS:

1. Toppings - ½ cup (125 mL) shredded cheese
½ cup (125 mL) buttered bread crumbs
½ cup (125 mL) crushed potato chips
Add any of these toppings after step 3 and microwave on HIGH for just 1 minute to melt cheese or heat crumbs.

2. Add 1 cup (250 mL) of leftover vegetables or chopped broccoli.

3. Serve over biscuits, patty shells, noodles, rice or leftover mashed potatoes.

Your Time: _____

TURKEY DIVAN

Turkey, broccoli & cheese — sure to be a favourite.

1	head broccoli	1	
1-10 oz.	can cream of mushroom soup	284	mL
½ cup	mayonnaise	125	mL
¼ cup	milk	60	mL
1 tsp.	lemon juice	5	mL
½ tsp.	curry powder	2	mL
4 cups	chopped cooked turkey	1	L
½ cup	shredded cheddar cheese	125	mL
½ cup	buttered bread crumbs	125	mL

1. Arrange broccoli in a shallow 2-qt. (2 L) casserole dish with stems toward the outside and flowers toward the centre. Cover with matching lid or plastic wrap and microwave on HIGH 5 to 7 minutes. Drain.

2. Meanwhile in a small mixing bowl, combine soup, mayonnaise, milk, lemon juice and curry powder. Microwave on MEDIUM-HIGH for 2 to 3 minutes, just until hot. Stir once during cooking time to distribute heat more evenly.

3. Spread turkey over broccoli. Pour soup mixture over turkey and broccoli. Spread cheese on top. Cover and microwave on MEDIUM-HIGH for 5 to 6 minutes, just until heated through.

4. Sprinkle bread crumbs on top and microwave on HIGH for 1 minute.

Your Time: _____

FISH & SEAFOOD

The microwave oven is an excellent choice of cooking mode for fish and seafood. The speed and moisture retention of microwave cooking are decided advantages in cooking them. They cook quickly and remain moist and tender with a mild, pleasant flavour. Steamed or poached fish and seafood are more easily prepared in the microwave oven, since the large quantities of water necessary in conventional cooking are not required. Weight-watchers will love microwave prepared fish and seafood because cooking oil can be eliminated.

THE KEY TO SUCCESS WITH FISH

Fish and seafood are delicate foods which need to be cooked carefully. To preserve their delicate flavour and texture they should be cooked for a minimal time — usually just until heated through. They are naturally tender, but toughen quickly when overcooked. If you are in doubt as to whether or not they are cooked, let them stand covered on the counter for 3 to 5 minutes. This standing time may be all that is needed to finish the cooking process whereas microwaving them for an extra minute or two may toughen them.

PLANNING MEALS WITH FISH & SEAFOOD

Cook fish last when preparing an entire meal. Standing time is just about as long as it takes to carry it from the oven to the table. Fish and seafood won't reheat as easily as some foods, and overcooking can occur during reheating. Other foods, such as vegetables, will keep a better texture longer after cooking and can be reheated more easily.

UTENSILS & COVERS

- Always cook fish and seafood in a covered utensil, so that the moisture will be retained. The use of coverings decreases the cooking time as well as prevents dehydration. Plastic wrap and casserole covers can be used interchangeably. Both hold in the steam which promotes even cooking. Leave fish uncovered only when there is a topping or coating on the fish that you wish to keep crisp. Even here, a covering of paper toweling is often desirable.

- Cover all fish and seafood during standing time to keep it moist and prevent dehydration while it completes its cooking process. (For example, the center may need to finish cooking.)

- Glass casseroles, baking pans or plates cook fish very well, however, if you cook fish often, you may want to purchase a special glass fish baking dish. Most dishes are too small to hold a large fish, but a fish dish will solve that problem. It also makes a very attractive serving dish.

- Shellfish may be cooked in its shell since the shell is transparent to microwave energy. Wrap it tightly with plastic wrap. You can purchase special shells or shell shaped dishes for serving seafood. Check to see if these shells are microwave safe as the materials they are made of vary.

FOODS THAT DON'T WORK & WHY

Don't deep fry fish in the microwave oven. The fat becomes dangerously hot.

Don't cook battered or "pan fried" fish, it does not become crisp and brown, not even when using a browning tray.

Don't microwave live shellfish. They are best cooked conventionally in a large pot of boiling water.

HOW TO KNOW WHEN FISH IS DONE

Fish cooks fast. Most fish and seafood require a cooking time on HIGH or 3 - 4 minutes per pound (7 - 9 minutes per kg). Always cook fish and seafood for the minimum amount of time. Avoid overcooking by checking and rearranging fish after half the cooking time. Allow a standing time of 2 to 3 minutes to completely cook. Fish is done when it is opaque and can be easily flaked with a fork. Make certain that the center of a large fish flakes easily as well as the edges.

Shellfish meat will look opaque, and the shell will have a pink or pinkish orange color when it is completely cooked. It is recommended that many seafoods, especially the meatier types, be cooked until outer areas appear opaque but the centers are still slightly translucent. These areas will finish cooking as the seafood stands, while the outer areas remain tender. The flesh of all seafood, such as shrimp, crab and lobster, will look opaque and firm.

Be careful not to overcook. Overcooking dries and toughens fish.

DEFROSTING FISH

Fish should be completely defrosted before cooking. Fish defrosts rapidly so be careful not to over defrost. It should be rearranged and turned over halfway through the defrost time. Thawed fish should not feel warm, even the corners and edges should feel cold. Fillets frozen in a block should begin to loosen when defrost time is finished. Whole fish should still be icy inside the cavity. It is best to finish defrosting by running under cold water until fish softens and is no longer icy.

FROZEN BREADED OR BATTERED FISH PIECES

Frozen breaded fish are best heated on a preheated browning tray. Microwaving food brings the moisture to the surface of the food, causing the crisp exteriors to turn soggy when heated in a glass or plastic dish. The hot surface of the browning tray will preserve most of their original crispness. Carefully turn them over halfway through the cooking time. They will be quite fragile and not as crisp as when conventionally baked but they are satisfactory. Sacrificing a bit of crispness may be worth the time saving (5 to 7 minutes on HIGH for an 8 oz. or 250 g pkg.).

Breaded or battered shellfish and battered fish will not be crispy, even if you do heat them on a browning tray.

REHEATING FISH

If it is necessary to cook fish ahead of time, leave it slightly underdone so that the reheating will not overcook the fish. Be certain to cover during reheating.

ADAPTING CONVENTIONAL FISH RECIPES FOR MICROWAVE COOKING

- Most fish and seafood recipes, especially casseroles, adapt easily to microwave cooking. Find a recipe which contains similar types and quantities of ingredients in this book or the manual that came with your oven. It can be a guide for the required cooking time.
- Eliminate the fat called for in the recipe. Microwaved foods do not stick to their cooking dishes as they do conventionally. The exception to this is when a dab of butter is added for flavour.
- Poached fish does not need to be cooked in liquid unless the liquid is used as a vehicle for seasonings or a base for a sauce. Reduce any liquid required; use just enough to fill the dish to a half inch depth.
- When adding fish to a stew or creole which requires a long cooking time, add the fish at the end of the cooking time. Cook on MEDIUM-LOW just until the fish is slightly translucent. The heat of the other ingredients will finish cooking it during standing time.

HINTS

- Place larger and thicker pieces of fish and seafood near the edge of the dish for more even cooking.
- One kind of fish required in a recipe can easily be substituted for another. For example, snapper, flounder, perch, halibut and sole can be used interchangeably in most recipes. Fish steaks can also be substituted for fillets, but they may require slightly longer cooking and defrosting times.
- If someone in your household likes to fish, freeze your catch for fresh-tasting fish all year 'round. Seal fillets or steaks in a plastic bag with a small amount of water and freeze. Clean whole fish, then dip them in water and freeze on a baking dish. The icy coating will protect fish from freezer burn. Package for freezing after it is frozen.
- Seafood can be attractively garnished with lemon slices, parsley, almonds, tomato slices or spices.
- Most seafood casserole recipes can be prepared ahead of time and refrigerated. Remember to allow 4 to 7 minutes of extra cooking time, due to the refrigerator temperature. The cooking time of a refrigerated casserole will vary slightly, depending upon the size and ingredients of the casserole.

COOKING WHOLE FISH

- Cook a whole fish covered with plastic wrap or a well fitting glass lid to retain the steam.
- It may be necessary to turn the fish over halfway through cooking if it is being cooked in liquid.
- The head and the tail of the fish tend to cook more quickly than the rest of the meat on a whole fish. It is best to wrap these areas with light weight aluminum foil during the first two thirds of cooking time.
- Filling the cavity of the fish with stuffing, vegetables or seasonings adds flavour to the fish without adding a significant increase in the cooking time.

FISH STEAKS

Fish steaks can be used in recipes calling for fish fillets, however they will take almost twice as long to cook.

FISH FILLETS

- Fish cooks in about the same time it requires to become hot. Usually the pieces are cut thinly enough to allow the microwaves to readily penetrate throughout. For fillets and thinly-cut steaks, allow about 4 minutes cooking time per lb. (9 minutes per kg.) of fish. Cook just until it can be flaked apart easily with a fork. Then allow to stand covered a minute or two to finish cooking. Be careful about overcooking fish, as this gives a dry texture and strong flavour.
- Fillets can be cooked in lemon juice (¼ cup or 60 mL) or for a flavour change use apple juice, white grape juice or pear nectar. Sprinkle with paprika, lemon pepper, parsley, chopped green onions or any combination of these.
- Create Scalloped Fillets — Cook 1 lb. (500 g) fish fillets for half the suggested cooking time. Sprinkle with any of the following: salt and pepper, parmesan cheese, paprika, parsley or thyme. Cover with 2 cups (500 mL) of buttered crumbs and ⅓ cup (75 mL) milk or cream and microwave for the other half of cooking time. Dress this up by adding sauteed mushrooms (or canned), celery or onions with the seasonings. This takes about 8 minutes, total cooking time.

SHELLFISH

- Arrange peeled and deveined shrimp around edge of glass pie plate, tails toward center. Cover and cook on HIGH for 4 minutes per pound.

- Small pieces of frozen fish, like shrimp, can be thawed and cooked at the same time. Larger pieces, like lobster tails and fillets, are best thawed before cooking.

- Shellfish can be prepared right in the shell. Shells make very attractive and unusual serving "dishes." Shellfish cooked in the shell will have the same cooking time as fish cooked out of the shell since shells do not absorb microwaves.

- Fresh clams steam in their shells. Set a dozen well scrubbed clams in a shallow dish (with just enough water to cover the bottom of the dish, if desired.) Cover with plastic wrap and microwave on HIGH for 1 minute and MEDIUM for 5 to 6 minutes or until shells open.

- To eliminate unpleasant cooking odours when cooking unpeeled shrimp, cook in water with a bit of vinegar and a bay leaf.

CANNED FISH

Canned fish is already cooked, so needs only to be heated. Add it last to a casserole. Often the heat of the other ingredients will heat the fish.

FRESHWATER FILLETS

This recipe demonstrates the superb results you get when you cook fish in the microwave.

1 lb.	freshwater fish fillets — jackfish, pickerel, perch	500 g
	salt & pepper to taste	
2 tbsp.	lemon juice	30 mL
2 tbsp.	butter	30 mL

1. Lay fillets in a shallow 2-qt. (2 L) casserole dish, arranging them so that thin parts are toward the centre and thick parts toward the outside. Sprinkle with salt, pepper and lemon juice. Dot with butter.

2. Cover with matching lid or plastic wrap (remember to leave a vent in plastic wrap). Microwave on HIGH for 7 minutes.

3. Rearrange and turn fillets over. Cover and microwave on HIGH for another 3 minutes, or until fish flakes easily.

VARIATION: Sprinkle with ½ cup (125 mL) buttered bread crumbs after step 3 and microwave uncovered on HIGH for 1 minute.

Your Time: _____

STUFFING FOR FISH

The savory flavour of this stuffing permeates the fish.

¼ cup	butter	60 mL
¼ cup	onion, chopped	60 mL
2	stalks celery, chopped	2
1 cup	fresh mushrooms, sliced	250 mL
2 cups	bread crumbs	50 mL
1 tsp.	parsley	5 mL
1 tsp.	sage	5 mL
	dash of thyme	

1. Place butter in a 2-qt. (2 L) casserole dish. Microwave on HIGH for 45 seconds or until melted. Stir in vegetables. Cover and microwave on HIGH for 5 minutes.

2. Add remaining ingredients and stir to moisten. Stuff fish.

Your Time: _____

FISH STEAKS

So moist and tender when cooked in the microwave.

2	¾ inch (7 cm) thick fish steaks, halibut or salmon	2
2 tbsp.	lemon juice	30 mL
2 tbsp.	butter	30 mL

1. Place fish steaks on glass plate. Sprinkle with lemon juice and dot with butter. Cover with plastic wrap.

2. Microwave on HIGH for 6 to 8 minutes.

VARIATION: Sprinkle ¼ cup (50 mL) slivered almonds or sesame seeds over steaks before cooking.

SERVING SUGGESTION: For an extra special touch, serve steaks with Hollandaise Sauce, page 160.

Your Time: _____

STUFFED FILLET ROLLS

A savory stuffing is rolled up in fillets. Assemble ahead, microwave just before serving.

2 lbs.	fish fillets (sole, flounder, turbot) — about 8 fillets	1 kg
2 tbsp.	lemon juice	30 mL
1	recipe Stuffing for Fish, page 120	1
2 tbsp.	butter	30 mL
	snipped parsley	

1. Thaw fillets, if frozen. Sprinkle with lemon juice.

2. Spoon about ¼ cup (60 mL) of fish stuffing onto each fillet. Roll up and secure with a wooden toothpick. Place in a shallow 2-qt. (2 L) casserole dish with seams down.

3. Cover with matching lid or plastic wrap (leave a vent in plastic wrap). Microwave on HIGH for 8 to 10 minutes. Let stand, covered for about 5 minutes to complete cooking.

4. During standing time, microwave butter on HIGH for 30 seconds, or until melted.

5. Just before serving, brush rolls with melted butter and sprinkle with parsley.

Your Time: _____

STUFFED RAINBOW TROUT

An attractive meal for a special occasion.

2	whole trout (about 12 oz. or 375 g each)	2
	salt & pepper to taste	
	juice of one lemon	
	Stuffing for Fish (page 120)	

1. Wash trout and sprinkle with salt and pepper — inside and out.

2. Sprinkle lemon juice inside trout cavity. Fill with stuffing.

3. In a 2-qt. (2 L) shallow casserole dish, place trout with heads at opposite ends of dish. Sprinkle with lemon juice. Cover with wax paper. Microwave on HIGH for 7 to 8 minutes. Let stand covered for approximately 5 minutes to complete cooking.

Your Time: _____

WHOLE BAKED SALMON

A most impressive dish.

1	whole salmon — without the head	1
1	lemon	1
¼ cup	butter	60 mL

1. Wash fish inside and out. Place in an 8 x 12-inch (1.5 L) glass baking dish.

2. Cut lemon into wedges. Squeeze lemon juice all over fish — inside and out. Place lemon wedges inside the cavity.

3. Cut butter into small pieces. Place pieces of butter inside and on top of the fish. Cover with plastic wrap, leaving a small vent and microwave on HIGH for about 4 to 6 minutes per pound. Let stand covered for about 5 to 10 minutes to complete cooking. Fish should flake easily with a fork when done.

Your Time: _____

CHEESY CREAMED SALMON

You will enjoy this unusual recipe.

¼ cup	finely minced onion	60	mL
3 tbsp.	butter	45	mL
3 tbsp.	flour	45	mL
1 cup	milk	250	mL
	juice from the salmon		
	salt & pepper to taste		
½ cup	whipping cream	125	mL
2-7 oz.	cans salmon	198	g
1-10 oz.	can sliced mushrooms, drained	284	mL
¼ cup	grated Swiss cheese	60	mL
1 tbsp.	butter	15	mL
2	hard-boiled eggs, sliced	2	

1. Place onion and butter in a 2-qt. (2 L) casserole dish. Cover and microwave on HIGH for 3 minutes.

2. Stir in flour and salt and pepper. Gradually stir in milk and salmon juice. Microwave on MEDIUM-HIGH for 3 minutes, stirring every 30 seconds to keep flour suspended.

3. Stir in cream. Add salmon and mushrooms.

4. Spread over toast points, noodles or rice. Microwave on MEDIUM for 3 to 5 minutes — just until heated through.

5. Top with sliced egg. Sprinkle grated cheese over top and dot with 1 tbsp. (15 mL) butter. Microwave on MEDIUM for 1 to 2 minutes — just until cheese melts.

Your Time: _____

SALMON MORNAY

An easy dress up for canned salmon.

1 head	broccoli, cut up	
2 tbsp.	butter	30 mL
2 tbsp.	flour	30 mL
2 tsp.	chicken bouillon mix	10 mL
½ tsp.	dry mustard	2 mL
1½ cups	milk	375 mL
¾ cup	shredded Swiss cheese	175 mL
2-7¾ oz.	cans salmon, drained	213 g

1. Arrange broccoli in a shallow 2-qt. (2 L) casserole dish, placing stalks toward the outside and flowers toward the centre. Cover and microwave on HIGH 8 to 10 minutes, or until tender crisp. Drain off water and rearrange pieces so that the flowers are toward the outside and stalks in centre. Set aside.

2. In a 4-cup (1 L) deep casserole dish or measure, microwave butter on HIGH for 30 seconds or until melted. Stir in flour, chicken bouillon mix and dry mustard. Using a fork or wire whisk, gradually stir in milk. Microwave on MEDIUM-HIGH for 6 to 8 minutes, stirring after each minute of cooking time, until sauce thickens.

3. Stir in cheese. Keep stirring until cheese is melted. Break up salmon and stir into sauce. Pour over broccoli. Microwave on MEDIUM for 2 to 3 minutes, just until heated through.

Your Time: _____

JIFFY TUNA CASSEROLE

When I got married, my mother told me if I ever had "one of those days" and forgot to get supper made on time, I should fry up an onion. That way my husband would smell something cooking as he entered the house and be more patient to wait for supper. This casserole is a way to turn that "fried onion" into a meal in a hurry.

2 tbsp.	butter	30 mL
1	small chopped onion	1
1	apple, cored and diced	1
3 tbsp.	flour	45 mL
½ tsp.	curry powder	2 mL
½ cup	milk	125 mL
1 cup	chicken broth	250 mL
2-6 ½ oz.	cans light tuna, drained	184 g

1. Place butter, onion and apple in a 2-qt. (2 L) casserole dish. Cover and microwave on HIGH for 2 minutes.

2. Stir in flour and curry powder. Gradually stir in milk and chicken broth. Microwave on MEDIUM-HIGH for 3½ to 4 minutes, or until thickened.

3. Add tuna, breaking it up with a fork. Microwave on MEDIUM-HIGH for 3 to 4 minutes, until heated through.

SERVING SUGGESTION: Serve over noodles or rice.

Your Time: _____

TUNA MAC

This simple casserole is a hit with my children.

2 cups	cooked macaroni	500 mL
1-6 ½ oz.	can tuna, drained	184 g
1-10 oz.	can cream of mushroom soup	284 mL
1 cup	grated mozzarella cheese	250 mL
2 tbsp.	chopped green onion	30 mL
½ cup	peas	125 mL
1 tsp.	paprika	5 mL
⅛ tsp.	dry mustard	.5 mL

1. In a 2-qt. (2 L) casserole dish, combine all ingredients. Cover and microwave on MEDIUM-HIGH for 5 to 7 minutes, just until cheese is melted and casserole is heated through. Stir 2 or 3 times during cooking.

Your Time: _____

QUICK SEAFOOD SCALLOP

Your company will think you worked all day, (but you haven't).

1-10 oz.	can cream of celery soup	284 mL
¼ cup	milk	60 mL
1	egg, beaten	1
2 tbsp.	Parmesan cheese	30 mL
1-5 oz.	can flaked crab meat	140 g
1-4¼ oz.	can shrimp, rinse and drain	113 g
1-10 oz.	can sliced mushrooms	284 mL
1 tbsp.	butter, melted	15 mL
¼ cup	bread crumbs	60 mL
2 tbsp.	Parmesan cheese	30 mL

1. In a 2-qt. (2 L) casserole dish, combine soup, milk, beaten egg and Parmesan cheese. Microwave on MEDIUM-HIGH for 2 to 3 minutes, until hot.

2. Stir in crab meat, shrimp and mushrooms. Microwave on MEDIUM-HIGH for 4 to 6 minutes, just until heated through.

3. Microwave butter on HIGH for 30 seconds, til melted. In a small bowl, combine bread crumbs, 2 tbsp. (30 mL) Parmesan cheese and butter. Sprinkle crumb mixture over casserole dish. Microwave on HIGH for 1 minute to heat crumbs.

Your Time: _____

SHRIMP STIR FRY

Stir fry without much stirring.

2-7 oz.	pkg. frozen, small shelled shrimp	200	g
2 tsp.	soy sauce	10	mL
¼ cup	chicken broth	60	mL
½ tsp.	ground ginger	2	mL
⅛ tsp.	garlic powder	.5	mL
2 cups	fresh broccoli, cut into small pieces	500	mL
2	small onions, quartered	2	
1 cup	diagonally sliced celery	250	mL
1	green pepper, cut into squares	1	
1 cup	sliced fresh mushrooms	250	mL
	a small handful of snow peas		
8	cherry tomatoes, halved		

1. Marinate shrimp in mixture of soy sauce, chicken broth, ginger and garlic while you cut up the vegetables.

2. Place broccoli, onions, celery and green peppers in 3-qt. (3 L) casserole dish. Cover and microwave on HIGH for 5 to 6 minutes. Stir once or twice during cooking time.

3. Stir in shrimp mixture and mushrooms. Microwave on HIGH for 4 to 5 minutes or until shrimp are firm but cooked.

4. Stir in snow peas and tomatoes. Cover and let stand for 3 to 4 minutes to heat through. It may be neccesary to microwave for another minute or two.

Your Time: _____

SHRIMP CREOLE

The shrimp in this recipe thaw and cook while the rest of the ingredients are heated.

2 tbsp.	butter OR margarine	30 mL
1	medium green pepper, chopped	1
1	medium onion, chopped	
1 cup	thinly sliced celery	250 mL
2 tbsp.	flour	30 mL
1-14 oz.	can tomatoes	398 mL
1 tsp.	sugar	5 mL
5 drops	Tabasco sauce	
1	bay leaf	1
1 tsp.	salt	5 mL
⅛ tsp.	pepper	.5 mL
2-7 oz.	pkg. frozen shrimp, shelled and cleaned	200 g

1. Place butter in 2½-qt. (2.5 L) casserole dish. Microwave on HIGH for 30 seconds or until melted.

2. Stir in green pepper, onion and celery. Microwave on HIGH for 6 to 8 minutes, or until vegetables are tender. Stir once or twice during cooking time.

3. Stir in flour. Mix in tomatoes, sugar and spices. Microwave on HIGH for 4 to 6 minutes, or until heated through. Stir halfway through cooking time.

4. Add shrimp. Microwave, covered, on HIGH for 5 to 6 minutes or until shrimp are fully cooked. Stir twice during cooking time. Remove bay leaf before serving.

Your Time: _____

1. Vegetable Rice Pilaf, page 134.
2. Chicken Velvet, page 108.
3. Quick Seafood Scallop, page 126.
4. Coffee Pecan Creamy Pudding, page 211.

RICE, PASTA & CEREALS ◼◼◼◼◼◼◼

Rice, pasta and cereals are easy to prepare in the microwave oven. They can be cooked directly in the serving dishes, eliminating hard-to-clean pans. Also, cooking can be done without scorching. Microwaved cereals are very quick, however, the time needed for microwaving rice and pasta is about the same as conventional cooking. Rice and pasta require a certain amount of time to absorb the water to soften or become tender. Microwave energy cannot speed up this process.

⊙━ THE KEY TO SUCCESS WITH GRAINS & PASTA

The key to success with grains and pasta is to simmer them gently in moisture. The starch in these foods makes them prone to boil over easily, losing the moisture they need to tenderize, not to mention making a mess. First, choose a dish that is large enough to allow for the exaggerated boiling of starchy foods. Bring the water to a boil before adding rice, pasta or cereal. Adding oil to the water helps to prevent boilovers, as does greasing the rim of the dish. If they are cooked on a lower power level, like MEDIUM they will boil more slowly and require less attention. HIGH power can be used if you watch the food closely and stir it once during cooking time. When cooking rice on HIGH, the cooking time should be divided into two segments with 10 minutes standing time between them.

STANDING TIME

Standing time is very important to allow rice and pasta to absorb moisture and finish cooking. The covers should be left on during this time. Rice needs 5 to 10 minutes of standing time. Pasta needs about 3 minutes, covered, standing time.

UTENSILS & COVERS

When preparing rice in the microwave oven, the size of the dish is an important consideration. Choose a glass cooking dish which is large enough to allow water to boil vigorously. A good rule of thumb is to fill the dish only half full.

It is necessary to cook rice and pasta in a covered dish. This allows for faster cooking. Glass lids or heavy-duty plastic wrap are the best coverings to use since they are the most water-vapour-proof.

REHEATING RICE & PASTA

Microwaving is the perfect way to reheat rice and pasta. Reheated conventionally, rice and pasta will dry out unless you add more water, which makes them mushy. It is not necessary to add liquid for reheating in the microwave oven. Tightly covered with plastic wrap, pasta and rice reheat to "fresh cooked" flavor and texture. Microwave on HIGH, until steaming hot, about

1 to 2 minutes per cup (250 mL). This is so handy, you can cook rice ahead and reheat it later or add to a casserole. You can even freeze it in serving size portions. 2 cups (500 mL) of cooked, frozen rice will heat on HIGH in 4 to 5 minutes.

RICE
TO COOK RICE IN THE MICROWAVE OVEN
METHOD A:

This method is for ovens that do not have variable power levels. It is also a good method to use when you are cooking a whole meal in the microwave oven as it frees the oven long enough to cook another dish while the rice stands.

1. Combine 1 cup (250 mL) converted or long grain rice, and 2 cups (500 mL) water in a 2 qt. (2L) casserole dish. Add salt to taste and 2 tbsp. (30 mL) oil or butter. Cover.
2. Microwave on HIGH for 6 to 8 minutes or until mixture boils.
3. Let stand 10 minutes.
4. Microwave on HIGH for 3 to 4 minutes.
5. Let stand 5 minutes. Fluff with a fork and serve.

METHOD B:

This method works well for all types of rice. They slowly simmer to fluffy perfection.

1. In a 2 qt. (2L) casserole, microwave water on HIGH until boiling — about 5 to 6 minutes.
2. Add 1 cup (250 mL) rice, salt to taste and 2 tbsp. (30 mL) oil.
3. Cover and simmer on MEDIUM-LOW for times listed below:

   CONVERTED RICE & LONG GRAIN RICE: 1 cup (250 mL) rice plus 2 cups (500 mL) boiling water simmers for 14 to 16 minutes.

   BROWN RICE: 1 cup (250 mL) rice plus 3 cups (750 mL) boiling water simmers for 19 to 25 minutes.

   WILD RICE: 1 cup (250 mL) rice plus 2½ (625 mL) cups boiling water simmer for 45 to 60 minutes. If a softer product is desired, presoak wild rice before cooking.
4. Let stand 5 minutes. Fluff with a fork before serving.

TRICKS WITH RICE

- Substitute meat broth for water.
- Substitute juice for water — tomato or orange.
- Add 2 envelopes (78 g) of dry onion soup mix to boiling water.
- Add chopped raw onion and butter — 2 tbsp. (30 mL) each.
- Microwave 4 slices of bacon on HIGH for 4 minutes. Crumble and add to rice.
- Add 1 or 2 tbsp. (15 or 30 mL) chopped chives or green onion.

HINTS FOR RICE

- Rice should require virtually no stirring during cooking. In fact, less stirring is better since over-stirring can cause a "mushy" texture. Even after rice is cooked, avoid too much tossing.
- The standing time, after cooking, allows the rice to finish its own cooking and to absorb all of the moisture.
- Long grain white rice begins cooking at HIGH, but finishes cooking at a lower setting. This slower cooking helps to give rice a fluffier texture.
- Quick-cooking rice can be simply rehydrated. Bring the required amount of water to a boil in the serving dish. Stir in quick-cooking rice, cover with glass lid or heavy-duty plastic wrap, and let stand according to the amount of time required on the package.
- Slightly undercook pasta and rice that will be cooked in a casserole.

PASTA

Advocates of microwaved pasta maintain that they have a better flavor and firm "al dente" texture. Other people prefer to cook them conventionally because this leaves the microwave oven free to cook the sauce or main dish. I find it more convenient to cook lasagna noodles and spaghetti in the microwave oven because I can place whole pieces in a glass 8 x 12-inch (20 x 30 cm) baking dish for cooking.

TO COOK PASTA IN THE MICROWAVE OVEN:

1. Place 8 oz. (250 g) pasta in a 2½ to 3 qt. (3L) capacity casserole or baking dish.
2. Cover with 1½ to 2 qts. (2L) of BOILING water. Add 2 tbsp. (30 mL) oil.
3. Cover with matching glass lid or heavy plastic wrap.
4. Microwave on HIGH for times listed below:
   LASAGNA NOODLES: 13 to 15 minutes
   SPAGHETTI: 7 to 8 minutes
   MACARONI, BOWS, SHELLS OR NOODLES: 7 to 8 minutes

HINTS FOR PASTA

- Pasta should be stirred or turned over during cooking time.
- Drain and rinse pasta before serving.
- Slightly undercook pasta that is to be added to a casserole.
- If you like, you can add uncooked lasagna noodles to lasagna. Be sure to cover it with plastic wrap during cooking time.
- Pasta in sauce reheats very well.
- When cooking pasta casseroles containing delicate ingredients like cheese or cream, use a lower power setting.

CEREAL

A microwave oven can solve a common breakfast problem for busy families who eat at different times. Now each person can make his own breakfast favourite in a serving bowl. It saves on morning hassles, and best of all, no one gets stuck with scrubbing a sticky porridge pot.

You do not have to boil the water before adding the cereal, you can mix it all together before cooking. However, I prefer to boil the water first because it is faster and there is less likelihood of a boilover.

TRICKS WITH CEREAL

- Top it with maple syrup and walnuts.
- Mix in fruit flavoured yogurt.
- Mix in plain yogurt and applesauce. Sprinkle with cinnamon.
- Top it with fresh fruit and cream.
- Garnish with chopped, dried fruit like dates or apricots.
- Sprinkle with cinnamon and nutmeg.
- Sprinkle granola on top of cereal.

CURRIED RICE

A unique combination of textures and flavours.

1½ cups	boiling water	375 mL
1	chicken bouillon cube	
2 tbsp.	butter	25 mL
1 or 2 tsp.	curry powder	5-10 mL
¾ cup	uncooked rice	175 mL
1	small onion, chopped	
¼ cup	peanuts	50 mL
¼ cup	raisins	50 mL

1. In a 2 qt. (2 L) casserole dish, dissolve bouillon cube in water. Stir in butter, curry powder, rice and onion.

2. Cover and microwave on HIGH for 5 to 7 minutes and then on MEDIUM-LOW for 10 minutes. Let stand for 5 minutes.

3. Stir in raisins and peanuts. Let stand another 5 minutes. You may want to microwave it on HIGH for 1 or 2 minutes just before serving.

VARIATION: Substitute slivered almonds for peanuts.

Your Time: _____

AUNT SUE'S "FRIED" RICE

It really does taste like fried rice — without the work.

2 cups	uncooked rice	500 mL
4 cups	water	1 L
1 pkg.	onion soup mix	1
2 tbsp.	soy sauce	25 mL

1. Combine ingredients in a 3-qt. (3 L) casserole dish. Cover and microwave on HIGH for 7 to 8 minutes. Let stand covered for 10 minutes.

2. Microwave on HIGH for another 7 to 8 minutes. Let stand for 10 minutes. If rice is not fluffy, microwave for another on HIGH 2 to 3 minutes and allow another 5 minutes standing time.

Your Time: _____

SPICED RICE & PEAS

Adds zip to a meal.

1 cup	uncooked rice	250 mL
2 cups	water	500 mL
2 tbsp.	butter	25 mL
½ lb.	mushrooms	250 g
1 cup	peas, fresh OR frozen	250 mL
½ tsp.	Tabasco sauce	2 mL
⅛ tsp.	black pepper	.5 mL

1. Place rice and water in a 1½ qt. (1.5 L) casserole dish. Cover and microwave on HIGH for 10 minutes. Let stand on counter for 10 minutes.

2. Meanwhile, slice mushrooms. Place butter in a 1-qt. (1 L) casserole dish and microwave on HIGH for 30 seconds. Stir in mushrooms. Microwave on HIGH for 2½ to 3 minutes. Stir once or twice during cooking time.

3. Stir mushrooms, peas, tabasco sauce and pepper into rice. Microwave on HIGH for 3 to 4 minutes, just until peas are done.

VARIATION: This recipe is nice with brown rice, but the times in step 1 would be changed to microwave on HIGH for 12 minutes. Let stand for 20 minutes, then microwave on HIGH for 3 to 4 minutes.

Your Time: _____

VEGETABLE RICE PILAF

A versatile way to dress up rice.

1½ cups	boiling water	375 mL
1	chicken bouillon cube	1
2 tbsp.	butter	25 mL
¾ cup	uncooked rice	175 mL
1	small onion, chopped	1
¼ cup	finely diced celery	50 mL

1. In a 2 qt. (2 L) casserole dish dissolve bouillon cube in water. Stir in remaining ingredients.

2. Cover and microwave on HIGH for 5 to 7 minutes and then on MEDIUM-LOW for 10 minutes. Let stand 5 or more minutes, until rice is fluffy.

VARIATIONS: Add any or all of the following: ¼ cup (50 mL) chopped red or green pepper, ¼ cup (50 mL) slivered almonds, ¼ cup (50 mL) raisins.

Your Time: _____

BROCCOLI & RICE CASSEROLE

A tempting blend of textures.

1 tbsp.	butter	15 mL
1	small onion, chopped	1
2	stalks celery, chopped	2
2 cups	chopped broccoli	500 mL
1-10 oz.	can cream of mushroom soup	284 mL
1 cup	grated cheddar cheese	250 mL
2 cups	cooked rice	500 mL

1. Place butter in a 3-qt. (3 L) casserole dish and microwave on HIGH for 30 seconds.

2. Stir onion and celery into butter. Microwave on HIGH for 3 to 4 minutes, or until tender.

3. Stir in broccoli. Cover and microwave on HIGH for 6 to 8 minutes, just until tender crisp but not quite done.

4. Stir in remaining ingredients. Cover and microwave on HIGH for 6 to 8 minutes, just until heated through.

Your Time: _____

SPANISH RICE

Delicious as a side dish or as a meal in itself.

6	slices bacon	
1 cup	uncooked long grain rice	250 mL
1	medium onion, chopped	1
¼ cup	green pepper, chopped	50 mL
1-19 oz.	can tomatoes	540 mL
1 cup	water	250 mL
¼ cup	ketchup	50 mL
1 tsp.	salt	5 mL
½ tsp.	chili powder	2 mL
⅛ tsp.	pepper	.5 mL

1. Place bacon in a glass pie plate. Cover with paper towel. Microwave on HIGH for 6 minutes.

2. Remove bacon and set aside. Stir rice, onion, and green pepper into drippings. Spread around pie plate. Microwave on HIGH for 4 minutes or until lightly toasted.

3. In a 2-qt. (2 L) casserole dish combine remaining ingredients and add rice, green pepper and onion to this. Cover and microwave on HIGH for 7 to 8 minutes.

4. Let stand 10 minutes. Microwave on HIGH for 7 to 8 minutes.

5. Crumble bacon and stir into rice. Serve.

VARIATION:

WHOLE MEAL DEAL: Microwave 1 lb. (500 g) of crumbled lean ground beef on HIGH for 5 minutes. Drain and stir this into mixture in step 3.

JIFFY SPANISH RICE: Substitute Minute Rice for long grain rice. Do not brown it with the onion and green pepper, add it to the remaining ingredients. Microwave on HIGH for 8 to 10 minutes. Let stand, covered, for 5 to 10 minutes. Stir halfway through cooking time.

Your Time: _____

PLANNED-OVER PORK & RICE CASSEROLE

Your family will never identify this as leftovers.

4	slices bacon	4	
1	small onion, chopped	1	
1	small green pepper, chopped	1	
1 cup	uncooked rice	250	mL
1-14 oz.	can tomatoes	398	mL
1¼ cup	pork OR chicken broth stock	300	mL
1¾ cup	cubed cooked pork	425	mL
⅛ tsp.	pepper	.5	mL
1 tsp.	salt	5	mL
¼ cup	grated Parmesan cheese	50	mL

1. Place bacon slices in a 2-qt. (2 L) casserole dish. Microwave on HIGH for 4 minutes or until crisp. Crumble and set aside.

2. Stir onion and green pepper into bacon drippings. Microwave on HIGH for 2 minutes.

3. Add rice, tomatoes, stock, cooked pork, salt and pepper. Cover and microwave on HIGH for 10 to 12 minutes. Let stand for 10 minutes.

4. Microwave on HIGH for 10 to 12 minutes. Let stand 10 minutes.

5. Just before serving, stir in crumbled bacon. Top with Parmesan cheese.

Your Time: _____

FETTUCINE PAPALINA

This scrumptious pasta dish is similar to the one I always order in my favourite Italian restaurant — I could enjoy this often.

6	slices bacon OR ham	6
¼ cup	chopped onion	60 mL
1 cup	sliced mushrooms	250 mL
1 cup	Parmesan cheese	250 mL
¼ cup	butter	60 mL
½ cup	whipping cream	125 mL
	salt and pepper to taste	
2 cups	cooked fettucine OR broad noodles	500 mL

1. Chop bacon or ham. Place in a 1½-qt. (1.5 L) casserole dish with onion and mushrooms. Cover and microwave on HIGH for 6 to 8 minutes, or until vegetables are tender. Stir several times during cooking time. Drain.

2. Stir in cheese, butter, cream, salt and pepper. Microwave on MEDIUM for 4 to 5 minutes or until butter is melted and sauce is hot. Stir several times during cooking time.

3. Stir in noodles. It may be necessary to microwave on MEDIUM for 2 or 3 more minutes to heat.

Your Time: _____

SOUR CREAM GRAVY

I use this sauce on noodles, perogies, potatoes and even macaroni.

6	slices bacon, ham or smoked sausage	6
1	large onion	1
2 tsp.	flour	10 mL
1 cup	sour cream	250 mL
	salt & pepper to taste	

1. Place bacon in a 9-inch (24 cm) glass pie plate. Cover with paper towel and microwave on HIGH for 6 minutes.

2. Remove bacon from drippings, crumble and set aside.

3. Slice onion into drippings and stir to coat. Microwave on HIGH for 2 minutes, or until tender. Remove and set aside with bacon.

4. Stir flour into drippings and then stir in sour cream, salt and pepper. Add onions and meat and microwave on MEDIUM-HIGH for 2½ to 4 minutes, just until hot and thickened.

Your Time: _____

PASTA & SALMON MEDLEY

Salmon is unforgetable when combined with pasta in this delicious vege-table sauce.

1	clove garlic, minced	1
1	bunch broccoli, cut into 2-inch (5 cm) pieces	1
½ lb.	mushrooms, quartered	250 g
2	medium carrots, sliced	
2	green onions, cut into 1-inch (2.5 cm) pieces	
1-12 oz.	pkg. fettucine noodles	350 g
2 tbsp.	butter OR margarine	25 mL
2 tbsp.	flour	25 mL
2½ cups	milk	625 mL
1	chicken bouillon cube	1
¼ cup	grated Parmesan cheese	50 mL
1-7¾ oz.	can salmon, drained	213 mL

1. In a 3-qt. (3 L) casserole dish combine garlic, broccoli, mushrooms, carrots and onions. Cover and microwave on HIGH for 8 to 10 minutes or until vegetables are tender. Stir several times. Let stand, covered.

2. Meanwhile, cook fettucine noodles. Place 1½-qt. (1.5 L) of boiling water in a 3-qt. (3 L) casserole dish. Add noodles, cover and microwave on HIGH for 6 to 8 minutes. Stir and let stand for 5 to 7 minutes. Drain, rinse and set aside.

3. Microwave butter in a 4-cup (1 L) glass measure on HIGH power for 30 seconds. Stir in flour. Gradually stir in milk. Add bouillon cube and stir until dissolved. Microwave on HIGH for 4 to 5 minutes, stirring every 30 seconds, or until thickened. Stir in cheese, until melted.

4. Flake salmon and stir into vegetable mixture along with the cheese sauce. Serve over noodles or stir noodles into salmon mixture before serving. It may need to be reheated by microwaving, covered, on MEDIUM for 3 to 4 minutes.

Your Time: _____

139

LASAGNA

Now that's Italian!

1½ lb.	lean ground beef	750 g
½ cup	chopped onion	125 mL
1-14 oz.	can tomato sauce	398 mL
1 tsp.	salt	5 mL
2 tsp.	oregano	10 mL
½ tsp.	basil	2 mL
1 tsp.	Italian seasoning	5 mL
1	clove garlic, minced OR ¼ tsp. (1 mL) garlic powder	1
⅛ tsp.	black pepper	.5 mL
½ lb.	lasagna noodles	250 g
1	egg	1
1 pt.	dry cottage cheese	500 mL
1 lb.	mozzarella cheese	500 g
¼ cup	Parmesan cheese	50 mL

1. Combine ground beef and onion in 2-qt. (2 L) casserole dish. Microwave on HIGH for 8 to 10 minutes. Stir once or twice during cooking time. Drain.

2. Blend in tomato sauce and seasonings. Microwave, covered, on HIGH for 10 minutes. Stir once or twice during cooking time. Set aside. (For extra "cooked in" flavour, if I have time, I let it sit on a stove burner at LOW while I prepare the rest.)

3. Lay lasagna noodles in a glass 8 x 12-inch (1.5 L) pan. Cover with boiling water and add 1 tbsp. vegetable oil. Microwave on HIGH for 8 to 10 minutes. Rearrange halfway through cooking time. Drain.

4. Meanwhile combine cottage cheese and egg in a bowl.

5. In the 8 x 12-inch (1.5 L) baking dish, layer ⅓ at a time, the meat sauce, Parmesan cheese, noodles, cottage cheese and mozzarella cheese.

6. Microwave on MEDIUM-HIGH for 14 to 16 minutes.

VARIATION:

NO COOK NOODLE LASAGNA: Add ¼ cup (60 mL) water to meat sauce and skip step 3. Just layer raw noodles. Cover with plastic wrap while cooking.

Your Time: _____

GRANOLA

Yummy! not overly sweet.

4 cups	oatmeal	1 L
¾ cup	unsweetened coconut	200 mL
½ cup	wheat germ	125 mL
½ cup	sesame seeds	125 mL
½ cup	chopped filberts, walnuts OR pecans	125 mL
½ cup	liquid honey	125 mL
½ cup	vegetable oil	125 mL
½ tsp.	salt	2 mL
1 tsp.	vanilla	5 mL
2 tbsp.	water	25 mL

1. Combine dry ingredients in a large bowl. Set aside.

2. In a 2-cup (500 mL) glass measure, microwave honey on HIGH for 45 seconds. Stir in vegetable oil, salt, vanilla and water.

3. Stir into dry ingredients. Spread evenly in a glass 8 x 12-inch (2 L) baking dish. Microwave on HIGH for 10 minutes. Stir twice during cooking time.

4. Microwave on HIGH for another 5 minutes. Stir and check it for crispness every 2 minutes. Stop when slightly crisp.

5. Cool and store in an airtight container.

TIP: If you like a sweeter granola, and more honey or ½ cup (250 mL) raisins.

Your Time: _____

PORRIDGE BY THE BOWL

So quick and so easy and best of all, there's no pot to scrub.

1 cup	water	250 mL
	pinch of salt	
½ cup	quick oats	125 mL

1. Place water and salt into a 10-oz. (300 mL) cereal bowl. Microwave on HIGH for 2 to 2½ minutes, until it boils.

2. Stir in quick oats. Microwave on HIGH for 20 seconds. Let stand for 1 minutes.

CREAM OF WHEAT CEREAL: 1¼ cups (310 mL) boiling water plus 2½ tbsp. (65 mL) cereal.

VARIATION: When Daddy makes this for my kids, he tops it with a spoon of butter and a sprinkling of brown sugar and raisins. They eat it up in record time.

Your Time: _____

VEGETABLES

Of all the wonders a microwave oven can perform, cooking vegetables is by far the best: vibrant colour, bright fresh taste, natural tender crisp texture and maximum nutrition are the benefits of the easiest cooking method.

⊙━┱ THE KEY TO SUCCESS WITH VEGETABLES

Most vegetables are cooked without the addition of water so the colour, flavour and water-soluble nutrients are not lost in the water. Until you taste microwaved vegetables, you won't realize how much flavour you discarded with the water. The only time that I add water when cooking vegetables is when they are old and somewhat dried out — the water can often revitalize them.

Water softens vegetables so if you prefer them quite soft (green beans, asparagus, potatoes, carrots, and other root vegetables are sometimes better this way), adding a bit may be desirable — 2 tablespoons of water is usually sufficient, but definitely don't use more than it takes to cover the bottom of your pan — do not cover them completely in water. Water can also promote even cooking in a full dish of vegetables.

SEASON BUT DON'T SALT

The addition of salt is unnecessary; in fact, it is undesirable because salt draws out the moisture, leaving the vegetables tough, dry and flavourless. It is best to add the salt to the water before adding the vegetables or sprinkle the salt onto the vegetables after microwaving. However, you will not likely miss using salt because the flavour of microwaved vegetables is so fresh.

VEGETABLES COOK QUICKLY

Vegetables are usually cooked on HIGH power and for a very short time. The speed of cooking prevents nutrients from being cooked out. Timing varies with each vegetable, depending on how dense it is, how large the pieces are and of course, how much you are cooking at a time. Most microwave oven manuals have very good timing charts and I recommend you consult them for accurate cooking times. However, as a general rule of thumb, 4 to 6 servings of most fresh vegetables take about 6 to 9 minutes.

COOK VEGETABLES COVERED

For best results, cover vegetables tightly with plastic wrap leaving a small vent to allow excess steam to escape. If you are cooking in a casserole dish, cover with the matching lid. Covers also speed up the cooking process and promote even cooking. Leaving the cover on during the standing time allows vegetables to finish cooking. Whole vegetables can be cooked in their own skins, but don't forget to pierce them.

STIRRING VEGETABLES

When stirring vegetables, stir in such a way as to move the cooler inner vegetables to the outer edge and the warmer outer vegetables to the middle.

STANDING TIME

Vegetables have almost no standing time — usually about as long as it takes you to bring them from the microwave oven to the table. When preparing a whole meal with your microwave oven, you should usually cook your vegetables last. However, if you leave the cover on there is more standing time. If vegetables are a bit underdone to your taste, I recommend you let them stand, covered, for about five minutes rather than cooking them longer.

VEGETABLE COMBINATIONS & CASSEROLES

When microwaving vegetable casseroles or combinations several microwave techniques become important. Whenever possible, vegetables should be cut into uniform pieces. When combining different sizes of vegetables, place larger pieces towards the outside of the dish or add smaller pieces later. Likewise in combining vegetables of varying densities — dense, slow cooking vegetables are placed around the outside of the dish and quicker cooking vegetables are placed in the centre or added later. Stir the casserole once or twice during cooking time, if possible. Fresh or frozen vegetables can usually be interchanged without any changes in cooking times. Salt and seasonings should not be sprinkled on top but should be mixed into the sauce or liquid part of the vegetable dish or sprinkled on top after cooking.

FROZEN VEGETABLES

When microwaved, the taste of frozen vegetables is hard to distinguish from fresh. Normally, they do not need to be defrosted prior to cooking unless they are frozen in a large solid pack. DO NOT ADD WATER when microwaving frozen vegetables, there is usually enough moisture on the vegetable. However, they should be covered with a glass lid or plastic wrap to keep in that moisture. Frozen vegetables packaged in plastic cooking pouches can be cooked right in the pouch — be sure to pierce the pouch on the top so that steam can escape. A 10-oz. (284 g) package or 1½ cups (375 mL) of frozen vegetables usually cooks on HIGH power for 6 to 9 minutes.

FROZEN VEGETABLE HINTS

To prepare frozen vegetables for a casserole, cook them right in the box! Remove the outer wrapping and pierce box with a fork; then follow microwave directions on package. Gently squeeze package to get rid of extra water before opening.

Because the printed wax paper covering can mark the oven floor, you may wish to remove this covering or place the package on a paper towel.

CANNED VEGETABLES

Canned vegetables are already cooked and need only to be heated to serving temperature. I usually drain them or leave just a bit of the liquid and warm them in a serving dish — a 14-oz. can (398 mL), drained, fits in a soup bowl. They should be covered with a lid, overturned plate or wax paper.

BLANCHING VEGETABLES

Blanching vegetables in the microwave keeps the kitchen cool during those hot harvest days. It can even save some time. However, for best results, cook in small amounts as indicated in the following chart. Microwave blanching is especially convenient for putting up a day's picking immediately. When buying bulk fresh vegetables, you may find conventional methods quicker. The times given in the chart are accurate for my test ovens but a general rule of thumb that will help you with your oven is to blanch vegetables for one quarter to one third of their microwave cooking time.

STEPS TO QUALITY FROZEN VEGETABLES:

1. Select vegetables that are at their peak.
2. Blanch and freeze them immediately — the quicker they reach the freezer, the sweeter their flavour.
3. Prepare vegetables as indicated in the chart.
4. Measure amount to be blanched accurately and place in a glass casserole dish. Add water as directed in the chart and cover dish.
5. Have plenty of ice water ready for quick cooling. Also lay out toweling to absorb excess moisture before packing vegetables in freezer containers.
6. Microwave vegetables for the minimum time given on the chart. Stir or rearrange halfway through cooking time.
7. After total minimum cooking time, stir and check for doneness. The colour of the vegetables should be evenly bright throughout. If they are not, cover and cook until they are evenly bright throughout or for the maximum time. Stir and check after each minute of added time.
8. Immerse vegetables in ice water immediately to stop further cooking. Once the vegetables feel cold, spread them on the toweling to absorb excess moisture.
9. Package in freezer containers or bags. Seal, label and freeze quickly. To speed freezing, place in single layers against freezer walls or in the coldest part of your freezer. They can be stacked after they are completely frozen.
10. Frozen vegetables should be used within one year. After this time they will dry out and deteriorate. Maintain a freezer temperature of 0°F (-18 C) or below for best results.

BLANCHING CHART

All vegetables are blanched in a covered 1½-qt. (1.5 L) casserole dish unless otherwise noted.

Vegetables	Preparation	Amount of Vegetable	Amount of Water	Time (in minutes) on HIGH
Asparagus**	Trim. Cut into 2-inch pieces	1 lb. (.5 kg)	¼ cup (60 mL)	2 to 4
Beans**	Remove ends. Cut into 1" lengths	1 lb. (.5 kg)	½ cup (125 mL)	4 to 6
Broccoli	Soak in salt water to remove insects. Rinse. Remove woody parts. Chop or cut into spears.	1 - ¼ cup (310 mL)	4 to 6	
Carrots	Wash and remove tops of young tender carrots	1 lb. (.5 kg)	¼ cup (60 mL)	3½ to 6
Cauliflower*	Wash and break into flowerets.	1½ to 1¾ lb. (.7 - .8 kg)		3½ to 5
Corn on the Cob*	Remove husk and silk.	4 ears	none	3½ to 5
Corn, Kernel	Cut from cob.	4 cups (1 L)	none	3½ to 4
Peas	Wash and shell.	4 cups (1 L)	¼ cup (60 mL)	3½ to 4
Spinach*	Remove tough stems. Wash.	4 cups (1 L)	none	1½ to 3
Turnips**	Cube.	1 lb. (.5 kg)	¼ cup (60 mL)	3 to 5
Squash or Zucchini	Wash. Peel if desired. Cut in ¼-inch cubes			3 to 5

* These vegetables may need a larger casserole dish like a 2 to 3-qt.

** Depending on your taste, you may not like these blanched with so little water. Do a test batch to see how you like them. You may prefer to blanch these vegetables completely covered with water. Of course they will need the maximum amount of time if you use the extra water.

MOM'S HARVARD BEETS

An attractive side dish that just needs reheating.

½ cup	sugar	125 mL
2 tbsp.	cornstarch	30 mL
½ cup	vinegar	125 mL
½ cup	boiling water	125 mL
	salt & pepper to taste	
2 cups	sliced OR diced cooked beets	500 mL

1. Combine all ingredients EXCEPT beets in a 1½-qt. (1.5 L) casserole dish. Microwave on HIGH for 3 minutes or until thickened. Stir twice during cooking time.

2. Stir in beets. Cover and microwave on HIGH for 2 minutes, just until hot.

Your Time: _____

BRUSSELS SPROUTS MEDLEY

Colourful and pungent.

3 tbsp.	butter	45 mL
2 cups	brussels sprouts, halved	500 mL
1	leek, cut into ½-inch (1 cm) slices	1
2	large carrots, cut into 1/2-inch (1 cm) slices	2
¼ tsp.	caraway seeds	1 mL
⅛ tsp.	pepper	.5 mL
	sour cream	

1. Place butter in a 2-qt. (2 L) casserole dish. Microwave on HIGH for 45 seconds.

2. Stir in vegetables and seasonings. Cover and microwave on HIGH for 10 to 12 minutes or until tender when pierced with a fork. Stir twice during cooking time.

3. Serve with a dollop of sour cream on each serving.

Your Time: _____

BROCCOLI AND CAULIFLOWER SALAD

Microwave cooking leaves vegetables salad crisp.

2 cups	fresh broccoli flowerets	500 mL
2 cups	fresh cauliflower flowerets	500 mL
1 cup	fresh sliced mushrooms	250 mL
2 tbsp.	lemon juice	30 mL
¼ tsp.	mustard seed	1 mL
⅛ tsp.	pepper	.5 mL
1 tbsp.	finely chopped fresh dill	15 mL
1 tbsp.	vegetable oil	15 mL
¼ tsp.	salt	1 mL

1. Cook broccoli and cauliflower on HIGH for 5 to 7 minutes or until tender crisp. Rinse under cold water. Drain.

2. Place in a large salad bowl. Add mushrooms.

3. Combine remaining ingredients. Pour over vegetables and toss. Cover and chill for 1 hour before serving.

Your Time: _____

BROCCOLI IN CHEESE

An old favourite takes on a new glow.

12	spears of fresh broccoli OR 1-10 oz. (300 g) pkg. broccoli spears	12
1 cup	shredded Swiss cheese	250 mL
⅓ cup	mayonnaise	75 mL
½ tsp.	Dijon mustard	2 mL
2 tbsp.	grated onion	30 mL
¼ tsp.	salt	1 mL
⅛ tsp.	pepper	.5 mL

1. Arrange broccoli spears in a glass 8 x 12-inch (1.5 L) baking dish with stalks toward outside edges of dish and flowers toward centre. Cover with plastic wrap, leaving a small vent. Microwave on HIGH for 7 to 9 minutes or until tender crisp.

2. Meanwhile, combine remaining ingredients. Spread mixture over broccoli. Cover and microwave on MEDIUM for 2 to 4 minutes, until cheese is melted.

Your Time: _____

CREAMED CABBAGE

Cabbage cooks well in the microwave and with a minimal odour, too.

1 tbsp.	butter	15	mL
2 tsp.	cornstarch	10	mL
1 tsp.	salt	5	mL
¼ cup	whipping cream	60	mL
	dash of nutmeg		
½ tsp.	fresh dill, chopped	125	mL
4 cups	shredded cabbage	1	L

1. Place butter in a 2-qt. (2 L) casserole dish. Microwave on HIGH for 30 seconds. Stir cornstarch and salt into butter. Gradually stir in cream. Add remaining ingredients and mix well.

2. Microwave, covered, on HIGH for 12 to 14 minutes. Stir twice during cooking time.

Your Time: _____

RED CABBAGE

Adds a zippy flavour to any meal.

6	slices bacon	6	
4 cups	shredded red cabbage	1	L
2	cooking apples, peeled and cubed	2	
1 tsp.	salt	5	mL
⅛ tsp.	pepper	.5	mL
¼ tsp.	allspice	1	mL
2 tbsp.	brown sugar	30	mL
¼ cup	vinegar	60	mL

1. In a 2-qt. (2 L) casserole dish, microwave bacon on HIGH for 6 minutes. Crumble.

2. Add remaining ingredients and mix well. Cover and microwave on HIGH for 8 to 10 minutes. Stir twice during cooking time.

Your Time: _____

CORN ON THE COB

Cooking the corn in the husk retains the flavour of fresh picked corn.

1. Remove outer husk and silk from corn. If desired, place a bit of butter on the cob. Pull remaining husk over cob of corn and hold in place with a rubber band.

2. Place cobs of corn in a spoked wheel pattern with tips of the ears toward the centre and stem ends towards the outside. Microwave on HIGH for 2 to 3 minutes per cob of corn.

3. Carefully remove husk, after 3 minutes standing time, by holding stem end with a napkin or towel and pulling husk down and away from you. Watch out for steam.

VARIATION: Remove husk and silk and wrap in plastic wrap.

Your Time: _____

LEAH'S SCALLOPED CORN

Simply delicious!

1½ cups	kernel corn	325	mL
¾ cup	milk	175	mL
1	egg, slightly beaten	1	
½ cup	dry bread crumbs	125	mL
1	small onion, chopped	1	
¼ cup	green pepper, chopped	50	mL
	salt & pepper to taste		
2 tbsp.	butter	30	mL

1. Combine corn, milk and eggs in 1½-qt. (1.5 L) casserole dish. Stir in crumbs, onion, green pepper, salt and pepper. Dot with butter.

2. Microwave on MEDIUM for 15 to 18 minutes, or until knife inserted in center comes out clean.

Your Time: _____

LEAH'S GREEN BEAN CASSEROLE

Cooked in two steps to keep the crumbs crisp.

3-10 oz.	**pkg. frozen french-style green beans, thawed**	**300 g**
1-10 oz.	**can cream of mushroom soup**	**284 mL**
1	**small onion, chopped**	**1**
1 cup	**buttered bread crumbs OR slivered almonds**	**250 mL**

1. Separate beans into 1½-qt. (1.5 L) casserole dish. Stir in soup and onion.

2. Cover and microwave on HIGH for 7 to 10 minutes or until warmed. Stir.

3. Top with butter crumbs or almonds. Microwave, uncovered, on HIGH for 3 to 4 minutes, or until heated through.

Your Time: _____

GREEN BEANS & BACON

The dressing adds zest to the beans.

3	**slices bacon**	**3**
1-14 oz.	**can green beans, drained**	**398 mL**
1	**small onion, chopped**	**1**
2 tbsp.	**red wine vinegar**	**30 mL**
1 tsp.	**sugar**	**5 mL**
1 tsp.	**Worcestershire sauce**	**5 mL**
¼ tsp.	**salt**	**2 mL**

1. Place bacon slices on glass plate between paper towels. Microwave on HIGH for 3 minutes. Crumble.

2. Combine remaining ingredients in 1½-qt. (1.5 L) casserole dish. Top with bacon. Cover and microwave on HIGH for 3 to 4 minutes, until heated through.

Your Time: _____

WHOLE CAULIFLOWER

An easy way to impress company. Pour sauce over the top just before serving.

1	**medium head of cauliflower**	1
	Cheese sauce or sauce of your choice	

1. Wash head of cauliflower. Trim off outer leaves. Remove core, leaving a cone shaped hollow.

2. Place cauliflower on a glass plate and cover with plastic wrap.

3. Microwave on HIGH for 8 to 10 minutes, or until tender.

4. Remove plastic wrap and drain off excess water. Pour sauce over top of the head and serve.

Your Time: _____

PARSLEY BUTTERED CARROTS

A lovely way to do carrots.

2 tbsp.	butter	30 mL
2 cups	carrots, cut into ½ inch (1 cm) pieces	500 mL
1 tbsp.	chopped parsley	15 mL

1. Place butter in 1-qt. (1 L) casserole dish. Microwave on HIGH for 30 seconds. Stir in carrots and parsley.

2. Cover and microwave on HIGH for 6 to 8 minutes, or until tender. Stir twice during cooking time.

Your Time: _____

STUFFED MUSHROOMS

This is extremely tasty as a side dish or appetizer.

1 lb.	fresh mushrooms	500 g
4	slices bacon, chopped	4
2 tbsp.	finely chopped onion	30 mL
½ cup	soft bread crumbs	125 mL
2 tbsp.	grated Parmesan cheese	30 mL
⅛ tsp.	pepper	.5 mL

1. Remove mushroom stems and chop. Set aside.
2. Place bacon and onion in a medium glass bowl. Microwave on HIGH for 4 minutes or until bacon is crisp. Stir once during cooking time.
3. Add chopped stems, bread crumbs, cheese and pepper. Mix well.
4. Stuff mushroom caps with crumb mixture. Arrange in a circular pattern on a glass tray. Cover with plastic wrap and microwave on HIGH for 8 to 10 minutes.

Your Time: _____

SOUTHERN STYLE GREENS

Leaves stay a bright green when cooked to tender perfection.

4	slices bacon, chopped	4
1	small onion, chopped	1
1 qt.	fresh spinach, chard, turnip OR collard greens	1 L

1. Place bacon and onion in a 1½-qt. (1.5 L) casserole dish. Microwave on HIGH for 3 to 4 minutes.
2. Add greens. Cover and microwave on HIGH for 4 to 6 minutes, or until tender. Stir once or twice during cooking time.

Your Time: _____

PEAS & MUSHROOMS

A quick and easy complement for any meal.

2 tbsp.	butter	30 mL
1	small onion, chopped	1
1 cup	sliced mushrooms	250 mL
2 cups	peas, fresh or frozen	500 mL
1 tsp.	sugar	5 mL
1 tbsp.	chopped pimento	30 mL

1. Place butter in 1½-qt. (1.5 L) casserole dish. Microwave on HIGH for 30 seconds. Add onion and mushrooms. Stir well to coat vegetables with butter.

2. Microwave on HIGH for 4 to 6 minutes. Add remaining ingredients. Cover and microwave on HIGH for 3 to 4 minutes, or until vegetables are tender.

Your Time: _____

TATER BOATS

One thing every new microwave oven owner discovers quickly is the speed and convenience of baked potatoes. Tater boats are an interesting way to make a baked potato into a meal.

1. Slice each baked potato in half, lengthwise. Scoop out the centre to make a hollow. Set aside hollowed shells or boats.

2. Mash the potato centre with milk, seasonings and grated cheese if you like and fill the "boat" with this mixture. Microwave for 1 minute — just to reheat OR use the centre for another recipe like potato salad or hash-browns and fill the boat with any of the following:

CHEESE BOAT: Fill with hot cheese sauce and top with grated cheese.

BROCCOLI & CHEESE BOAT: Mix cooked, chopped broccoli with cheese sauce and fill potato boat. Top with grated cheese.

CHILI & CHEESE BOAT: Place a slice of cheddar cheese on each half of potato boat. Scoop ½ cup (125 mL) chili into the cavity and top with grated cheese.

HAM & CHEESE BOAT: Cube cooked ham and cream cheese. Mix with chopped green onion and fill "boat".

Each tater boat requires about ½ cup (125 mL) of filling and cooks on HIGH for 1 minute — just to reheat.

Your Time: _____

SCALLOPED POTATOES

Making scalloped potatoes in the microwave is a treat because cleanup is a snap.

2 tbsp.	butter	30 mL
2 tbsp.	flour	30 mL
1 cup	milk	250 mL
1½-qt.	potatoes, peeled and sliced	1.5 L
1	medium onion, chopped	1
	salt & pepper to taste	
	butter	

1. Place butter in a 2-cup (500 mL) glass measure. Microwave on HIGH for 30 seconds. Stir in flour. Gradually stir in milk, using a wire whisk. Microwave on MEDIUM-HIGH for 1½ to 2 minutes, until slightly thickened.

2. In a shallow 2½-qt. (2.5 L) casserole dish layer ⅓ of the potato, onion, seasonings and the sauce. Dot with butter. Repeat layers.

3. Cover with glass lid and microwave on MEDIUM-HIGH for 20 to 25 minutes. Stir two or three times during cooking time.

TIP: Be sure your casserole dish is only about half full to prevent a boilover.

VARIATIONS:

EASIEST SCALLOPED POTATOES: Use 1-10 oz. (284 mL) can of cream soup plus ½ can milk in place of the white sauce.

HAM & SCALLOPED POTATOES: Add 2 cups (500 mL) of diced cooked ham.

POTATOES AU GRATIN: Add ½ cup (125 mL) grated cheddar cheese to the white sauce and sprinkle ½ cup (125 mL) grated cheddar cheese on top before cooking.

Your Time: _____

MICRO CHIPS

Like oven fried potatoes but done more quickly in the microwave oven.

3	potatoes	3	
2 tbsp.	vegetable oil	30	mL
¼ cup	water	60	mL
¼ tsp.	Tabasco sauce	.5	mL
1	envelope Shake & Bake coating mix	1	
4 tbsp.	Parmesan cheese	60	mL
1 tsp.	salt	5	mL

1. Slice the potatoes thinly.

2. In a small bowl, combine vegetable oil, Tabasco sauce, and water.

3. Pour Shake & Bake mix into a plastic bag. Add cheese to Shake & Bake.

4. Dip potatoes in water mixture and then coat in Shake & Bake.

5. Spread the potato slices on a dinner plate. Microwave on HIGH for 6 to 7 minutes, or until lightly browned. Sprinkle lightly with salt.

Your Time: _____

CRUMB TOPPED TOMATOES

These tomatoes make an attractive garnish for any platter.

4	medium tomatoes	4	
⅓ cup	dry bread crumbs	75	mL
2 tbsp.	grated Parmesan cheese	30	mL
¼ tsp.	basil leaves	.5	mL

1. Slice tomatoes in half and arrange on a platter.

2. Combine remaining ingredients. Sprinkle on top of tomato halves.

3. Microwave, uncovered, on HIGH for 2 to 3 minutes or until tomatoes are warm. Serve immediately.

VARIATION: Sprinkle with crumbled bacon (3 slices microwaved on HIGH for 3 minutes).

Your Time: _____

AUNT EVA'S ZUCCHINI CREOLE

A spicy blend for a special treat.

6	strips bacon, chopped	6
1	large onion, chopped	1
2 cups	diced, unpeeled zucchini	500 mL
2	ribs celery, cut into ¼-inch (.5 cm) pieces	2
1	green pepper, cut into ½-inch (1 cm) squares	1
2	large tomatoes, peeled and chopped OR 1-14 oz. (398 mL) can of tomatoes	2
⅛ tsp.	sage	.5 mL
1	clove garlic, minced OR ⅛ tsp. garlic powder	.5 mL
	dash nutmeg	
	Dash Worcestershire sauce	
	salt & pepper to taste	

1. Place bacon and onion in a 3-qt. (3 L) casserole dish. Microwave on HIGH for 4 minutes or until onion is tender.

2. Add remaining ingredients and mix well. Cover and microwave on HIGH 8 to 10 minutes or until vegetables are tender.

3. Serve over cooked rice. This recipe keeps well in the refrigerator and tastes even better reheated. Reheat on MEDIUM-HIGH for about 5 minutes.

Your Time: _____

MARSHMALLOW FILLED SQUASH

The fluffy filling adds a festive touch to squash.

1	acorn squash	1
¼ cup	melted butter	60 mL
¼ cup	brown sugar	60 mL
8	large marshmallows	8

1. Halve the squash and remove seeds. Set each half on a glass plate — you may need to slice a bit off the bottom to make it sit steady.

2. Fill each squash half with half of the remaining ingredients. Cover with wax paper and microwave each half on HIGH for 4 to 6 minutes or until squash is tender. Allow it to stand for 3 to 5 minutes to complete cooking.

Your Time: _____

COLOURFUL VEGETABLE PLATTER

An impressive addition to any meal, pictured on the cover.

1	head broccoli, cut into 3-inch (6 cm) spears	1
1	head cauliflower, cut into floweretes	1
½ lb.	fresh mushrooms	250 g
2	large tomatoes, cut into 6 wedges each	2
¼ cup	butter	60 mL
¼ tsp.	garlic powder	2 mL
¼ cup	grated Parmesan cheese	2 mL

1. Arrange broccoli spears around outside edges of a round 13-inch (33 cm) glass platter with flowers toward the centre and stalks toward the outside. Repeat with cauliflower flowerets. Place mushrooms in centre of ring. Cover with plastic wrap, leaving a small vent. Microwave on HIGH for 8 to 10 minutes.

2. Carefully pull plastic wrap off of vegetables. Arrange tomato wedges around the platter.

3. Place butter in a glass measuring cup and microwave on HIGH for 45 seconds or until melted. Stir in garlic powder. Drizzle garlic butter over vegetables.

4. Sprinkle with Parmesan cheese. Re-cover with plastic wrap and microwave on HIGH for 1 minute or until tomatoes are heated through.

Your Time: _____

VEGETABLE SAUCES

One of my favourite ways to dress up vegetables or add variety is to serve them with a sauce. Before I had a microwave, this was a lot of fuss and bother but sauce is so quick and easy to make in the microwave (no scorching!) that I no longer wait for a special occasion to make sauce for vegetables.

I usually make sauces in a glass measuring cup. This saves dishes because I can cook and pour from the same dish; but it also promotes even cooking since the microwaves can penetrate the sauce from all sides. They don't need to be covered during cooking; covers make stirring awkward.

⊙—ⱬ THE KEY TO SUCCESS WITH SAUCE

As in conventional cooking, stirring is the key to a good sauce; however, they do not need the constant stirring and attention in the microwave. Generally they need to be stirred only about 3 or 4 times, just enough to keep the thickening agent (flour or cornstarch) suspended. If you forget to stir, the thickener will settle at the bottom of the dish and form a thick, gummy layer at the bottom of the liquid. To help myself to remember to stir, I usually set the timer for 30 seconds or a minute at a time — whenever the stirring should take place, rather than for the total cooking time. I also find that stirring with a fork or a wire whisk works the best.

SAUCES THICKENED WITH FLOUR OR CORNSTARCH

Sauces thickened with flour or cornstarch are best if allowed to stand for 2 minutes after they are thickened and then reheated for just a minute before serving. Remember to stir once during this standing time and again after the reheat time.

SAUCES THICKENED WITH EGG YOLK

Sauces thickened with egg yolk need to be beaten frequently to prevent lumps. They should not be boiled, just heated until thickened. Because this can happen so quickly, I usually cook them on MEDIUM or DEFROST and stir every 30 seconds. This may sound tedious, but it isn't really, because the sauce usually takes only 2 to 4 minutes cooking time.

WHITE SAUCE

This basic sauce dresses up almost any dish.

2 tbsp.	butter	30	mL
2 tbsp.	flour	30	mL
	salt & pepper to taste		
¼ tsp.	dry mustard, optional	2	mL
1 cup	milk	250	mL

1. Place butter in a 2-cup (500 mL) glass measure. Microwave on HIGH for 30 seconds or until melted. Stir in flour, salt, pepper and mustard. Gradually stir in milk.

2. Microwave on MEDIUM-HIGH for 2 minutes, or until thickened. Stir and check every 30 seconds.

VARIATIONS:

THIN WHITE SAUCE — Prepare white sauce as above using only 1 tablespoon (15 mL) each of butter and flour instead of the 2 tbsp. (30 mL) as stated above.

CHEESE SAUCE — Prepare white sauce as above until slightly thickened. Stir in ½ cup (125 mL) grated cheddar, processed or Swiss cheese. Continue stirring until cheese is melted and sauce is smooth. If cheese doesn't melt during stirring time, microwave on MEDIUM-HIGH for 1 minute on and stir again. I like to serve this sauce on macaroni as well as vegetables.

Your Time: _____

159

ALLEMANDE SAUCE

Lemon juice and mustard give this sauce a sharp taste. Serve it with any strong flavoured vegetable like brussels sprouts, broccoli and cabbage.

2 tbsp.	butter	30 mL
3 tbsp.	flour	45 mL
1 tsp.	chicken bouillon concentrate	5 mL
	pinch of dry mustard	
1 cup	water	250 mL
	salt & pepper to taste	
1	beaten egg yolk	1
1 tsp.	lemon juice	5 mL
2 tsp.	cream OR milk	10 mL

1. Place butter in 2-cup (500 mL) glass measure. Microwave on HIGH for 30 seconds. Stir in flour, chicken bouillon concentrate and mustard. Gradually stir in water.

2. Microwave on HIGH for 2½ to 3 minutes, or until mixture comes to a boil. Stir after each minute of cooking time. Microwave on LOW for 2 more minutes.

3. Stir a bit of the hot mixture into the egg yolk and then add warmed yolk into the hot sauce. Stir in the lemon juice and then the cream.

Your Time: _____

HOLLANDAISE SAUCE

This delicate, rich sauce adds a gourmet touch to vegetables and fish, yet does not require gourmet skills of the microwave cook.

	Dash of cayenne pepper	
2 tsp.	lemon juice	10 mL
1 cup	butter (DO NOT USE MARGARINE)	250 mL
4	egg yolks	4
1 tbsp.	light cream OR milk	15 mL

1. Place cayenne pepper, lemon juice and butter in 2-cup (500 mL) glass measure. Microwave on HIGH for 45 seconds. Stir butter until melted. Beat until smooth.

2. Add egg yolks and cream. Beat until well blended.

3. Microwave on MEDIUM for 15 seconds at a time, beating well after each. Continue this pattern until mixture thickens (about 1 to 1½ minutes) Do not overcook! or allow to boil. If mixture should curdle, add a few more drops of cream and beat until smooth.

Your Time: _____

1. Whole Wheat Muffins, page 182.
2. Citrus Marmalade, page 272.
3. Bacon & Tomato Tart, page 174.

BEARNAISE SAUCE

This sauce is traditionally served with meat but it can dress up a combination of green vegetables and meat. It goes well with strong flavoured vegetables like green beans or cabbage.

1 tbsp.	**finely chopped green onion**	15 mL
	salt & pepper to taste	
	dash of cayenne	
1 tsp.	**tarragon**	5 mL
½ cup	**butter**	125 mL
3 tbsp.	**wine vinegar or cider vinegar**	45 mL
4	**egg yolks, beaten**	4

1. In a glass 1-cup (250 mL) measure, combine all ingredients, except egg yolks. Microwave on HIGH for 2 to 3 minutes, just until the butter is all melted.

2. Beat egg yolks in a 2 cup (500 mL) glass measure. Using a wire whisk, gradually beat in the warm butter mixture.

3. Microwave on MEDIUM power for 10 seconds at a time, beating well after each 10 seconds, until sauce starts to thicken. This will take about 1 minute. Do not let sauce get too hot or it will curdle - microwave only until it starts to thicken. If you continue beating after this time, it will finish thickening out of the oven. Do not reheat. This sauce is usually served warm and will curdle if you reheat it.

MORNAY SAUCE

Mustard and chicken bouillon give this cheese sauce a distinctive flavour. It makes an elegant addition to vegetables like asparagus, cauliflower, cabbage, celery. It is also delicious with eggs.

2 tbsp.	butter	30 mL
2 tbsp.	flour	30 mL
	salt & pepper to taste	
½ tsp.	chicken bouillon concentrate	2 mL
¼ tsp.	dry mustard	1 mL
1½ cups	milk	325 mL
¼ cup	grated Parmesan cheese	60 mL
½ cup	grated Swiss OR Gruyere cheese	125 mL

1. Place butter in 4-cup (1 L) glass measure. Microwave on HIGH for 30 seconds. Stir in flour, salt, pepper, chicken bouillon and mustard.

2. Using a wire whisk, gradually stir in milk. Microwave on MEDIUM-HIGH for 5 to 7 minutes, stirring every minute, until the sauce thickens and boils.

3. Stir in cheese and continue stirring until cheese is melted and sauce is smooth. It may be necessary to microwave on MEDIUM-HIGH for another 30 seconds to 1 minute to completely melt the cheese.

Your Time: _____

SAUCE MOUSSELINE

Save this sauce for a special occasion. It is a fluffy, very rich Hollandaise sauce.

1	recipe Hollandaise Sauce (above)	1
¼ cup	whipping cream	60 mL

1. Whip cream until stiff peaks form.

2. Just before serving, fold whipped cream into warm Hollandaise sauce. Microwave on MEDIUM-LOW or DEFROST for 1 to 2 minutes - JUST UNTIL WARM.

VARIATION: I've also seen this sauce made with 2 beaten egg whites instead of cream. It would add the "fluff" without the calories.

Your Time: _____

EGGS & CHEESE

Eating a good breakfast no longer requires getting out of bed an hour earlier. You can cook a breakfast of bacon and eggs in the microwave oven faster than your coffee maker can brew your coffee. And your quick breakfast menu is not limited to that one entree. Eggs are so versatile that with each recipe they take on a new character, yet all are quick and easy to prepare with the help of the microwave oven. You won't even be slowed down by scrubbing sticky pans.

O—: THE KEY TO SUCCESS WITH EGGS & CHEESE

A delicate touch is needed when microwaving eggs and cheese. Both are sensitive to overcooking. When eggs are overcooked they become tough and rubbery; when cheese is overcooked, it becomes tough and stringy. Cooking eggs and cheese on MEDIUM power will help to prevent this toughness. Remove eggs and egg dishes while they are still slightly moist and slightly underdone. Let them stand a few minutes, covered, to complete the cooking process.

Because egg yolks are high in fat, they cook faster than the whites. Cooking eggs at MEDIUM power will allow the whites time to set without toughening the edges or overcooking the yolks. A cover of plastic wrap will also help to compensate for this difference. If sauce or water surrounds eggs, the whites cook before the yolks get too hard.

PREPARATION

It is important to pierce the yolk of an egg before cooking. This should be done with a fork or the pointed tip of a knife. This is necessary to keep the yolk from bursting during cooking. The membrane of the yolk holds in the steam but piercing it allows the steam to escape.

UTENSILS & COVERS

Eggs can be prepared in individual serving dishes or casserole dishes. Or for easy cleanup, use plastic coated paper bowls. I recommend you grease glass cooking dishes to make clean up easier.

Use the exact utensils recommended for cooking eggs in the recipes. Cooking times can vary due to the types and shapes of utensils.

Cook eggs covered. Glass lids or plastic wrap are the best coverings to use since they hold steam in better than other coverings. Since egg yolks cook faster than egg whites, a yolk can become tough or may "pop," while the white is is still undercooked. A cover will retain steam which cooks the egg white and keeps the yolk tender. A cover will also contain the mess if the egg does happen to burst!

HOW TO KNOW WHEN EGGS ARE COOKED

Remove eggs when slightly underdone. The whites should be slightly runny, they will firm during standing time. Standing time is important to complete cooking without toughening. Err on the side of caution; you can always let it stand another minute or two.

Overcooked eggs sometimes pop, even if you have pierced the yolk.

FOODS THAT DON'T WORK & WHY

DO NOT try to hard-boil eggs in the microwave. There is no way for the steam that builds up inside the egg to escape because you can't pierce shell or membrane. The pressure of this steam will burst the shell. It makes a real mess!

Hard-boiled eggs should not be reheated whole, they can be reheated if they are sliced or chopped first. They may still explode because the membrane of the yolk has not been pierced. Eggs sometimes become rubbery when reheated.

Souffles, unless they are specially formulated for microwave cooking will rise beautifully and then fall flat when the microwave oven shuts off. They need special ingredients to stabilize them for microwave cooking.

ADAPTING

Egg and cheese recipes convert easily for microwave cooking. When converting your own favourite egg recipes, select a similar recipe in this chapter or the manual that came with your microwave oven and use approximately the same amount of cooking time. Check eggs early during cooking to see if they are done. If not, cook slightly longer. Be careful not to overcook. Make a note of the correct time for your recipe for future reference.

HINTS FOR COOKING EGGS

- The size, temperature and age of the eggs can affect cooking times. Large eggs require a slightly longer cooking time than small eggs. Most recipes in cookbooks, including this one, use large eggs. If you are using medium or small eggs, less time will be needed. Room temperature eggs cook faster than refrigerator temperature eggs. Recipes in this chapter are based upon refrigerator temperature eggs.
- Older eggs should be used for scrambling, rather than for poaching or frying. Yolk membranes become weak in older eggs and tend to break during cooking when fried or poached. Use fresh eggs for frying and poaching.
- Before frying or poaching eggs, gently pierce or puncture the yolk membrane with a knife or the tines of a fork. This will slightly break the membrane and prevent the yolk from bursting during cooking.

- Be careful not to overcook eggs. Overcooking can cause eggs to become tough and "rubbery". Check eggs at the minimum amount of cooking time recommended in the recipe to see if they are done.
- For fluffier meringue, warm egg whites on MEDIUM HIGH (15 seconds for 2 egg whites) to bring chilled egg whites to room temperature. Room temperature egg whites whip to a greater volume.

CREATIVE TRICKS WITH EGGS

Add any of the following to omelets or scrambled eggs mixture:

- 1 or more slices of process cheese
- grated cheese — cheddar, mozzarella, swiss
- cubed cream cheese
- sliced sausage or wiener
- diced, cooked potato
- crumbled bacon
- chopped onion and/or green pepper
- chopped ham
- chopped tomato — sliced mushrooms

Any of the above can be combined. Use your imagination and add your favourite foods, or leftovers from your fridge.

OMELETS

French omelets do not crust or brown in the microwave. Puffy omelets are lovely.

QUICHE

Quiche is a savory custard pie rather than a sweet one. It is served as an appetizer in French meals, but it makes a great meal at breakfast, lunch or even supper.

Warm milk before adding to remaining ingredients or partially cook the custard before adding to shell. It will help the quiche to set more evenly.

When converting your favourite quiche recipe for microwave cooking use evaporated milk rather than cream for a more stable set.

Bake the pie shell before adding the custard or it will become soggy.
When done, a knife inserted should come clean but this test should be done AFTER the standing time. When you remove it from the microwave oven it should still be moist on top and may have begun to pull away from the edges of the pan. It will finish setting on its standing time.

CHEESE

- Processed cheese can be microwaved on HIGH. It melts to a creamier consistency than natural cheeses — an advantage when added to sauces and casseroles.

- Speedy cheese sauce — Spoon processed cheese spread from a jar into a glass measuring cup. Microwave on HIGH for 1 minute at a time, stirring after each minute, until liquid.

- Micro-melt cheese to top vegetables, casseroles, sandwiches, or even apple pie. Simply top cooked food with sliced or grated cheese. Microwave on MEDIUM HIGH for 20 seconds per slice — just until melted. Cheese melts fast.

- Soften cream cheese on LOW or DEFROST for even texture throughout. An 8 oz. package takes 1 minute.

- Cheese experts say that for fuller flavour natural cheeses should be served at room temperature. Microwave on LOW for 30 seconds at a time until it reaches the desired temperature.

- Quick "grilled" cheese sandwiches — Place a slice of cheese on a piece of buttered toast. Set on a napkin and microwave on MEDIUM HIGH for 20 seconds or until cheese starts to melt.

- For smooth sauce, add shredded cheese rather than chunks of cheese. If you add shredded cheese to hot sauce, the heat from the sauce is usually enough to melt the cheese.

- Cheese is added to a dish at the beginning only if the dish is cooking just to heat through. If the dish will cook longer than this, it is best to add the cheese near the end of the cooking time. This will prevent cheese from becoming tough and rubbery.

- The time cheese takes to melt varies depending on hardness, aging and type of storage.

POACHED EGGS

1. In a 10 oz. (284 mL) microwave safe bowl place ¼ cup (50 mL) water plus a dash each of vinegar and salt. Microwave on HIGH for 1 minute, or until boiling.

2. Break an egg into the boiling water. Cover and microwave on MEDIUM for 45 to 60 seconds. Let sit in water until completely set.

Your Time: _____

SPANISH POACHED EGGS

These spicy eggs will perk up breakfast or brunch.

1 tbsp.	butter	30	mL
1	small onion, chopped	1	
1-7 ½ oz.	can tomato sauce	213	mL
1	clove garlic, minced OR ⅛ tsp. garlic powder	.5	mL
¼ cup	chopped green & red peppers OR 1 tsp. (5 mL) chili powder	125	mL
¼ tsp.	oregano	1	mL
¼ tsp.	basil leaves	1	mL
2 tsp.	brown sugar	10	mL
4	eggs	4	

1. In a 1 ½-qt. (1.5 L) casserole dish, microwave butter on HIGH for 30 seconds to melt. Stir in chopped onion. Microwave on HIGH for 2 minutes or until onion is tender.

2. Stir in remaining ingredients except for eggs. Microwave on HIGH for 1½ minutes or until boiling.

3. Carefully break or slide eggs into sauce. Using a sharp tipped knife, give each egg yolk a sharp poke. Cover and microwave on MEDIUM-HIGH for 3 to 4 minutes. Egg whites should be set but moist. Let stand covered for 3 to 5 minutes to complete cooking.

4. Serve over tortillas or toast.

Your Time: _____

EGGS BENEDICT

An elegant breakfast with little fuss.

4	eggs, poached	4
½ cup	Hollandaise Sauce (Page 160)	125 mL
4	thin slices ham OR back bacon	4
2	English muffins, halved	2

1. Place ham or back bacon on plate. Microwave on HIGH for 45 seconds.

2. Arrange muffin halves, cut side up, on each serving plate. Top each half with a slice of ham or back bacon. Place 1 poached egg on each slice of bacon. Spoon Hollandaise Sauce over eggs.

3. Heat one plate at a time. Microwave on HIGH for 15 seconds or until heated through.

Your Time: _____

BAKED EGGS

1. Butter custard cups or each cup of a microwave muffin pan. Break 1 egg into each cup. Pierce yolk gently, with sharp tip of a knife or a fork.

2. Cover with plastic wrap.

3. Microwave on MEDIUM for 1 minute per large egg. 2 eggs take about 40 seconds to 1 minute; 4 eggs take 2 to 2½ minutes. If you hear a popping sound, you may be overcooking.

4. Let stand 1 to 2 minutes before eating. The longer the eggs remain in covered dishes, the more they will cook. Rely on this standing time to complete cooking process rather than microwaving for a longer time.

SPEEDY EGG SALAD: Prepare eggs as above, cooking each egg about 20 seconds longer than for baked eggs. When cool, mash and mix with salad dressing, salt and pepper and chopped onion.

Your Time: _____

BAKED EGGS MORNAY

A flavoursome way to delicately coddle eggs.

2 tbsp.	butter	30 mL
2 tbsp.	flour	30 mL
	salt & pepper to taste	
½ tsp.	prepared Dijon mustard	2 mL
½ tsp.	chicken bouillon mix	2 mL
1½ cups	mllk OR dairy half & half	325 mL
¼ cup	grated Parmesan cheese	60 mL
½ cup	shredded Swiss cheese	125 mL
4	eggs	4

1. In a 1½-qt. (1.5 L) round casserole dish, microwave butter on HIGH for 30 seconds or until melted. Stir in flour, salt, pepper, mustard and chicken bouillon mix. Using a wire whisk, gradually mix in the milk. Microwave on MEDIUM-HIGH for 4 to 5 minutes, or until slightly thickened. Stir every half minute to prevent lumps.

2. Reserve 2 tbsp. (30 mL) each of Parmesan cheese and Swiss cheese. Stir remaining cheese into sauce.

3. Carefully, break in the 4 eggs — just as for poaching eggs. Using a sharp tipped knife, give each egg yolk a quick poke. Sprinkle with reserved cheese.

4. Microwave covered on MEDIUM for 4 to 5 minutes. Egg whites should be set but still moist. Let stand, covered, for 4 to 5 minutes to complete cooking.

Your Time: _____

SCRAMBLED EGGS

Scrambled eggs are one of the foods that cook better in the microwave oven than conventionally. Not only do they take less time and need less stirring, but they are fluffier and greater in volume.

1. Beat eggs. Add 1 tbsp. (30 mL) milk per egg. Season to taste. Pour into greased dish.

2. Microwave on MEDIUM HIGH for 30 to 60 seconds at a time. Stir after each. Stand 1 minute.

   2 eggs — 1½ to 2 minutes
   4 eggs — 3 to 3½ minutes
   6 eggs — 4½ to 5½ minutes
   8 eggs — 5½ to 7½ minutes

Your Time: _____

DENVER SCRAMBLE

8	eggs	8
½ cup	milk	125 mL
1	medium tomato, chopped	1
1 cup	chopped ham	250 mL
¼ cup	chopped green pepper	50 mL
¼ cup	chopped onion	50 mL

1. Beat eggs and milk. Stir in remaining ingredients.

2. Pour into a greased 9-inch (22 cm) round cake dish. Microwave on MEDIUM HIGH for 1 minute at a time, stirring after each minute, for 6 to 8 minutes.

Your Time: _____

MORNING B.E.T. SANDWICH

Bacon, egg and tomato — an easy breakfast version of a popular sandwich.

1-3 oz.	pkg. cream cheese	125 g
4	eggs	4
	salt & pepper to taste	
1 tbsp.	butter OR vegetable oil	15 mL
8	bacon slices	8
4	slices toast	4
8	tomato slices	8
4	olives, sliced	4

1. Place cream cheese in a small mixing bowl. Microwave on DEFROST for 1 minute to soften.

2. Preheat a 10-inch (25 cm) browning tray on HIGH for 5 minutes. Meanwhile, beat together cream cheese, eggs, salt and pepper.

3. Grease surface of hot browning tray with butter or vegetable oil. Pour cream cheese and egg mixture onto tray. Microwave on MEDIUM-HIGH for 2 to 3 minutes, just until omelet is set — it should still look a bit moist on top. Set on a heat safe surface on the counter to finish cooking. When done, cut in half.

4. Place bacon slices on a glass plate between paper towels. Microwave on HIGH for 6 to 7 minutes or until crisp.

5. To assemble sandwiches: Place each half of omelet on a slice of toast. Top each with 2 slices tomato, 2 slices bacon and 2 olives, sliced. Top with another piece of toast. If neccessary, reheat assembled sandwiches on paper towels on MEDIUM-HIGH for 20 seconds each.

VARIATION: These can be made as open faced sandwiches if you prefer.

Your Time: _____

TOMATO SURPRISE

A nice change for brunch.

1	medium tomato	1
1	large egg	1
	sprinkle of pepper & salt	
2 tbsp.	grated cheese, bread crumbs OR crumbled bacon	30 mL

1. Cut top off tomato and remove meat of tomato. Set aside for use in another recipe. Place tomato shell in greased custard cup.

2. Break egg into tomato shell. Pierce yolk with sharp knife or fork. Sprinkle with remaining ingredients.

3. Cover with plastic wrap and microwave on MEDIUM for 2 to 2 ½ minutes. Let stand for 1 to 2 minutes before serving. The longer you let it stand with the cover on, the more it will cook. Rely on this standing time to complete cooking rather than microwaving for a longer time or your tomato will turn to mush.

Your Time: _____

POPEYE EGG

Kids love this. They can even make it themselves.

1	slice toasted bread, buttered	1
1	large egg	1

1. Cut a 3-inch (6 cm) diameter circle in toast with cookie cutter or knife. Place toast on plate. Break egg into hole. Pierce yolk with knife or fork. Cover with paper towel.

2. Microwave on MEDIUM-HIGH for 30 to 60 seconds.

Your Time: _____

AMAZING MUSHROOM QUICHE

Forms its own crust.

1 cup	shredded Swiss cheese	250 mL
1 cup	sliced mushrooms	250 mL
½ cup	flour	125 mL
	salt & pepper to taste	
4	eggs	4
1½ cups	milk	325 mL
2 tsp.	Worcestershire sauce	10 mL
½ cup	sliced green onion	125 mL

1. In a large bowl, mix together cheese, mushrooms, flour, salt and pepper.

2. In a small mixing bowl, beat together eggs, milk and Worcestershire sauce. Stir into mixture from step 1. Mix well.

3. Grease a 9-inch (24 cm) pie plate. Pour mixture into greased pie plate. Cover with plastic wrap, leaving a vent.

4. Microwave on MEDIUM for 9 to 12 minutes. Remove cover and sprinkle green onions over top. Microwave on MEDIUM for 2 or 3 more minutes or until it looks set, yet moist on top. If it starts pulling away from the edge of the pan, it is done. To complete cooking, let stand for 5 minutes on the counter.

Your Time: _____

PLAIN OMELET

1 tsp.	butter	5 mL
2	eggs	2
2 tbsp.	water or milk	30 mL
¼ tsp.	salt	1 mL
8	eggs	8
	dash pepper	

1. Melt butter in a 9-inch (22 cm) glass pie plate on HIGH for 20 seconds. Spread over the bottom of the plate.

2. Beat together remaining ingredients and pour into prepared plate. Cover plate with plastic wrap, leaving a small vent, and microwave on MEDIUM for 2 to 3 minutes or until set but still moist on top. Stir after 1 minute.

3. Let stand, covered, until moisture has disappeared, about 2 minutes.

4. Fold in half using a spatula and slide onto serving plate.

Your Time: _____

QUICHE LORRAINE

This delicious quiche can be served with or without the crust.

1-9-inch	baked pie shell	24	cm
½ lb.	bacon, cooked and crumbled	500	g
1 cup	shredded Swiss cheese	250	mL
¼ cup	minced onion	60	mL
4	eggs	4	
1 cup	evaporated milk	250	mL
½ tsp.	salt	2	mL
¼ tsp.	sugar	1	mL
⅛ tsp.	cayenne pepper	.5	mL

1. Sprinkle bacon, cheese and onion into pie shell.

2. Beat eggs, milk and seasonings in large mixing bowl until well blended. Pour into pie shell.

3. Microwave on MEDIUM-HIGH for 9 to 12 minutes, or until knife inserted in center comes out clean. If it starts to pull away from the edges, it is done. Let stand 1 to 3 minutes before serving.

Your Time: _____

BACON & TOMATO TART

Try this for supper or lunch. The flavour combination is delicious.

8	slices bacon	8	
2	medium tomatoes, chopped	2	
1¼ cups	shredded Swiss cheese	310	mL
1-10 oz.	can cream of mushroom soup	284	mL
3	eggs, slightly beaten	3	
¼ cup	milk	60	mL
1	baked 9-inch pie shell	24	cm

1. Place bacon slices between paper towels on a glass plate. Microwave on HIGH for 6 to 8 minutes, until crisp. Chop.

2. Spread tomatoes and 1 cup (250 mL) of the cheese in bottom of pie shell.

3. Mix together soup, eggs and milk until smooth. Pour into pie shell.

4. Sprinkle bacon and remaining cheese on top. Microwave on MEDIUM for 12 to 14 minutes or until set but still moist on top. Let stand on counter for 5 minutes more to complete cooking.

Your Time: _____

BREADS

Your microwave oven offers flexibility for bread preparation. You can use the microwave oven to proof yeast bread dough or defrost frozen bread dough. It can bake fresh bread, reheat it or thaw frozen bread. Whatever your needs, the microwave can help you to make light, moist breads with a minimum of time and effort.

○━━ THE KEY TO SUCCESS WITH BREADS

Patience is the key to success with breads in the microwave oven. They do cook quickly in the microwave oven, but rushing them by microwaving them on HIGH power usually results in a tough, dry product. Breads require a lower power setting to allow time for the rising and expansion that causes a nice, light bread.

Breads usually look moist when they first come out of the microwave oven and novice cooks are tempted to return them to the oven until they become dry on top. Resist that temptation because the moisture will disappear very rapidly during standing time. Cooking bread until it looks dry on top usually makes it dry throughout.

TOPPINGS

In the microwave oven, all breads are quick, whether from scratch or from a mix. However, this speed means no browning takes place. Recipes using dark spices (like cinnamon), dark flours (like whole wheat or rye), brown sugar or molasses have a more appealing colour when microwaved. To give an attractive appearance to the unbrowned microwave breads, microwave cooks coat them with a variety of toppings which enhance their appearance and often add flavour.

To coat breads, brush tops and sides of bread with butter or milk and roll in topping mixture. Use up all of the topping specified in the recipe or cover generously because breads expand as they rise and cook, and will need the extra coating to completely cover the finished expanded product. The baking dish can also be greased and covered with the topping mix. In the case of quick breads and muffins, generously sprinkle the topping on top of each loaf or muffin just before baking.

Choose any of the following toppings to enhance the flavour and appearance of microwaved breads:

* Cinnamon and sugar.
* Crumbs: cookie, cracker, bread, cake, chips, or graham. Season with cinnamon and sugar, or herbs.
* Streusal: 1/2 cup (125 ml) flour, 3 tbsp. (45 ml) brown sugar, 1/4 tsp.(1 ml) cinnamon, and 2 tbsp.(30 ml) butter.
* Nut crunch: 1/4 cup (60 ml) flour, 2 tbsp.(30 ml) butter, and 1/4 cup (60 ml) nuts.

- Oatmeal, cornmeal, dark flour, wheat germ, wheat flakes, or cracked wheat.
- Dried grated cheese.
- Poppy seeds, sesame seeds, caraway seeds, herbs.
- Toasted coconut: Spread 1/2 cup (125 ml) in a dinner plate. Microwave on HIGH for 2 to 3 minutes, stir every minute.
- Crushed French onions or onion soup mix.
- Crumbled bacon and shredded cheddar cheese.
- Taco seasoning or mix.
- Frosting or glaze.

COOK BREADS COVERED

A pourous cover like paper toweling promotes even reheating of breads. A loose covering like wax paper can help quick breads to cook more evenly and eliminate moist patches. Plastic or glass retain too much moisture and cause bread to become soggy.

PREPARING MICROWAVED BREADS FOR SERVING

Breads can be kept warm by wrapping them in cloth or paper towel. Microwaved breads are delicate when warm or fresh; an electric knife slices the best at this time. A serrated knife can be used on cooled breads.

BREADS THAT DON'T WORK AND WHY

Popovers, French Bread, crusty Rolls do not form a crisp crust.

Waffles and Pancakes need to be cooked on hot surface. However, leftover or frozen waffles and pancakes reheat well in the microwave oven.

Donuts cannot be deep fried in the microwave oven because fat becomes dangerously hot.

REHEATING

Breads reheat well but novice microwave cooks tend to overheat them and consequently get tough, rubbery or even hard results. If severely overdone, breads will even toast or burn on the inside. For best results, microwave each piece on MEDIUM or MEDIUM-HIGH for 10 to 15 seconds. Reheat only as much as you'll use at one time. The lower power level prevents the gluten in the flour from toughening and also ensures more even heating.

In bread products containing fruit or some kind of filling, the filling becomes hotter faster than the rest. This leads people to believe that foods cook "inside out" in microwave ovens but, in fact, the porous composition of the bread allows the microwaves to pass through to the center. Sugary substances attract microwave energy, consequently the sugary fillings become hotter than the bread.

Reheated breads should feel just warm on the surface. The center is hotter and in the few seconds of standing time between the microwave and table, the heat will even out. If you heat them until they are hot to touch on the surface, they will be tough or hard and dry inside.

Covering breads loosely in a napkin or paper towel helps promote even heating without retaining moisture. Day old breads can be heated in a plastic bag, but for fresh bread, a plastic bag retains so much moisture that they become soggy.

When reheating several items, arrange them in a circle for even heating.

STORING MICROWAVED BREADS

For optimum freshness, store muffin batter in the fridge and bake them up as you are ready to eat them. If you bake a loaf or a whole batch of muffins, store leftovers in the freezer. When needed, you can thaw them in seconds with results that equal freshly baked bread.

HINTS

- Recycle stale bread: Place it in a plastic bag, or wrap in a paper towel and set in the microwave oven with a glass of hot water. Microwave for 15 to 30 seconds.

- To prevent sogginess, place breads on a folded paper towel or napkin or on a plastic rack.

- Overcooking takes place in centre — not outside, so beware.

- Make bread crumbs quickly and easily. Place bread slices on plastic rack and microwave on HIGH for 45 seconds per slice. Let stand to cool. Crumble.

MUFFINS

Muffins are marvelous in the microwave. A batch of 6 cook in about 2 1/2 to 5 minutes — about as long as a couple of slices of toast. Most batters will keep in the fridge for a week so you can bake fresh muffins each day as you need them.

PREPARATION OF MUFFINS

When preparing the batter, blend just to moisten all particles. For fluffier muffins, beat liquid ingredients together before adding them to dry ingredients. Microwaved muffins rise higher, so fill containers only half full. If the batter is light-coloured, sprinkle each muffin with a topping before baking. Remember to coat each muffin heavily, because they expand when cooked.

UTENSILS FOR MUFFINS

There are various types of muffin containers on the market. Some have holes on the bottom to prevent sogginess. Of course, these should be lined with paper cups. Muffin pans without holes are more versatile and can be used for individual quiche or poached eggs. If you don't have a muffin pan, use custard cups or cut off the tops of paper cups and arrange them in a circle in your oven.

Paper liners absorb moisture which helps to prevent soggy bottoms. Use 2 liners per muffin if extra absorption is needed. Also, remove muffins from the pan immediately and allow them to cool on a rack to prevent soggy bottoms.

HOW TO KNOW WHEN MUFFINS ARE DONE

Microwave muffins are done when the top looks set and has lost most of its stickiness. It may still appear moist, but that moisture will dry up during standing time. When touched lightly with a finger, the surface of the muffins should spring back. A toothpick inserted into the centre should come out clean or with just a few crumbs on it. Microwave muffins are moist and sometimes moist crumbs cling to the toothpick. This DOES NOT indicate that a few more seconds of cooking time are needed. Extra time is needed when the toothpick comes out doughy.

ADAPTING MUFFINS

Most conventional muffin recipes can be cooked in the microwave oven with little adjustment, depending on the recipe. Muffins with a rich batter work the best. Microwave muffins usually require 1 to 2 tbsp. (15 to 25 ml) shortening per cup (250 ml) of flour. Thin batter may need liquid reduced by 1/4 (ie. 1 cup becomes ¾ cup or 250 ml becomes 175 ml). If crumbly; add another egg.

When trying a favorite muffin recipe, prepare as usual and test 1 muffin in a custard cup on MEDIUM-HIGH for 30 seconds. If it is dry or crumbly you may need to alter the recipe by adding shortening or another egg. If too moist; lower power level to MEDIUM-LOW and increase time to 1 minute per muffin. If none of these work to your satisfaction, you've lost only 3 muffins and you can still bake the rest conventionally.

QUICK BREADS

Quick breads really are quick when baked in the microwave. Microwaved quick breads rise higher and faster and have more even texture than when conventionally baked. When preparing recipes calling for chopped nuts or fruit, chop them finely as batters thin during cooking time and large pieces would sink to bottom.

UTENSILS FOR QUICK BREADS

Because they have greater volume, quick breads are often baked in a 6½ (1.5 L) or 12-cup (3L) tube pan. If you don't have a tube pan, set a 4-oz. (125 ml) custard cup or drinking glass in a 2 to 3-qt. (2-3 L) casserole dish. If using a loaf pan, a recipe calling for 1¼ to 1⅓ cup (150 - 160 mL) flour makes 1 loaf. If larger, make a few muffins with the extra batter.

You may grease your pans but DO NOT FLOUR! You may also line the bottom of the pan with wax paper. Run a knife around the edge of the dish before removing.

HOW TO KNOW WHEN QUICK BREADS ARE DONE

Quick breads should be cooked until the top looks set and loses most of its stickiness or when a toothpick, inserted in center, comes out clean. When touched, the surface springs back. When it pulls away from the edges of pan, remove immediately or it will overcook. Surface moisture will disappear during standing time and at this time, quick breads will pull away from edges of pan.

Allow quick breads to have 3 to 5 minutes standing time in the pan and then invert on cooling rack or a plate to finish cooling.

Sometimes bottoms are moist or soggy. Elevating the dish on a rack or inverted pan may help. Likewise, cooking for a longer time on a lower power level will help. If it happens, place loaf upside down on a rack or paper towel lined plate and microwave on HIGH for an additional 30 seconds to 1 minute. This should finish cooking the bottom of the loaf, and chances are, you'll be the only one to know what happened.

COFFEECAKES

- Coffeecakes cooked in plastic pans cook more quickly than in glass pans.
- You may grease pans to keep from sticking, but DO NOT FLOUR! as it forms a gummy coating on pan. You may however coat pans with topping. Wheat germ absorbs the excess moisture which forms between dishes and bread during baking, as well as adding colour and texture.
- Microwaved coffeecakes look best when prepared with an upside down topping before cooking, or glazed or drizzled with icing before serving.
- Elevate the coffecake when baking by setting it on a plastic rack or an overturned casserole dish.
- To adapt a favourite coffeecake recipe for microwave cooking you may need to add 1 to 2 tbsp. (15 - 25 ml) more shortening.

YEAST BREADS

The microwave can be used to speed up the preparing of yeast breads which normally take several hours. You can use it to defrost frozen bread dough, proof dough as well as to bake it, if you like. Microwave baked breads, however, are different from conventional. They do not brown or form a crust because there is no hot, dry air to dry out surfaces. This is an advantage if you are using the bread for sandwich loaves as there is no crust to trim. Breads can be coated with seeds or wheat germ, oatmeal or crumbs to enhance their appearance.

PROOFING (RISING) YEAST DOUGH

This can be done in a microwave oven, even if you intend to bake the bread conventionally. Most doughs require two risings; first in bowl and second in the pan. If you do the second rising in the microwave, be sure to use non-metal pans which can be used in both ovens. If you don't have such pans you can still speed up the first rising in the microwave.

Prepare dough according to the recipe. Place in a greased large glass or plastic bowl. Grease top of dough. Microwave on WARM for one third of the suggested rising time (eg. 1 hour becomes 20 minutes).

Check by lightly pressing finger into dough. If impression remains, it is ready. Punch down and shape into loaves. Bake according to recipe directions.

UTENSILS FOR YEAST BREADS

Higher rising microwave breads require that you use a larger pan than for conventional loaves or form smaller loaves. Glass or ceramic pans are the best.

BAKING YEAST BREADS IN THE MICROWAVE OVEN

Microwaved breads also rise higher than conventional breads because there is no crust to stop them. Because of this, microwaved breads must be cooked slowly, using MEDIUM (50%) power to prevent the formation of large air pockets which later collapse causing an uneven shape.

When trying a recipe for the first time, use the minimum time given and check every minute after that (record your time for the next time you make it).

Sometimes bottoms are moist or soggy. Elevating the dish on a rack or inverting the pan may help. Likewise, cooking for a longer time on a lower power level may help. If it happens, place loaf on a rack or paper towel lined plate — upside down and microwave on HIGH for an additional 30 seconds to 1 minute.

HOW TO KNOW WHEN YEAST BREADS ARE DONE

Breads should be cooked until the top looks set and loses most of its stickiness. When touched; the surface springs back. Surface moistness will disappear during standing time.

Allow breads to have 3 to 5 minutes of standing time in pan and then invert on cooling rack or a plate to prevent sogginess.

ADAPTING YEAST BREAD RECIPES

- To microwave yeast breads in the microwave, they need to be rich in shortening to keep them from drying out. For richer dough; use ¼ cup (60 ml) shortening for 2½ to 3 cups (625 - 750 ml) of flour.

- Because they do not brown in the microwave oven, each loaf should be brushed with milk and rolled in crumbs or wheat germ to coat it heavily. This gives a more attractive, brown coating.

- Choose a recipe in this book or the manual that came with your microwave oven that is similar to the recipe you wish to adapt. Follow the sample recipe's quantities, instructions and cooking times.

- Microwaved buns can be frozen fresh and browned and crisped just before serving by baking them for 8 to 10 minutes in a preheated oven at 425°F (220°C).

REFRIGERATOR BRAN MUFFINS

With this recipe you can serve fresh, homemade muffins to your family every morning.

4 cups	whole wheat flour	1 L
3 cups	natural bran	750 mL
¾ cup	brown sugar	175 mL
1 tsp.	salt	5 mL
2 tsp.	baking soda	10 mL
1 cup	raisins	250 mL
4	eggs	4
¾ cup	vegetable oil	175 mL
1½ cups	molasses	325 mL
2¼ cups	sour milk OR buttermilk	560 mL

1. Combine dry ingredients in mixing bowl.

2. Blend together eggs, vegetable oil, molasses and milk and add all at once to dry ingredients. Stir just until moistened.

3. Refrigerate for 24 hours before using. Fill paper-lined muffin containers half full with batter. Microwave on MEDIUM-LOW for 45 seconds per muffin.

TIP: These will keep, if covered, for 6 weeks in the refrigerator.

Your Time: _____

WHOLE WHEAT MUFFINS

A tasty, wholesome treat.

1 cup	whole wheat flour	250 mL
¼ cup	molasses	60 mL
2 tbsp.	brown sugar	30 mL
1½ tsp.	baking powder	7 mL
⅓ cup	milk	75 mL
¼ cup	vegetable oil	60 mL
1	egg	1
¼ cup	raisins	30 mL

1. Combine all ingredients in mixing bowl. Stir only until particles are moistened.

2. Fill paper-lined muffin containers half full with batter. Microwave on MEDIUM-HIGH for 20 seconds per muffin or 2 minutes for 6 muffins.

Your Time: _____

JAM MUFFINS

A treat for breakfast or tea time. Be sure to let them cool a bit before serving as the jam gets very hot.

⅓ cup	butter	75	mL
2	eggs	2	
⅔ cup	milk	150	mL
1 tsp.	lemon rind	5	mL
1¾ cups	flour	425	mL
½ cup	sugar	125	mL
4 tsp.	baking powder	20	mL
½ tsp.	salt	10	mL
	Jam — about 1/2 cup	125	mL
½ cup	finely chopped walnuts	125	mL

1. In a 1-cup (250 mL) glass measure, microwave butter on HIGH for 1 minute or until melted.

2. In a medium mixing bowl, beat eggs. Beat in milk, butter and lemon rind.

3. Sift flour, sugar, baking powder and salt into egg mixture and stir just until moistened.

4. Spoon 1 tbsp. (15 mL) of batter into each muffin cup. Spoon a scant teaspoon of jam on top and then another tablespoon of batter, just enough to make muffin cups half full. Spread to cover jam. Place another dab of jam on top of each muffin and sprinkle surface of each muffin with about 1 tsp. (5 mL) chopped walnuts.

5. Microwave on MEDIUM-LOW for 45 seconds per muffin or 4½ minutes for 6 muffins.

Your Time: _____

BANANA CHOCOLATE CHIP MUFFINS

These scrumptious muffins are Marianne's favourite.

⅓ cup	butter	75 mL
2	eggs	2
1 cup	mashed very ripe banana	250 mL
½ cup	chocolate chips	125 mL
¼ cup	chopped nuts	60 mL
1¾ cup	flour	425 mL
½ cup	sugar	125 mL
4 tsp.	baking powder	20 mL
½ tsp.	salt	2 mL

1. In a 1-cup (250 mL) glass measure, microwave butter on HIGH for 1 minute or until melted.

2. In a medium mixing bowl, beat eggs. Mix in butter, banana, chocolate chips and nuts.

3. Combine remaining ingredients and add to banana mixture. Stir just to moisten.

4. Fill paper-lined muffin containers half full with batter. Microwave on MEDIUM-HIGH for 30 seconds per muffin or about 2½ minutes for 6.

Your Time: _____

BLUEBERRY MUFFINS

When you bite into these muffins, you'll marvel at the fresh blueberry flavour.

2 cups	flour	500 mL
½ cup	sugar	125 mL
3 tsp.	baking powder	15 mL
½ tsp.	salt	2 mL
2	eggs	2
½ cup	vegetable oil	125 mL
½ cup	milk	125 mL
½ cup	blueberries	125 mL

1. Combine dry ingredients in mixing bowl. Make a well in center.

2. Mix together eggs, vegetable oil and milk. Add all at once to dry ingredients and stir just to moisten. Add blueberries.

3. Fill paper-lined muffin containers half full with batter. Sprinkle sugar and cinnamon heavily on top of each muffin. Microwave on MEDIUM-HIGH for 20 seconds per muffin or 2 minutes for 6 muffins.

Your Time: _____

AUNT EDNA'S BLUEBERRY OAT MUFFINS

A nutritious, fresh flavoured muffin.

1 cup	rolled oats	250	mL
1 cup	buttermilk OR sour milk	250	mL
1 cup	whole wheat flour	250	mL
1 tsp.	baking powder	5	mL
½ tsp.	soda	2	mL
½ tsp.	salt	2	mL
¾ cup	brown sugar	175	mL
1	egg	1	
¼ cup	melted butter OR margarine	60	mL
1 cup	blueberries	250	mL

1. Combine oats and buttermilk in a bowl and set aside.

2. Combine flour, baking powder, soda, salt and brown sugar in a large bowl.

3. Add egg and melted butter to oat mixture. Stir this mixture into the dry ingredients. Stir just until moistened. Fold in blueberries.

4. Fill paper-lined muffin cups half full with batter. Microwave on MEDIUM-HIGH for 25 seconds per muffin or 2½ minutes for 6 muffins.

* Yield: 1½ dozen muffins

Your Time: _____

PEANUT BUTTER & BANANA MUFFINS

The flavours of a teatime favourite baked into a muffin.

2 cups	flour	500 mL
½ cup	brown sugar	125 mL
1 tbsp.	baking powder	15 mL
½ cup	peanut butter	125 mL
2 tbsp.	vegetable oil	30 mL
2	eggs	2
¾ cup	milk	175 mL
2	medium bananas, mashed	2

1. Combine flour, brown sugar and baking powder in a mixing bowl.

2. Combine remaining ingredients in another mixing bowl. Stir into dry ingredients. Stir just until moistened.

3. Fill paper-lined muffin cups half full with batter. Microwave on MEDIUM-HIGH for 20 seconds per muffin.

* **Yield:** 2 dozen muffins

Your Time: _____

NANCY'S PINEAPPLE MUFFINS

These delicious muffins won't last long.

½ cup	butter OR margarine	125 mL
¾ cup	sugar	175 mL
1 cup	crushed pineapple, drained	250 mL
1½ cups	flour	325 mL
1	egg	1
1 tsp.	baking soda	5 mL
⅛ tsp.	baking powder	.5 mL
1 tsp.	vanilla	5 mL
1 tsp.	cinnamon	5 mL

1. Soften butter by microwaving on DEFROST for 1 minute. Mix all ingredients together.

2. Fill paper-lined muffin containers half full with batter. Microwave on MEDIUM-LOW for 45 seconds per muffin or 4½ minutes for 6 muffins. Check with a toothpick for doneness. Let stand for 5 minutes — moisture will dry during standing time.

Your Time: _____

PUMPKIN BREAD RING

By baking the loaf in a ring shaped pan, we eliminate the slow-to-cook centre.

2 cups	sugar	500	mL
¾ cup	vegetable oil	175	mL
2 cups	cooked OR canned pumpkin	500	mL
4	eggs	4	
3 cups	flour	750	mL
2 tsp.	baking powder	10	mL
1 tsp.	salt	5	mL
½ tsp.	nutmeg	2	mL
1 tsp.	cinnamon	5	mL
1 cup	chopped walnuts	250	mL
1 cup	raisins	250	mL

1. Beat together sugar, vegetable oil, pumpkin and eggs.

2. Mix in remaining ingredients. Pour into a 12-cup (3 L) tube pan.

3. Cover with wax paper and microwave on MEDIUM for 18 to 20 minutes or until toothpick inserted in centre comes out clean.

4. Let bread ring stand, uncovered, in pan for about 10 minutes before unmolding.

Your Time: _____

AUNT EDNA'S DATE LOAF

Freezes well — pleases well, too.

1 tsp.	baking soda	5	mL
½ cup	orange juice	125	mL
1 cup	boiling water	250	mL
¾ lb.	dates, chopped	325	g
1 cup	brown sugar	250	mL
2 cups	flour	500	mL
1 tsp.	baking powder	5	mL
½ cup	chopped nuts	125	mL
1	egg	1	
1 tsp.	vanilla	5	mL

1. Combine baking soda, orange juice and boiling water. Pour over dates and let stand for 10 minutes.

2. Meanwhile, combine dry ingredients in a large mixing bowl. Mix in egg, vanilla and the date mixture.

3. Pour batter into a 12-cup (3 L) tube pan. Elevate by setting it on an inverted empty dish or a plastic rack in the microwave oven.

4. Cover with wax paper and microwave on MEDIUM for 14 to 18 minutes, or until toothpick inserted in centre comes out clean. Let it stand in the microwave oven for one or two minutes if you are not sure whether or not it is done. During this time, the moisture on top should begin to dry up and the loaf may begin to pull away from the edges of the pan. If not, microwave it for a bit more time.

Your Time: _____

BANANA BREAD

Marianne says this is the best banana bread she's ever tasted.

½ cup	shortening	125 mL
1 cup	sugar	250 mL
2	eggs	2
1 tsp.	baking soda	5 mL
¾ cup	buttermilk OR sour milk	175 mL
2	mashed bananas	2
½ tsp.	vanilla	2 mL
2 cups	flour	500 mL
1 tsp.	baking powder	5 mL
¼ tsp.	salt	1 mL
½ cup	chopped walnuts	125 mL

1. Cream shortening and sugar. Mix in eggs.

2. Stir baking soda into milk and add to creamed shortening. Mix in bananas and vanilla.

3. Sift together flour, baking powder, and salt. Stir into moist ingredients. Beat well. Add nuts.

4. Pour batter into a 12-cup (3 L) tube pan. Set on an inverted dish or a plastic rack in the microwave oven. Cover with wax paper and microwave on MEDIUM for 15 to 18 minutes, or until toothpick inserted in center comes out clean. Let it stand in the microwave oven for one or two minutes if you are not sure whether or not it is done. During this time, the moisture on top will begin to dry up and the loaf may begin to pull away from the pan if it is done. If not, microwave it for a bit more time.

Your Time: _____

APPLESAUCE SPICE LOAF

This moist and spicy loaf will be a microwave hit.

2 cups	flour	500	mL
1 tsp.	baking powder	5	mL
1 tsp.	baking soda	5	mL
1 tsp.	cinnamon	5	mL
1 tsp.	ginger	5	mL
½ tsp.	salt	2	mL
½ tsp.	ground cloves	2	mL
½ cup	butter OR margarine, softened	125	mL
1 cup	brown sugar, packed	250	mL
2	eggs	2	
1 cup	applesauce	250	mL
1 cup	chopped walnuts	250	mL

1. Combine flour, leavening and spices. Set aside.

2. Beat together butter and sugar until light and fluffy. Beat in eggs one at a time.

3. Mix in flour mixture alternately with applesauce, just until blended. Stir in walnuts.

4. Pour batter into a 12-cup (3 L) tube pan. Place on an inverted dish or plastic rack. Cover with wax paper and microwave on MEDIUM for 9 to 12 minutes, or until toothpick inserted in center comes out clean. Let it stand in the microwave oven for one or two minutes if you are not sure whether or not it is done. During this time, the moisture on the top should begin to dry up and the loaf will pull away from the edges of the pan. If not, microwave it for a bit more time.

Your Time: _____

ZUCCHINI NUT BREAD

A choice way to use up some of that extra zucchini from your garden.

2	eggs	2
2 cups	sugar	500 mL
2 cups	unpeeled grated raw zucchini	500 mL
1 cup	vegetable oil	250 mL
1 tbsp.	vanilla	15 mL
1 tsp.	pumpkin pie spice	5 mL
1 tsp.	salt	5 mL
3 tsp.	cinnamon	15 mL
1 tsp.	baking powder	5 mL
1 tsp.	baking soda	5 mL
3 cups	flour	750 mL
1 cup	chopped nuts	250 mL

1. Beat eggs until fluffy. Blend in sugar, zucchini, vegetable oil and vanilla.

2. Combine dry ingredients. Add zucchini mixture to dry ingredients, stirring just until all particles are moistened. Stir in nuts.

3. Pour into a 12-cup (3 L) tube pan. Place on an inverted dish or a plastic rack in the microwave oven. Cover with wax paper and microwave on MEDIUM for 14 to 18 minutes or until toothpick inserted in the center comes out clean. Let it stand in the microwave oven for one to two minutes if you are not sure whether or not it is done. During this time, the moisture on top will begin to dry up and the loaf may begin to pull away from the edges of the pan if it is done. If not, microwave it for a bit more time.

Your Time: _____

BUBBAT

This is actually a poultry stuffing that my Mennonite grandmothers used to put inside the cavity of chicken. I've always had it served as a bread with a roast chicken dinner. You can try it either way.

1 cup	flour	250 mL
1½ tsp.	baking powder	7 mL
½ tsp.	salt	2 mL
2 tbsp.	sugar	30 mL
2 tbsp.	lard OR margarine	30 mL
⅓ cup	milk	75 mL
1	egg, beaten	1
1 cup	raisins	250 mL

1. Combine dry ingredients in mixing bowl.

2. In a glass 1-cup (250 mL) measure, microwave lard or margarine on HIGH for 30 seconds.

3. Stir lard, milk and beaten egg into dry ingredients. Add raisins. Mix and pour into a 9 x 3-inch (2 L) round cake dish.

4. Microwave on HIGH for 4 to 6 minutes, or until toothpick inserted in center comes out clean. Let it stand in the microwave oven for one to two minutes if you are not sure whether or not it is done. During this time, the moisture on top will begin to dry up and the loaf may begin to pull away from the edges of the pan if it is done. If not, microwave it for more time.

Your Time: _____

PEACH COFFEECAKE

A tasty delight.

⅓ cup	butter OR margarine	75	mL
1 cup	brown sugar	250	mL
1½ cups	flour	325	mL
½ cup	buttermilk OR sour milk	125	mL
1	egg	1	
½ tsp.	baking soda	2	mL
½ cup	chopped nuts	125	mL
2 cups	sliced peaches	500	mL

1. Cream butter or margarine with sugar. Mix in flour. Remove 1/2 cup (125 mL) of mixture and set aside for use as a topping.

2. Add buttermilk, egg and baking soda to remaining flour mixture. Mix well. Stir in nuts.

3. Pour batter into a 9 x 3-inch (2 L) round cake dish. Arrange peach slices on top of batter. Sprinkle with reserved topping.

4. Microwave on MEDIUM-HIGH for 8 to 10 minutes, or until a toothpick inserted into the centre comes out clean.

Your Time: _____

THEL'S CORNBREAD

This is a recipe from my mother-in-law, who lives in Georgia. When you taste this moist, delicious cornbread you'll know why it's a staple food in her house.

1 cup	cornmeal	250	mL
¼ cup	vegetable oil	60	mL
3	eggs, well beaten	3	
1 cup	sour cream	250	mL
1-10 oz.	can cream style corn	284	mL

1. Combine cornmeal, vegetable oil, eggs and sour cream. Beat until smooth.

2. Stir in cream style corn.

3. Pour into 9 x 3-inch (2 L) round cake dish. Microwave on MEDIUM-HIGH for 8 to 10 minutes.

Your Time: _____

CRISSCROSS COFFEECAKE

Pretty to look at and good to eat.

2 cups	flour	500	mL
¾ cup	milk	175	mL
½ cup	sugar	125	mL
½ cup	butter OR margarine, softened	125	mL
2 tsp.	baking powder	10	mL
½ tsp.	salt	2	mL
2	eggs	2	
1 cup	fruit preserves OR sauce	250	mL
½ cup	finely chopped nuts OR ¼ cup (60 mL) sugar mixed with 1 tsp. (5 mL) cinnamon	125	mL

1. Combine flour, milk, sugar, butter, baking powder, salt and eggs in a mixing bowl and beat with electric mixer on medium speed until well blended.

2. Pour batter into a 9 x 3-inch round cake dish (2 L).

3. Spoon preserves over top in rows to make a lattice top. Sprinkle nuts or sugar cinnamon mixture all over top.

4. Place dish on a rack or inverted bowl in microwave oven. Cook on ME-DIUM for 14 to 20 minutes.

5. Let stand for 20 minutes or until cool, before serving.

Your Time: _____

CARAMEL BISCUIT RING

This is a favourite in my classes. There's usually a volunteer to clean off the serving plate.

2 tbsp.	butter	30	mL
½ cup	brown sugar, packed	125	mL
2 tbsp.	corn syrup	30	mL
½ cup	pecan halves	125	mL
¼ cup	marischino cherry halves	60	mL
1 pkg.	(10) refrigerator buttermilk biscuits		

1. Place butter in 12-cup (3 L) tube pan and microwave on HIGH for 30 seconds or until melted. Stir in brown sugar and corn syrup. Spread evenly on bottom of pan.

2. Arrange pecan halves and cherry halves on top of sugar mixture. Place biscuits around ring on top of mixture.

3. Microwave on MEDIUM for 4 to 7 minutes.

VARIATIONS:

CINNAMON RING: Add ¼ tsp. (1 mL) cinnamon to syrup-sugar mixture and substitute coconut for the pecans.

MAPLE RING: Substitute maple syrup for corn syrup and walnuts for pecans.

Your Time: _____

EASY CINNAMON RING

I don't believe there's an easier way to make cinnamon twists.

1 pkg.	(10) refrigerator buttermilk biscuits	1
2 tbsp.	butter	30 mL
¼ cup	brown sugar	125 mL
1 tsp.	cinnamon	5 mL
1 tbsp.	finely chopped nuts	15 mL

1. Separate biscuits. Roll each biscuit into a 4-inch rope.

2. Place butter in a small bowl and microwave on HIGH for 30 seconds. In another small bowl mix together brown sugar and cinnamon and nuts.

3. Dip each rope into the melted butter to coat and then into the sugar mixture to coat. Tie each rope into a knot and place in a tube pan or around the edges of a 9 x 3-inch (2 L) round cake dish.

4. Microwave on MEDIUM for 5 to 6 minutes.

Your Time: _____

CABBAGE PATCH BREAD

A bread with a unique and savory flavour. This recipe is requested often.

1 pkg.	active dry yeast	1
⅓ cup	warm water	75 mL
1-5 oz.	can evaporated milk	160 mL
½ cup	vegetable oil	125 mL
1	egg	1
¾ cup	coarsely chopped cabbage	175 mL
1	sliced carrot	1
¼ cup	sliced celery	60 mL
¼ cup	snipped parsley	60 mL
2 tbsp.	honey OR molasses	30 mL
1 tsp.	salt	5 mL
3 cups	whole wheat flour	750 mL
1¼ cups	all-purpose flour	310 mL
3 tbsp.	melted butter	45 mL

1. In a large mixing bowl prepare yeast and warm water according to package directions. Set in microwave oven to rise but DO NOT TURN IT ON!

2. Meanwhile, place remaining ingredients EXCEPT for the flours, butter and crumbs into a blender or food processor. Cover and blend until smooth. Stir into yeast mixture.

3. Stir in whole wheat flour and then as much all-purpose flour as you can. Turn out onto a lightly floured surface. Knead in enough of the all-purpose flour to make a moderately stiff dough that is smooth and elastic. (This will take about 6 to 8 minutes.)

4. Shape dough into a ball. Place into a greased bowl and cover with damp cotton cloth. Place in microwave oven with a 1-cup (250 mL) glass measure of warm water. Microwave on the lowest setting of your microwave (WARM) for 20 minutes or until double in bulk.

5. Punch down dough. Shape into a ball and cover with the bowl. Sprinkle 2 well greased 10-inch (25 cm) pie plates or microwave baking trays with a light coating bread crumbs, wheatgerm, cornmeal or sesame seeds. Divide dough in half and roll each half to make a 24-inch (70 cm) long strip. Brush each strip with melted butter and roll in crumbs to coat well.

6. Form each strip into a ring in the pie plate. Pinch ends together. Place a greased glass, open end up, in the centre of the ring. Cover both rings with a damp cotton cloth. Place one bread ring in microwave oven with the measuring cup of water and microwave on WARM for 20 minutes. Place the other bread ring in a warm place to rise. When the first one is done, repeat with the other bread ring.

7. Microwave bread rings, one at a time (in the same order they were proofed) on MEDIUM for 9 to 11 minutes or until top springs back when touched lightly.

8. Let stand for 10 minutes before turning out onto a cooling rack. Eat one fresh and freeze the other.

TIP: Coat heavily with crumbs because as the bread rises and expands the coating will thin out.

SERVING SUGGESTION: Serve warm with cream cheese and onion spread.

Your Time: _____

WHOLE WHEAT BREAD

You'll love this moist honey nut flavoured bread. This recipe makes 1 loaf.

¼ cup	milk	60	mL
1 pkg.	dry yeast	1	
¾ cup	milk	175	mL
¼ cup	honey	60	mL
⅛ cup	wheat germ	25	mL
¼ cup	butter OR margarine, melted	60	mL
½ tsp.	salt	2	mL
1¼ cup	all purpose flour	310	mL
1¼ cups	whole wheat flour	310	mL
	wheat germ to coat pan		

1. In 1 cup (250 mL) measure, microwave ¼ cup (60 mL) milk on HIGH for 20 to 25 seconds or until lukewarm. Stir in yeast to dissolve. Set aside.

2. In 1-cup (250 mL) measure, microwave remaining milk on MEDIUM-HIGH for 1½ to 2 minutes, or until scalded. In large mixing bowl, combine honey, wheat germ, butter and salt. Stir in scalded milk. Set aside to cool to lukewarm.

3. Add yeast mixture to honey mixture. Beat in flours, one cup (250 mL) at a time, until stiff dough forms. Turn onto floured board. Knead until elastic, about 6 to 8 minutes. Form into ball.

4. Place dough in lightly greased bowl. Grease top of dough. Cover with damp cotton cloth. Microwave on WARM, or lowest setting on microwave, for 12 to 15 minutes, or until doubled in bulk.

5. Lightly grease a 1-qt. (1 L) glass loaf pan. Dust with wheat germ on bottom and sides. Shape dough to fit and place in dish.

6. Cover pan with damp cotton cloth and microwave on WARM for 8 to 12 minutes or until doubled in bulk.

7. Remove cloth and microwave on MEDIUM for 6 to 7 minutes or until top springs back when lightly pressed with a finger.

8. Remove from dish. Brush with butter. Sprinkle with wheat germ.

Your Time: _____

HERBED WHOLE WHEAT CROUTONS

A tantalizing accompaniment to soups or salads.

3 tbsp.	butter	45	mL
2	cloves garlic, minced	2	
½ tsp.	dried leaf basil	2	mL
½ tsp.	dried crushed oregano	2	mL
½ tsp.	dried parsley flakes	2	mL
	dash of freshly ground black pepper		
2 cups	whole wheat bread cubes	500	mL
	Crumbs for coating		

1. Place butter in a glass 8 x 12-inch baking dish (1.5 L). Microwave on HIGH for 45 seconds or until melted.

2. Stir in garlic, herbs and pepper. Microwave on HIGH for 30 seconds to 1 minute.

3. Stir bread cubes into butter to coat. Microwave on HIGH for 5 to 6 minutes or until bread cubes are crispy. Stir 2 or 3 times during cooking.

4. Let stand 10 minutes to finish crisping. Store in a covered container until ready to serve.

VARIATIONS:

PLAIN CROUTONS: omit spices.

CHEESE CROUTONS: omit spices. Sprinkle with 2 tbsp. (30 mL) Parmesan cheese in step 3.

* **Yield:** 13 cups (750 mL)

Your Time: _____

Desserts cooked in the microwave are usually superior in taste and appearance to conventionally cooked desserts. Indeed, they are a joy to make — such attractive and delicious results with so little effort. They offer significant time savings and generally require a minimum of attention. With microwave speed and convenience, desserts need not be reserved for special occasions. They can be an everyday treat, not only for your family but also for the cook!

Techniques vary with the type of dessert, therefore, they have been categorized by types in this section.

FOODS THAT DON'T WORK & WHY

Do not make double crust pies or cook filling in raw pastry because the steam from the filling makes pastry soggy.

Puff pastry or choux won't work. They do not become crisp.

FRUIT

Tempting to behold, microwaved fruit also comes out plump, juicy and bursting with flavour. Whether you are using fresh, canned or dried fruit, microwave cooking will improve your favourite fruit dessert recipes.

- Fruit desserts can be microwaved on HIGH unless they contain delicate ingredients like milk or eggs.
- Because microwave cooking causes very little evaporation, you may find it necessary to add a thickener, like cornstarch, to fruit desserts. Cornstarch is preferable to tapioca because microwave cooking is too fast to allow time for the tapioca to thicken.
- Whole pieces of fruit, such as baked apples, should be partially peeled or pierced to prevent them from bursting.
- Fruit should be cooked covered to keep in the moisture.

FRUIT COBBLER & CRISP

- Fruit cobbler and crisp turn out very well in the microwave with little adjustment.
- You may find it preferable to use dark brown sugar to give more colour to topping.
- Remember that toppings become crisp as they cool. The steam from the fruit makes them soft while they are hot.
- Crisps are cooked uncovered to keep the topping from becoming soggy but cobblers are sometimes covered with wax paper.
- Cook cake-type cobblers in a round 9 x 3-inch (2L) cake dish for best results.

DEFROSTING FROZEN FRUIT

Stir often during defrost time. Microwave just until outside feels a bit warm. Stir and let stand 5 minutes. It should feel cold, firm and slightly icy.

FRUIT HINTS

- To obtain more juice from lemons and other citrus fruits, heat on HIGH for 30 seconds.
- To soften dried fruits, place 1 cup (250 mL) raisins, prunes, apples or apricots in a bowl. Cover with water and heat on HIGH for 3 minutes. Let stand 5 minutes, then drain.
- To peel fruits, like peaches, microwave each piece of fruit on HIGH for 30 seconds. Let stand for 2 minutes, then peel.

PUDDING

- Puddings are terrific in the microwave, offering considerable convenience over stove cooking where they must be stirred constantly to prevent lumps and scorching. While it is still important to stir puddings, microwave cooks need only stir every minute or two until it begins to thicken. If you forget to stir, the thickener will form a gummy layer on the bottom of the dish.
- A wire whisk does a very good job of keeping the pudding mixed and preventing lumps.
- It is convenient to cook pudding in a 4-cup (1 L) measure from which it can easily be poured into serving dishes. Microwaved pudding is even quicker and easier if you heat the milk for 2 or 3 minutes before adding it to the pudding mix.

CUSTARD

- Because microwave cooking retains food's moisture, it is not necessary to set a custard in water to cook it; however, if the your oven does not cook very evenly, setting the dish of custard in a baking dish of hot water will improve the results.
- Custard is a delicate food and should be cooked on MEDIUM or MEDIUM-LOW. It must be kept below the boiling point or it will curdle and separate.
- Custard is usually cooked uncovered, but it may be cooked covered with a glass lid or wax paper to promote even cooking.
- Be careful not to overcook custard. Check to see if it is set by inserting a knife in the centre. It is done when it appears set but still moist on top. The moisture will dry up during standing time and the custard will begin to pull away from the edges of the dish. Overcooked custard becomes weepy, or watery.
- To caramelize sugar for making caramel custard or butterscotch sauce, place ½ cup (125 mL) sugar in a bowl and cook on HIGH for 2 to 3 minutes, until a golden brown liquid is formed.

PIE

THE KEY TO SUCCESS WITH MICROWAVED PIES

The key to success with pies is to precook the pie crust. Most pie fillings are moist and their moisture tends to keep the crust moist during cooking. However, an unfilled pie shell cooks very quickly and turns out tender and flaky. Once the pie crust is cooked, it can be filled and then cooked again, if necessary, until the filling is done. Even though it involves cooking in two steps, baking a pie in the microwave offers a significant time saving. Microwaving a pie shell is especially convenient when you do not wish to heat up the kitchen for just a pie shell.

PREPARATION OF PASTRY PIE CRUST

Because microwaved pie shells cook so rapidly, plain pastry does not brown. By adding coloured ingredients to the pie crust, or brushing a coating over the pie crust, the appearance becomes appealing. Some suggestions for colouring the crust are:

- Prepare the crust using half whole wheat flour and half all purpose flour. There is a commercially prepared mix of flour available, called a bread mix, which also works well for pies.
- Add yellow food colouring to the water before adding it to the shortening and flour mixture.
- Add 2 tbsp. (50 mL) cocoa plus 1 tbsp.(30 mL) sugar to the pie crust to make a chocolate crust.
- Add 1¼ tsp. (6 mL) spices such as cinnamon, nutmeg which add not only colour, but also flavour.
- Brush the unbaked crust with vanilla or beaten egg yolk.

HINTS FOR PREPARING FLAKY PASTRY PIE CRUST

- Follow the recipe carefully, being especially careful when measuring ingredients. Too much water will make a pie crust soggy; use only the amount listed. Too much flour will make it tough; and too much shortening, greasy and crumbly.
- When making a pie crust, handle the dough as little as possible.
- Make sure the crust is rolled to an even thickness.
- Grease pie plate before adding the pastry.
- To minumize shrinking during cooking, allow the dough to rest in the pie plate before final shaping.
- Prick bottom and sides with a fork, before microwaving the pie shell.
- To absorb moisture, place one or two layers of paper towel on top of the pastry shell during cooking time.

HOW TO KNOW WHEN MICROWAVED PASTRY PIE CRUST IS DONE

A pastry pie crust is done when the top looks dry and blistered. If it is only slightly moist, let it stand for a few minutes. During standing time, the moisture should dry up. If not, you can microwave the crust for a few more seconds until it is done. If you are using a clear glass pie plate, you should also check for doneness on the bottom of the crust. It should look opaque and dry.

CRUMB CRUSTS

Crumb crusts cook perfectly in the microwave oven, without any alterations. Because the crackers or cookies used to make the crust are already brown, there is no difference between the appearance of a microwaved crumb crust or a conventional crumb crust. There is, however, a significant difference in the time it takes to bake a crumb crust. Most crumb crusts are microwaved in less than two minutes compared with 10 minutes of preheating time and 10 minutes of baking time in the conventional oven. Microwaved crumb crusts are perfect for cool summer pies.

⊙━━➤ THE KEY TO SUCCESS WITH CRUMB CRUSTS

The key to success with crumb crusts is to melt the butter or margarine completely before adding the crumbs. The butter should be completely liquid. If there are any lumps of unmelted butter, they will cause burnt spots on the crust because microwave energy is attracted to that fat. The crumbs and butter should be well blended to prevent any concentration of butter or sugar which will also cause burnt spots.

CREAM PIES & REFRIGERATOR PIES

Excellent results are produced when these pies are prepared with the microwave oven. The crust and the filling should be prepared separately. Cook the crust first and by the time the filling is ready, the crust should be cool. See guidelines for puddings (page 201) to prepare cream pie fillings.

CUSTARD PIES

When preparing custard pies in the microwave oven, it is important to bake the crust first. Brush the baked crust with beaten egg yolks to fill any holes before adding the filling. Custard pies should be eaten the same day they are made or within 24 hours.

When both the crust and filling require cooking, it may be helpful to partially cook the filling as well as to precook the crust. In this way, the final time is shortened and the chances of overcooking the edges lessened. This method is best used in microwave ovens that do not have a turntable.

For more hints on cooking custard pies in the microwave oven, see the section on custards.

FRUIT PIES

Flavourful fruit pies can be cooked in the microwave oven with considerable time savings, however, they do require some special techniques:

- Both crusts should be baked before the fruit filling is added, so the best way to make a fruit pie is to top it with a crumb topping or with baked pastry cut outs rather than a full pastry crust.

- Add cornstarch or flour to raw fruit filling rather than tapioca because the pie cooks too quickly for the tapioca to thicken.

- Fruit pies work very well on combination cooking. Assemble a two-crust fruit pie as for conventional baking (use a glass pie plate). Microwave pie on HIGH for 7 to 8 minutes while you preheat the conventional oven to 450°F (230°C). Bake conventionally or on the convection mode of a combination microwave/convection oven for 12 to 15 minutes or until crust is golden.

DEFROSTING PIES

Do not use metal pie plate; transfer to glass pie plate if necessary. Defrost frozen pie until filling is thawed and fruit is tender, about 8 to 10 minutes. Frozen cream pies defrost in about 5 to 7 minutes.

Frozen unbaked two-crust pies need combination cooking. Use the microwave oven until filling is cooked; then put pie into conventional oven to brown.

REHEATING PIES

Pieces of fruit pie are easily reheated to a warm, freshly baked temperature just before serving. Just place on serving plates and microwave on HIGH about 15 seconds for each serving.

BAKED APPLES

An old favourite made easy with microwave cooking.

4	apples, halved and cored	4
	cinnamon	
¼ cup	brown sugar	125 mL
2 tbsp.	butter	30 mL

1. Arrange apples in a 9 x 3-inch (2 L) round cake dish. Sprinkle with cinnamon. Fill each apple cavity with brown sugar. Place a small piece of butter on top of each apple. Cover with plastic wrap.

2. Microwave on HIGH for 4 to 5 minutes, or until apples are tender.

Your Time: _____

APPLE CRISP

Plump, juicy, white apples under a crisp crumb crust — out of this world.

6	apples, peeled, cored and sliced	6
½ cup	white sugar	125 mL
1 tbsp.	cornstarch	15 mL
½ tsp.	cinnamon	2 mL
½ cup	butter OR margarine	125 mL
½ cup	brown sugar	125 mL
½ cup	flour	125 mL
1 cup	oatmeal	250 mL

1. Place apples in 1½-qt. (1.5 L) casserole dish. Mix together sugar, cornstarch and cinnamon. Add to apples and toss.

2. Place butter in a medium glass bowl. Microwave on HIGH for 1 minute. Add brown sugar, flour and oatmeal. Mix together. Pour on top of apple mixture.

3. Microwave on HIGH for 8 to 9 minutes.

VARIATION: Try it with peaches, nectarines, cherries, rhubarb, or saskatoons. It takes about 4 cups (1 L) of fruit.

Your Time: _____

PAM'S FRUIT COBBLER

This delightful fresh fruit dessert is a welcome additon to any meal.

1 qt.	sliced, sweetened fresh fruit	1	L
2 cups	flour	500	mL
1½ cups	brown sugar	375	mL
2 tsp.	baking powder	10	mL
½ tsp.	salt	2	mL
2	eggs	2	
½ cup	butter	125	mL
	cinnamon		

1. Line a shallow 9 x 3 inch (2 L) round cake dish with fruit.

2. Mix together flour, brown sugar, baking powder, salt and eggs. Spread over fruit.

3. In a 1-cup (250 mL) glass measure, microwave butter on HIGH for 1 minute or until melted. Dribble over fruit topping. Sprinkle with cinnamon.

4. Microwave on MEDIUM-HIGH for 9 to 11 minutes, or until topping is set.

Your Time: _____

CHUNKY APPLESAUCE

This tastes like fresh picked apples.

8-10	cooking apples	8-10	
½ cup	white or brown sugar	125	mL
⅓ cup	water	75	mL
½ tsp.	cinnamon	2	mL

1. Peel, core and slice the apples. Place in a 3-qt. (3 L) casserole dish.

2. Add remaining ingredients. Cover and microwave on HIGH for 8 to 10 minutes or until the apples are tender. Stir once or twice during cooking time.

3. Let the apples stand for about 7 minutes and then mash.

Your Time: _____

SOUTHERN AMBROSIA

This light and creamy ambrosia would make a delicately sweet addition to a barbecue buffet or summer picnic.

1-14-oz.	can pineapple tidbits	398 mL
¼ cup	sugar	60 mL
2 tbsp.	cornstarch	30 mL
2	apples	2
2	oranges	2
2	bananas	2
½ cup	flaked coconut	125 mL
1 cup	whipping cream, whipped	250 mL

1. Drain juice from pineapple into a 2-cup (500 mL) glass measure. Stir in sugar and cornstarch. Microwave on HIGH for 2 minutes or until clear and thickened. Set aside to cool.

2. Dice apples and oranges into a large serving bowl. Slice bananas. Mix well (the orange juice will keep the apples and bananas white). Add the pineapple and coconut.

3. Mix cooled pineapple juice into whipped cream. Pour over fruit. Mix and chill.

Your Time: _____

PLUMA MOOS

A fruit soup. My Mennonite grandmothers always served it at family occasions.

1 cup	washed raisins	250 mL
1-16 oz.	pkg. dried mixed fruit	450 g
4 cups	water	1 L
1-16 oz.	can bing cherries	450 mL
2 tbsp.	cornstarch	30 mL
1 tbsp.	water	15 mL

1. In a 3-qt. (3 L) casserole dish, combine raisins, mixed fruit and 1-qt. water. Cover and microwave on HIGH for 10 minutes. Stir once during cooking time.

2. Add cherries and juice. Microwave on HIGH for 6 minutes or until boiling.

3. Mix together cornstarch and 1 tbsp. (15 mL) water. Stir into fruit mixture and microwave on HIGH for 5 minutes, or until slightly thickened.

Your Time: _____

CHRISTMAS PUDDING

A moist pudding with a rich, full flavour

1 cup	seedless raisins	250	mL
1 cup	currants	250	mL
½ cup	mixed candied fruits & peels	125	mL
¼ cup	blanched slivered almonds	50	mL
1 cup	flour	250	mL
1 tsp.	baking soda	5	mL
½ tsp.	ground cloves	2	mL
½ tsp.	ground cinnamon	2	mL
½ tsp.	ground nutmeg	2	mL
½ cup	shortening	2	mL
1 cup	firmly packed brown sugar	250	mL
1	egg	1	
1 tsp.	vanilla	5	mL
1 cup	finely grated raw carrot	250	mL
1 cup	finely grated raw potato	250	mL

1. Combine raisins, currants, fruits and peels, and almonds in a large mixing bowl. Sift together the flour, baking soda and spices over the fruit. Stir to coat fruit evenly with flour mixture.

2. Cream shortening. Mix in sugar. Add egg and vanilla and beat until fluffy. Stir in carrot. Stir in half of the potato. Blend thoroughly.

3. Gradually blend the fruit and flour mixture into the shortening mixture. Add the remaining potato and stir just to blend. Spoon batter into a greased 12 cup (3 L) tube pan.

4. Set a plastic rack into a glass baking dish and add boiling water to a depth of ½ inch (1.3 cm). Set pudding on the rack; cover tube pan and glass baking dish completely with plastic wrap.

5. Microwave on HIGH for 5 minutes. Microwave on MEDIUM for 10 minutes or until a long pick inserted into the centre comes out clean. Let stand 10 minutes before serving.

TIP: This can be stored in the fridge and reheated by steaming as above on MEDIUM power for 5 minutes.

VARIATION: Substitute chopped walnuts for almonds and/or dates for candied fruits and peels.

Your Time: _____

CREAMY CHRISTMAS PUDDING SAUCE

This rich, fluffy sauce dresses up a Christmas pudding. It also tastes wonderful as a topping for mincemeat pie.

½ cup	butter	125 mL
½ cup	white sugar	125 mL
½ cup	brown sugar	125 mL
2	egg whites, beaten	2
½ cup	whipping cream	125 mL
½ tsp.	vanilla	2 mL

1. Combine butter and sugars in a 2-cup (500 mL) glass measure. Microwave on MEDIUM-HIGH for 3 to 4 minutes, or until hard ball stage is reached (This is when a drop forms a hard ball when dropped into ice water).

2. Meanwhile, beat egg whites until stiff peaks form. Slowly beat sugar mixture into egg whites. Continue beating until mixture thickens.

3. Whip the cream. Flavour with vanilla. Carefully fold whipped cream into egg white mixture. This sauce should look like a seven minute frosting. Serve over steamed pudding.

Your Time: _____

ORANGE SAUCE

This sauce is a light sauce for Christmas pudding.

2 tbsp.	cornstarch	30 mL
1 cup	sugar	250 mL
2 cups	boiling water	500 mL
	juice and rind (grated) of one orange	
1 tbsp.	lemon juice	15 mL
1 tsp.	butter	5 mL

1. Combine cornstarch, sugar and boiling water in a glass 4-cup (1 L) measure. Microwave on HIGH for 2½ to 3½ minutes, until clear and thickened.

2. Stir in remaining ingredients. Serve over Christmas Pudding or Gingerbread.

QUICK TIP: Cut the orange into chunks, then juice and grate in the blender.

Your Time: _____

CREAMY PUDDING

You'll never go back to cooking pudding on the stove. This pudding is fast, easy, and delicious — the creamiest you'll ever make, too.

2 cups	milk	500	mL
3 tbsp.	cornstarch	35	mL
⅔ cup	white sugar	150	mL
1 tsp.	vanilla	5	mL
2	eggs, slightly beaten OR 4 egg yolks	2	
2 tbsp.	butter	30	mL

1. Place milk in 2-cup (500 mL) glass measure. Microwave on MEDIUM-HIGH for 2½ minutes.

2. Combine cornstarch and sugar in a 4-cup (1 L) glass measure or 1½-qt. (1.5 L) casserole dish. Gradually stir milk into cornstarch mixture using a wire whisk. Microwave on MEDIUM-HIGH for 4 to 5 minutes, or until thickened and glossy. Stir two or three times during cooking time.

3. Mix some of the thickened milk into the beaten eggs to warm them. Stir warmed eggs into milk mixture. Microwave on MEDIUM for 1 minute or until boiling.

4. Stir in butter and vanilla. Pour into dessert dishes or baked pie shell.

VARIATIONS:

BUTTERSCOTCH PUDDING: Substitute brown sugar for white sugar

BANANA CREAM PUDDING: Add 2 sliced bananas

COCONUT CREAM PUDDING: Add ½ cup (125 mL) toasted coconut. (To toast: sprinkle on a 9-inch (24 cm) glass plate and microwave on HIGH 1 minute at a time, stirring well after each minute, until LIGHTLY toasted — about 2 minutes.)

FLAPPER PIE: Prepare pudding as above using 4 egg yolks instead of 2 whole eggs. Pour pudding into a 9-inch (24 cm) graham cracker crust. Beat egg whites until soft peaks form. Gradually add sugar ¼ cup (50 mL) and beat until stiff. Spread meringue onto pie; sprinkle with ¼ cup (50 mL) graham cracker crumbs. Microwave on HIGH for 3 to 3½ minutes, or until meringue is set.

SOUTHERN BANANA PUDDING: Prepare pudding as above, using 4 egg yolks instead of 2 whole eggs. Line a 2-qt. (2 L) casserole dish with vanilla wafers. Slice 2 bananas over wafers. Pour half of the pudding over bananas. Place a layer of vanilla wafers over pudding; layer 2 more sliced bananas and top with remaining pudding. Beat egg whites until soft peaks form. Gradually add ¼ cup (50 mL) sugar and continue to beat until stiff. Spread meringue onto pudding and top with ¼ cup (50 mL) crushed vanilla wafer crumbs. Microwave on HIGH for 3 to 3½ minutes, or until meringue is set or bake on the convection mode at 425°F (220°C) for 5 minutes.

CHOCOLATE PUDDING: Add 2 squares of melted chocolate with vanilla and butter or add 3 tbsp. (35 mL) cocoa to cornstarch and sugar.

COFFEE PECAN PUDDING: Add 2 tsp. (10 mL) instant coffee powder and ½ cup (125 mL) chopped pecans with the butter and vanilla.

RASPBERRY CREAM PIE: Substitute ½ tsp. (2 mL) almond extract for vanilla. Pour into baked pie shell. When set, top with sweetened raspberries and whipped cream. This would also work with any other fresh fruit.

PARFAITS: Alternate spoonsful of pudding with sweetened fruit in parfait glasses. Top with whipped cream.

PETITS POTS DE CREME — Prepare pudding as above, using dairy half & half (10% m.f.) instead of milk. Add 2 squares of melted chocolate. Blend well. Add ¼ cup (50 mL) chocolate chips or another square of chocolate, grated. The chocolate chips should not melt completely. Pour pudding into small dessert dishes. Top each with a spoonful of whipped cream and sprinkle with chopped nuts.

Your Time: _____

PACKAGED PUDDING

The ultimate in convenience!

1. In a 2-cup (500 mL) glass measure, microwave milk on MEDIUM-HIGH for 2 to 3 minutes. Stir into a 3 oz. (113 g) packaged pudding mix.

2. Microwave pudding on MEDIUM-HIGH for 3 to 5 minutes, or until mixture comes to a boil. Stir every 2 minutes.

Your Time: _____

MINUTE TAPIOCA PUDDING

Made even quicker with the microwave oven!

3 tbsp.	minute tapioca	35 mL
2	eggs, beaten	2
½ tsp.	salt	2 mL
2 cups	milk	500 mL
1 tsp.	vanilla	5 mL

1. Combine all ingredients in a 1-qt. (1 L) casserole dish. Let stand for 5 minutes.

2. Microwave on MEDIUM-HIGH for 6 to 8 minutes, or until it boils. Stir well every 2 minutes to keep egg from curdling.

Your Time: _____

MOM'S RICE PUDDING

A fluffy, old-fashioned pudding — a favourite from my childhood.

2 cups	cooked short grain rice	500 mL
¾ cup	milk	175 mL
⅓ cup	sugar	75 mL
2	eggs, separated	2
½ tsp.	vanilla	2 mL
4 tbsp.	sugar	50 mL
1 cup	raisins	250 mL

1. Combine rice, milk and sugar in a 2-qt. (2 L) casserole dish. Microwave on MEDIUM for 4 minutes, or until hot.

2. Beat egg yolks slightly. Stir a bit of hot rice mixture into yolks and then stir warmed yolks into rice mixture. Microwave on MEDIUM for 2 to 3 minutes, stirring every minute. Add vanilla.

3. Beat egg whites until stiff. Add 4 tbsp. (60 mL) sugar. Fold into rice mixture (you can use an electric mixer on low for this). Add raisins. Serve hot or cold.

TO COOK SHORT GRAIN RICE FOR THIS RECIPE: Combine 1 cup (250 mL) shortgrain rice and 2 cup (500 mL) water in a 1 ½ qt. (1.5 L) casserole dish. Cover and microwave on HIGH for 8 to 10 minutes. Let stand covered for 10 minutes to finish cooking.

Your Time: _____

FRENCH LEMON DESSERT

This is worth the effort to make — creamy, lemony and luscious.

½ cup	butter OR margarine	125	mL
2 cups	graham wafer crumbs	500	mL
2 tsp.	sugar	10	mL
2-3 oz.	pkg. lemon pudding mix	85	g
2¼ cups	hot water	550	mL
4	eggs separated	4	
2 cups	whipping cream	500	mL
1 cup	icing sugar	250	mL
1-8 oz.	pkg. cream cheese	250	g

1. In a glass 8 x 12-inch (1.5 L) pan, microwave butter on HIGH for 1 minute, or until melted. Stir in graham wafer crumbs and sugar. Press onto bottom of pan. Microwave on HIGH for 1½ minutes.

2. In an 8-cup (2 L) glass measure combine pudding mixes and hot water. Microwave on HIGH for 3 to 4 minutes, stirring after each minute, until glossy looking and thickened.

3. Beat egg yolks slightly. Gradually stir a bit of hot lemon pudding mix into egg yolks. Stir warmed egg yolks into pudding mix. Microwave on MEDIUM for 2½ to 3½ minutes, or until pudding comes to a boil. Stir after each minute. Stir in a tablespoon of butter if desired. Set aside to cool a bit.

4. Beat egg whites until stiff. Fold into cooled lemon pudding. Spread over graham crust.

5. Beat cream until stiff. Beat in icing sugar. Cream the cream cheese and mix into the whipped cream. Spread over lemon pudding. Chill.

Your Time: _____

BASIC CHEESECAKE

This recipe is not very sweet which makes it just right when topped with fresh fruit.

2 - 8 oz.	pkg. cream cheese	250 mL
4	eggs	4
1 cup	sugar	250 mL
¼ tsp.	salt	1 mL
2 tsp.	vanilla OR 2 tbsp. (30 mL) lemon juice	10 mL
1	9-inch crumb crust	24 cm

1. Soften cream cheese by microwaving on DEFROST for 1 to 2 minutes.

2. Beat eggs into cream cheese. Beat in sugar. Add remaining ingredients. Beat until smooth.

3. Pour over crumb crust and microwave on MEDIUM for 16 to 18 minutes. When cool, serve topped with sour cream or fresh fruit.

ALTERNATE COOKING METHOD: In mixing bowl, microwave batter on MEDIUM-HIGH for 4 minutes, stirring every 2 minutes. Pour over crust and microwave on MEDIUM for 10 to 15 minutes. This method works better for ovens that have no turntable.

TIP: Combine all ingredients at once in blender.

VARIATIONS:

CHOCOLATE CHEESECAKE: Add 2 squares of chocolate, melted (microwave 2 minutes on MEDIUM-LOW) and use vanilla extract rather than lemon juice.

MARBLE CHEESECAKE: After batter has been poured into the crust, add 2 squares of chocolate, melted. Swirl into batter.

BLACK FOREST CHEESECAKE: Add 2 squares of chocolate, melted. Substitute ½ tsp. (2 mL) almond extract for vanilla or lemon juice. Bake cheesecake in a chocolate crumb crust. When cool, serve topped with cherry filling and whipped cream.

CHOCOLATE CHIP CHEESECAKE: Pour batter into a chocolate crumb crust. Add ½ cup (125 mL) mini chocolate chips to batter and sprinkle another ½ cup (125 mL) on top of cheesecake. Bake as above.

APRICOT CHEESECAKE: Add 2 cups (500 mL) of canned apricot halves (drained) to batter and use ½ tsp. (2 mL) almond extract instead of vanilla or lemon juice. Bake as instructed. Thicken juice from apricots by adding 2 tbsp. (30 mL) cornstarch. Microwave on HIGH for 2 to 3 minutes, or until clear and boiling. When cheesecake is cooled, top with several apricot halves and the thickened juice.

MINI CHEESECAKES: Prepare basic cheesecake recipe above. Line micro-wave muffin pan with small paper liners. Place a vanilla wafer on the bottom of each paper and pour cheesecake batter over to fill ¾ full. Microwave on MEDIUM for 30 to 40 seconds per cheesecake or until set. When cool, top each cheesecake with a piece of fresh fruit or a teaspoon of fruit preserves.

Your Time: _____

CRUMB CRUST

This is so easy — perfect every time.

⅓ cup	**butter OR margarine**	75 mL
1 cup	**graham wafer crumbs**	250 mL
¼ tsp.	**cinnamon**	1 mL
2 tsp.	**sugar**	10 mL

1. In a glass 9-inch (24 cm) pie plate, microwave butter on HIGH for 1 minute or until melted.

2. Stir crumbs, cinnamon and sugar into butter. Mix well. Pat to line pie plate.

3. Microwave on HIGH for 1½ minutes.

TIP: Make sure that butter is completely liquid and that crumbs and butter are well mixed. If there is a lump of butter in the crust it will cause a black smoking spot in your crust.

VARIATIONS:

CHOCOLATE CRUST: use chocolate wafer crumbs instead of graham wafer crumbs and omit the cinnamon.

Substitute vanilla wafers, zwieback or cornflake crumbs for graham wafer crumbs.

Your Time: _____

BAKED CUSTARD

Pamper yourself with this light and delicate treat.

2 cups	milk	500 mL
3	eggs	3
⅓ cup	sugar	75 mL
⅛ tsp.	salt	.5 mL
¾ tsp.	vanilla	3 mL
	nutmeg	

1. In a 2-cup (500 mL) glass measure, microwave milk on MEDIUM-HIGH for 3 to 4 minutes, or until scalded.

2. In a 4 cup (1 L) glass measure or mixing bowl, beat eggs lightly. Mix in sugar, salt, vanilla. Add milk slowly, stirring constantly.

3. Pour into 6 greased 4-oz. (125 mL) custard cups. Sprinkle with nutmeg.

4. Place dishes in a circle on microwave oven turntable. Microwave on MEDIUM-LOW for 9 to 11 minutes, or until custard is set.

NOTE: If custard pulls away from the edges of the dish, it is set even if it looks a bit moist or runny on top. Moisture will dry up during standing time.

Your Time: _____

PAM'S NO ROLL PIE CRUST

This makes such a tender, flaky crust.

2 cups	whole wheat flour	500 mL
1 tsp.	salt	5 mL
½ cup	vegetable oil	125 mL
¼ cup	milk	60 mL

1. Combine flour and salt.

2. Combine vegetable oil and milk. Before vegetable oil and milk separate, quickly pour them into the flour. Stir with a fork until blended.

3. Divide dough in half. Pat each half dough into a greased 9-inch (24cm) pie plate.

4. Microwave each pie crust on HIGH for 3½ to 5 minutes or until it looks dry. If it has just a few moist spots, they will dry during standing time.

TIP: Handle this dough as little as possible as it becomes tough easily. Let it remain crumbly when you put it in the pan — treat it like a crumb crust.

Your Time: _____

216

SOUTH AFRICAN MILK TART

Alace brought the recipe for this special treat back from South Africa.

2½ cups	whole milk	625 mL
2	cinnamon sticks	2
½ cup	butter	125 mL
¼ cup	sugar	60 mL
1	egg	1
1 tsp.	baking powder	5 mL
1 cup	flour	250 mL
1 tbsp.	flour	15 mL
2 tbsp.	cornstarch	30 mL
½ cup	sugar	125 mL
2	eggs, beaten	2
1 tsp.	vanilla	5 mL
1 tsp.	butter	5 mL
	ground cinnamon	

1. Place cinnamon sticks into milk. Microwave on MEDIUM-HIGH for 3 to 4 minutes. Set aside for 10 minutes to allow cinnamon to flavour the milk.

2. Cut together ½ cup (125 mL) butter and ¼ cup (50 mL) sugar. Stir in egg. Combine baking powder and 1 cup (250 mL) flour. Mix into butter mixture. Press dough into a greased 10-inch (1.8 L) glass pie plate. Microwave on HIGH for 3 to 4 minutes.

3. Remove cinnamon sticks from milk. Combine 1 tbsp. (15 mL) flour, cornstarch and sugar. Stir in the milk. Microwave on MEDIUM-HIGH for 3 to 4 minutes, or until thick and glossy. Stir several times during cooking time.

4. Stir a bit of the thickened milk mixture into the beaten eggs. Stir warmed eggs into thickened milk mixture. Microwave on MEDIUM power for 1½ minutes or until mixture boils.

5. Stir in vanilla and butter. Pour into pie shell. Sprinkle with ground cinnamon and chill.

TIP: If milk mixture becomes lumpy beat with a wire whisk or hand mixer until smooth.

NOTE: Do not substitute ingredients.

Your Time: _____

SOUTHERN PECAN PIE

This rich dessert brings compliments every time.

3 tbsp.	butter	45 mL
⅔ cup	brown sugar	150 mL
3	eggs	3
½ cup	half & half (10% m.f.)	125 mL
¾ cup	corn syrup	175 mL
¾ tsp.	vanilla	3 mL
	pinch of salt	
1-10 inch	baked pie shell	1.8 L
1 cup	pecan halves	250 mL

1. Cream butter in medium mixing bowl. Slowly beat in sugar. Beat in eggs, one at a time.

2. Add salt, vanilla, half & half and corn syrup.

3. Pour into pie shell. Top with pecan halves.

4. Microwave on MEDIUM-HIGH for 7 to 8 minutes or until filling is set.

Your Time: _____

PUMPKIN PIE

A traditional favourite cooked a new, easy way.

1½ cups	pumpkin	375 mL
1 tsp.	flour	5 mL
1 tsp.	cornstarch	5 mL
⅓ cup	brown sugar	75 mL
⅓ tsp.	cinnamon	1 mL
	Dash of nutmeg	
⅛ tsp.	mace	.5 mL
	salt to taste	
1	egg	1
⅔ cup	milk	150 mL
1-9 inch	pastry shell, baked	24 cm

1. Mix together all ingredients in a mixing bowl.

2. Pour into baked 9-inch (24cm) pie shell

3. Microwave on MEDIUM for 14 to 16 minutes or until set.

Your Time: _____

LEE'S PEAR PIE

When you try this unusual pie it may just become your family favourite. The easy-to-make, crispy topping contrasts deliciously with the tender pear filling.

6 cups	sliced pears	1.5 mL
⅔ cup	white sugar	150 mL
1 tsp.	cinnamon	5 mL
2 tbsp.	flour	30 mL
1-10 inch	baked pie shell	1.8 L
½ cup	butter	125 mL
½ cup	brown sugar	125 mL
1 cup	flour	250 mL

1. Slice pears (don't peel if the skins are nice). Mix with white sugar, cinnamon and 2 tbsp. (30 mL) flour. Pour into baked pie shell.

2. Using a pastry cutter or two knives, cut butter into brown sugar and 1 cup (250 mL) flour to make crumbs. Spread over pears.

3. Microwave on HIGH for 8 to 10 minutes, or until pears are tender.

VARIATION: This recipe also works with apples.

Your Time: _____

EASY FUDGE PIE

Satisfy your chocolate craving with this devilish delight.

1-14 oz.	can sweetened condensed milk	300 mL
1-6 oz.	pkg. semi-sweet chocolate chips	175 g
1-10 inch	baked pie shell	25 cm
⅓ cup	sliced almonds	75 mL

1. In a 4-cup (1 L) glass measure, microwave milk on MEDIUM-HIGH for 2½ minutes, or until hot.

2. Stir in chocolate chips. Microwave on MEDIUM-HIGH for 30 seconds, if needed to melt chips. Pour into baked pie shell.

3. Sprinkle with almonds. Microwave on MEDIUM-HIGH for 3-1/2 to 4 minutes, or until set. Cool before serving.

Your Time: _____

CAKES & FROSTINGS

Cakes are traditionally baked for special occasions like birthdays, but microwave cooking is changing that. Because cakes can be microwaved in just minutes they can be served as a spur of the moment snack. In fact, if you keep a small cake mix and a few basic ingredients in the cupboard, you can bake a cake for drop-ins in the time it takes for the coffee maker to brew the coffee. With this speed, there will be no need for the refrain, "If I'd 'a known you were coming, I'd 'a baked a cake."

Not only will the speed please you, but you and your guests will be delighted with the delicious, light, moist results. The microwave produces cakes of greater volume than conventional cakes, so there will be more to pass around.

THE KEY TO SUCCESS WITH CAKES

The key to success with cakes is to maintain even cooking. Cooking with variable power levels promotes even cooking. Choosing an evenly shaped baking dish, such as a round or tube cake pan will also help. Cakes cooked in an oven without a turntable will need to be rotated. These techniques of microwave cooking all become particularly important when cooking cakes. However, one technique that works well, even without the others, is to cover the cake with wax paper or a microwave safe plate during cooking time. A cover keeps the heat inside the cake pan, resulting in an evenly cooked cake with a smooth top. Of course, the cover should be removed immediately after the cooking time to allow the surface of the cake to dry.

PREPARING CAKES FOR MICROWAVE COOKING

Prepare the batter according to the recipe instructions. Most cake recipes need no adjustment for microwave cooking. If you desire a lighter cake, substitute cake flour for all purpose flour; increase the amount by 2 to 3 tablespoons (30-45 ml) for each cup (250 ml) of flour. Allowing the batter to stand 5 to 10 minutes in the pan before baking will result in a fluffier cake.

It is not necessary to grease the cake pan since microwaved foods do not stick to the cooking dishes, however, you may wish to grease the pan with shortening if the cake is not being turned out of the pan while warm. Do not use oil and spray coatings, they make the cake uneven and sticky. DO NOT FLOUR the pan, it forms a tough coating.

COOKING CAKES IN THE MICROWAVE OVEN

Most cakes can be cooked on HIGH but lower power levels produce a cake with a more even top and finer texture. Some recipes call for a combination of HIGH and MEDIUM powers.

Rotation is necessary when cooking in an oven that has no turntable. Most cakes should be rotated two or three times during cooking. The recipes in this cookbook were tested in turntable ovens, so no rotating instructions are given in the recipes. If you open the door to your microwave oven to rearrange the cake or cupcakes; the cake will not "fall" as it would with a conventional oven.

ELEVATE LARGE CAKES

With some ovens, there is a tendency for cakes to remain doughy on the bottom. If you find this to be a problem, try elevating the cake on a plastic rack or an overturned casserole dish. Sometimes this changes the cooking pattern enough to eliminate the problem. Or, heat water in the baking dish for a few minutes while mixing the cake batter. Then, remove the water and grease the dish. The heat of the dish helps to cook the bottom of the cake.

If you discover this doughy bottom after you have turned the cake out of the pan, it can still be fixed. Just set the inverted cake on a microwave safe plate and microwave it for a minute or two, until set. Chances are, you will be the only one who knows what happened.

UTENSILS

Because cakes cook differently in the microwave than conventionally, the baking dishes are different. New microwave cake utensils made of plastic are designed to accomodate the greater expansion of cake batter. The round layer cake dishes, measuring 9 x 3 inches (22 x 6 cm) with a 2L capacity, hold half of batter from a 2-layer cake mix. Tube pans (12 cup or 3L) hold all of the batter from a 2-layer package. They are very convenient if you microwave cakes often.

This does not mean you can't use the glass baking dishes you have in your kitchen, it just means you will need to make a bit of an adjustment when using them. As a general rule, cake dishes should be filled only half full with batter. A cake recipe that calls for 1 cup (250 ml) of flour per layer will fit in an 8-inch (20 cm) round cake dish, however, most single layer cake mixes will not. If you are using a mix or recipe that is too large for an 8-inch (20 cm) dish, you can make cupcakes with the extra batter. You may have a 10 x 2 inch (1.8 L) pie plate in your cupboard. This will often be the right size for a single layer cake. If you are using a square or rectangular glass cake dish, it will be necessary to shield the corners with foil to prevent them from overcooking.

When cooking frosting in the microwave oven, use a large dish to allow for boiling. The same general rule for cakes applies also to frosting. Fill the dish only half full.

TOPPINGS

Little browning takes place on microwave cakes because they cook so fast. This is seldom a problem since most cakes are frosted and many of them have a brown coloured batter. However, for those light coloured cakes that need some enhancement, try any of the following:

- Make an upside down cake, by spreading the bottom of the pan with melted butter, brown sugar and fruit.
- Bundt cakes: lightly oil and sprinkle sugar or nuts to coat the pan.
- Frost with whipped cream or topping mix.
- Sprinkle with powdered sugar
- Combine coconut, nuts and brown sugar to sprinkle over top before baking
- Top with pie filling
- Consider using pudding as a topping!

HOW TO KNOW WHEN A CAKE IS DONE

The standard tests for doneness apply to microwaved cakes as well. Insert a toothpick into the centre of the cake. If it comes out clean, or just with crumbs sticking to it, the cake is done. Microwave cakes are moist, therefore, moist crumbs often do stick to the toothpick. The important thing is that it does not come out doughy. You can also touch the top of the cake lightly with your finger, if it springs back the cake is done. If you have any doubt as to its doneness, let it sit in the microwave oven for 3 to 5 minutes. During this time, a cake that is done will start to pull away from the edges of the pan. If not, you can give it another minute or so of cooking without worrying about it falling.

The surface of the cake should look moist, perhaps just glistening, but occasionally it will look like there is a "puddle" of batter on top. Resist the temptation to cook the cake until it looks dry, as it will then be dry throughout. The moist areas do not mean that the cake needs additional cooking. This situation happens quite frequently with cake-type products. When you notice this condition, touch it with a finger to see if it is only on the surface or if it extends into the cake. If it is only on the surface, additional cooking normally does not help and it may overcook other areas. Usually the moist areas will dry up during the standing time.

If the baking dish is made of glass, lift it up and check the bottom to make sure there are no wet, unbaked areas. This is especially important in large cakes. If it is still slightly doughy on the bottom, let it stand on the counter for 5 minutes. The counter may trap sufficient heat to finish cooking the bottom. If it is not cooked, you can continue cooking without concern about the cake falling. You may even wish to turn it out on a microwave safe plate to finish cooking the bottom.

TIPS FOR FROSTING MICROWAVED CAKES

Wait until the cake is completely cooled before frosting. When cool, lightly brush off crumbs with a pastry brush.

Use thin icing, foam icing or a glaze to frost microwaved cakes because their tops are fragile.

ADAPTING

Most cakes adapt well to microwave cooking without any alterations. Rich cakes like those made with oil or cakes that are high in sugar content work the best. A two-layer cake should have at least 3 eggs in it. Test the recipe by making one cupcake. If it seems too fragile, you may increase shortening by 2 tbsp. (30 ml) or add an extra egg. Some cake mixes require a reduction by one quarter of the water called for. Most major brands of cake mix now come with microwave instructions printed on the package.

Usually sponge, chiffon and angel food cakes are not recommended for microwave cooking, however, some recipes for these cakes have been specially formulated for microwave cooking. Some angel food cake mixes can be altered for microwave cooking by adding 2 tbsp. (30 ml) of flour to the mix.

GENERAL HINTS

- Cake Cones — Spoon cake batter into flat bottomed ice cream cones (fill each half full). Arrange cones in a circle in the microwave oven. Cook on HIGH for 20 to 25 seconds per cone. Serve at kids' parties topped with ice cream or frosting and decorated with candy or raisins.

- To soften refrigerated cake frosting, warm in the microwave oven on HIGH for 20 seconds.

- For best results when icing your cake, ice the sides first. When you do the top you can use up the extra icing.

- Cherry juice can be thickened with a little cornstarch to make a topping for cakes.

- When cutting a cake in half horizontally; mark a line with toothpicks.

- If you don't want the raisins to sink to the bottom of the cake, roll them in butter before adding to the batter.

PINEAPPLE UPSIDE DOWN CAKE

A quick, easy, and impressive dessert

1-9 oz.	yellow cake mix	250	g
1	egg	1	
½ cup	water or pineapple juice from slices	125	mL
2 tbsp.	butter	30	mL
¼ cup	brown sugar	60	mL
1-14 oz.	can pineapple slices	398	mL
	marischino cherries		

1. Combine cake mix, egg and pineapple juice in mixing bowl. Blend according to cake mix package directions. Set aside.

2. Place butter in a 9 x 3-inch (2 L) round cake dish and microwave on HIGH for 30 seconds or until butter is melted. Mix in brown sugar and spread to cover bottom of pan. Arrange pineapple slices and cherries on top of sugar mixture.

3. Pour batter over topping. Cover with wax paper and microwave on HIGH for 5 to 7 minutes or until cake springs back when lightly pressed with finger.

VARIATION: Use peaches, nectarines, or apricots instead of pineapple.

TIP: If you let your cake mix sit for 5 to 10 minutes before baking, you'll have a lighter cake.

Your Time: _____

1. Bonanzas, page 263.
2. Lee's Pear Pie, page 219.
3. Southern Ambrosia, page 207.
4. Apricot Upside Down Gingerbread, page 235.

WHITE CAKE

A good basic white cake from one of my students, Helen Marzolf.

¼ cup	margarine	60 mL
¾ cup	white sugar	175 mL
1	egg, well beaten	1
1 tsp.	vanilla	5 mL
3 tsp.	baking powder	15 mL
½ tsp.	salt	2 mL
1½ cups	cake flour	375 mL
⅔ cup	milk	150 mL

1. Cream margarine and sugar in large mixing bowl. Add egg and vanilla. Beat well.

2. Sift together dry ingredients.

3. Alternately add dry ingredients and milk to creamed mixture. Mix well and set aside.

4. In round 9 x 3-inch (2 L) round cake dish prepare upside down topping, if desired or line bottom of pan with wax paper. Pour in batter.

5. Cover with wax paper and microwave on HIGH for 5 to 7 minutes, or until top springs back when lightly pressed with finger.

TIP: If making an upside down cake; use fruit juice instead of milk.

COCONUT DELIGHT — Make 2 or 3 layers of White Cake. Fill layers with lemon pudding & pie filling. Frost with "Less Than 7 Minute Frosting" and sprinkle with coconut.

Your Time: _____

MICROWAVE LESS THAN 7 MINUTE FROSTING

This frosting is perfect for microwave cakes because it is so easy to spread and doesn't lift up the soft top of microwave cakes. With the many variations below it goes with almost any cake. And if that's not enough, it is EASY — less fuss and bother than Seven Minute Frosting on the stove.

1 cup	sugar	250 mL
⅓ cup	cold water	75 mL
⅓ tsp.	cream of tartar OR 1½ tsp. (7 mL) corn syrup	1 mL
2	egg whites	2

1. Place sugar, water and cream of tartar in a 4-cup (1 L) glass measure. Microwave on HIGH for 5 to 6 minutes or until soft ball stage is reached. (This is when the syrup slightly hardens into a soft ball when dropped into ice cold water.)

2. Meanwhile, in a large mixing bowl, beat the egg whites stiff.

3. SLOWLY, pour the hot syrup into the egg whites while beating with the electric mixer. Continue to beat until stiff peaks form. Spread on cake.

VARIATIONS:

SEAFOAM ICING: Use brown sugar instead of white; eliminate cream of tartar or corn syrup; reduce water to ¼ cup (60 mL).

PEPPERMINT: Add ¼ tsp. (1 mL) peppermint extract. Garnish with crushed peppermint candy, if desired.

TROPICAL: Use lemon, lime or pineapple juice instead of water. Add 1 tsp. (5 mL) grated lemon rind. Garnish with coconut or fruit. If you feel even more exotic, try it with grape juice.

CHOCOLATE: Microwave 3-1-oz. (30 g) squares of chocolate for 1 to 2 minutes. Stir to finish melting. Fold into icing. Do not beat or frosting will lose some of its fluffiness. It looks nice if it is just marbled, too.

COFFEE — Add 1 tsp. (5 mL) instant coffee and ⅛ tsp. (.5 mL) cinnamon to syrup mixture.

MOCHA — Add 1 tsp. (5 mL) instant coffee and ¼ cup (60 mL) cocoa to syrup mixture.

Your Time: _____

GELATIN DELIGHT CAKE

Kids love this special occasion cake.

1	single layer white cake mix OR White Cake recipe, page 225	
1 cup	water	250 mL
1-3 oz.	pkg. any flavour of jelly powder	85 g
1 cup	whipped cream OR whipped topping	250 mL

1. Prepare cake mix or recipe as directed. Place in a wax paper lined 9 x 3-inch (2 L) round cake dish and microwave on MEDIUM-HIGH for 7 to 9 minutes.

2. Place water in a 2-cup (500 mL) glass measure. Microwave on HIGH for 1½ to 2 minutes, or until boiling. Meanwhile, reserve 1 teaspoon (5 mL) of the jelly powder. Stir remaining jelly into boiling water. Stir until dissolved.

3. Turn cake out on a cooling rack. Place rack on a dinner plate. Poke holes in the cake with a fork. Pour jelly over cake. Refrigerate 1 hour.

4. Set cake on serving plate. Frost with whipped cream. Sprinkle with reserved jelly powder.

TIP: This is a good cake for holidays — use red jelly powder for Valentine's day or green jelly powder for St. Patrick's day.

Your Time: _____

BOSTON CREAM PIE

It's easier than you think.

1 cup	milk	250 mL
⅓ cup	sugar	75 mL
2 tbsp.	cornstarch	30 mL
¼ tsp.	salt	2 mL
1	egg, slightly beaten	1
2 tbsp.	butter OR margarine	15 mL
½ tsp.	vanilla	2 mL
2 tbsp.	butter OR margarine	30 mL
1 - 1 oz.	square unsweetened chocolate	28 g
1½ oz.	cream cheese	63 g
1 cup	icing sugar	250 mL
1 tbsp.	milk	15 mL
½ tsp.	vanilla	2 mL
2 layers	White Cake recipe, page 225	

1. Place milk in a glass 1-cup (250 mL) measure. Microwave on MEDIUM-HIGH for 1 minute. Combine sugar, cornstarch and salt in a 2-cup (500 mL) glass measure. Stir warm milk into sugar mixture. Microwave on MEDIUM-HIGH for 1 to 2 minutes or until slightly thickened and glossy looking. Stir and check it every 30 seconds.

2. Beat egg in a small dish. Stir in a bit of the hot milk mixture. Stir heated egg mixture into remaining milk mixture. Microwave on MEDIUM for 1 minute or until just to the boiling point. Stir in butter and ½ tsp. (2 mL) vanilla. Cool to lukewarm. Spread over bottom layer of white cake and top with second layer.

3. In a medium glass mixing bowl, microwave 2 tbsp. (30 mL) butter and chocolate square on HIGH for 1 minute, stir until melted. Add cream cheese. Beat until smooth. Gradually beat in icing sugar, milk and vanilla. Beat until smooth and of spreading consistency.

4. Frost top of cake with chocolate icing. Refrigerate until ready to serve.

Your Time: _____

CHOCOLATE LAYER CAKE

A moist cake with many possibilities.

½ cup	butter	125 mL
2 cups	sugar	500 mL
2	egg yolks	2
1 tsp.	vanilla	5 mL
2 cups	cake flour	500 mL
¾ cup	cocoa	175 mL
½ tsp.	salt	2 mL
1 tsp.	baking soda	5 mL
1¾ cup	milk	375 mL

1. In a large mixing bowl, cream butter and sugar. Beat in egg yolks and vanilla.

2. Combine dry ingredients. Alternately add dry ingredients and milk to butter mixture.

3. Line two 9 x 3-inch (2 L) round cake dishes with wax paper. Pour half of the batter into each pan. Microwave one layer at a time, covered, on MEDIUM-HIGH for 7 to 9 minutes.

Your Time: _____

CHOCOLATE UPSIDE DOWN CAKE

As delicious as it is efficient.

¼ cup	butter	60	mL
½ cup	brown sugar	125	mL
½ cup	flaked coconut	125	mL
½ cup	chopped pecans	125	mL
¼ cup	butter OR margarine	60	mL
1 cup	white sugar	250	mL
1	egg yolk	1	
½ tsp.	vanilla	2	mL
1 cup	cake flour	250	mL
⅓ cup	cocoa	75	mL
¼ tsp.	salt	1	mL
½ tsp.	baking soda	2	mL
¾ cup	milk	175	mL

1. Place ¼ cup (60 mL) butter in 9 x 3-inch (2 L) round cake dish. Microwave on HIGH for 45 seconds or until melted. Mix in brown sugar, coconut and pecans. Spread evenly to cover bottom of dish.

2. Cream butter and sugar in large mixing bowl. Add egg yolk and vanilla. Beat well.

3. Combine dry ingredients.

4. Alternately add dry ingredients and milk to creamed mixture. Pour batter over topping.

5. Cover with wax paper and microwave on HIGH for 6 to 8 minutes, or until top springs back when lightly pressed with finger.

Your Time: _____

SWISS ALMOND MOCHA DELIGHT

A spectacular cake for a special occasion.

½ cup	chocolate chips	125 mL
2 tbsp.	hot water	30 mL
2 tsp.	instant coffee	10 mL
2 tsp.	sugar	10 mL
2 cups	whipping cream	500 mL
	Chocolate Layer Cake in 3 layers	
1 cup	slivered almonds	250 mL

1. In a 2-cup (500 mL) glass measure, combine chocolate chips, hot water, coffee and sugar. Microwave on MEDIUM-HIGH for 2 to 4 minutes, or until melted and smooth. Stir after each minute of cooking time. Set aside to cool.

2. Whip the cream until just starting to thicken. Mix about ½ cup (125 mL) cream into chocolate mixture and then add all of the chocolate mixture to the cream. Whip until stiff.

3. Set aside ⅓ of the whipped mixture and ¼ cup (60 mL) of the slivered almonds. Stir remaining almonds into remaining whipped mixture and spread between cake layers. Frost top and sides of cake with plain whipped mixture and garnish with remaining almonds and cherries if you like.

Your Time: _____

FANCY IN A HURRY CHOCOLATE CAKE

Just what you need for those busy days that everyone has.

	Chocolate Layer Cake in 3 layers	
2 cups	whipped cream OR whipped topping	500 mL
1-4 oz.	jar marischino cherries, cut in halves	125 mL
1 cup	chopped walnuts	250 mL
	candied cherries	
	shaved chocolate	

1. On each layer of cake spread ⅓ of the whipped cream; top with cherries; sprinkle with walnuts. Do not frost sides of the cake. Chill until ready to serve.

DECADENT CHOCOLATE CAKE

The name says it all.

½ cup	butter	125 mL
3-1 oz.	squares unsweetened chocolate	30 g
1 cup	hot water	250 mL
2½ cups	SIFTED all-purpose flour	625 mL
1 tsp.	baking powder	5 mL
2 cups	sugar	500 mL
1 tsp.	vanilla	5 mL
2	eggs, separated	2
½ cup	sour cream	125 mL
1 tsp.	baking soda	5 mL

1. Place butter, chocolate and water in a large mixing bowl. Microwave on HIGH for 2 to 2½ minutes, or until boiling. Stir and set aside.

2. Sift flour and baking powder onto wax paper.

3. Stir butter mixture again. Mix in sugar and vanilla. Beat in egg yolks, one at a time, blending throughly.

4. Combine sour cream and baking soda. Beat into chocolate mixture. Mix in flour and baking powder mixture. Blend throughly.

5. With electric mixer, beat egg whites in a small bowl until soft peaks form. Stir a little of the egg whites into chocolate batter to lighten it. Fold remaining egg whites into chocolate mixture until no streaks of white remain.

6. Pour into a 12-cup (3 L) tube pan. Place tube pan on a rack or an inverted casserole dish in the microwave oven. Cover with wax paper and microwave on MEDIUM for 12 to 14 minutes or until top springs back when lightly touched. Let stand for 5 to 8 minutes to finish cooking.

7. Turn out on a cooling rack. When completely cooled, frost with Decadent Chocolate Frosting, page 233.

Your Time: _____

DECADENT CHOCOLATE FROSTING

¾ cup	semi-sweet chocolate chips	175 mL
6 tbsp.	whipping cream	90 mL
2 tbsp.	butter	30 mL
1 tsp.	vanilla	5 mL
1¼ cups	icing sugar	310 mL

1. Combine all ingredients in a medium size glass mixing bowl.

2. Microwave on MEDIUM-HIGH for 1 minute or until butter and chocolate have melted. Stir 2 or 3 times during cooking time.

3. With an electric mixer, beat until it thickens slightly, but is still runny. Frost Decadent Chocolate Cake. (Frosting is soft and runny but becomes firm on cake.) Decorate with crystalized sugar flowers.

Your Time: _____

TOMATO SOUP CAKE

Don't let the name stop you from trying this wonderful spice cake. It tastes especially good when frosted with caramel icing.

¼ cup	butter OR margarine	60 mL
1 cup	brown sugar	250 mL
1	egg, beaten	1
1-10 oz.	can tomato soup (undiluted)	284 mL
1½ cups	flour	375 mL
1 tsp.	nutmeg	5 mL
1 tsp.	baking soda	5 mL
½ tsp.	salt	2 mL
1 tsp.	cinnamon	5 mL
1 tsp.	baking powder	5 mL
1 cup	raisins	250 mL
½ cup	chopped walnuts	125 mL

1. Cream butter and sugar. Mix in egg and tomato soup.

2. Combine dry ingredients. Add to soup mixture and beat well.

3. Stir in raisins and walnuts. Pour into a 9 x 3-inch (2 L) cake dish which has been lined with waxed paper. Cover with wax paper and microwave on MEDIUM-HIGH for 9 to 10 minutes.

Your Time: _____

GINGERBREAD

Fragrant spices and light texture make this gingerbread hard to beat.

¼ cup	butter OR margarine	60 mL
½ cup	sugar	125 mL
1	egg	1
½ cup	molasses	125 mL
⅓ cup	milk	75 mL
1½ cup	flour	375 mL
1 tsp.	baking soda	5 mL
1 tsp.	cinnamon	5 mL
1 tsp.	ground ginger	5 mL

1. Cream butter and sugar. Mix in egg, molasses and milk. Blend well. Combine dry ingredients and stir into creamed mixture.

2. Pour batter into a wax paper lined round 9 x 3-inch (2 L) cake dish. Cover with wax paper and microwave on MEDIUM-HIGH for 6 to 8 minutes.

SERVING SUGGESTION: Top each serving with Orange Sauce, page 209.

Your Time: _____

APRICOT UPSIDE DOWN GINGERBREAD

3 tbsp.	butter OR margarine	45 mL
½ cup	brown sugar	125 mL
1-14 oz.	can apricot halves	398 mL
	batter for single layer Gingerbread	
	(recipe, page 234 OR prepared mix)	

1. Place butter in a 9 x 3-inch (2 L) round cake dish. Microwave on HIGH for 45 seconds or until melted.

2. Stir in brown sugar. Spread evenly over the bottom of the cake pan.

3. Drain the apricot halves well. Arrange apricot halves on top of the sugar mixture with the cut side up. Pour gingerbread batter over apricot halves.

4. Cover with wax paper and microwave on MEDIUM-HIGH for 7 to 10 minutes. Cake is done when a toothpick inserted in the centre comes out clean or when cake pulls away from the edges of the dish. Cake should still look moist and very slightly underdone when oven shuts off. It should dry up and/or pull away from the edges during the next 3 to 5 minutes of standing time.

Your Time: _____

APPLESAUCE GINGERBREAD

2 cups	applesauce	500 mL
1 tbsp.	cornstarch	15 mL
	batter for single layer Gingerbread (recipe	
	page 234 OR from a mix)	

1. Combine applesauce and cornstarch. Spread in the bottom of a 9 x 3-inch (2 L) round cake dish.

2. Pour gingerbread batter over applesauce.

3. Microwave on MEDIUM-HIGH for 7 to 10 minutes.

Your Time: _____

PINEAPPLE UPSIDE DOWN GINGERBREAD

1-14 oz.	can pineapple slices	398	mL
2 tbsp.	butter	30	mL
¼ cup	brown sugar	60	mL
¼ tsp.	cinnamon	1	mL
5 or 6	marischino cherries		
½ cup	shredded carrot	125	mL
	Batter for single layer Gingerbread		
	(recipe page 234 OR from a mix)		

1. Drain pineapple slices. If you like, you can use the juice to prepare the gingerbread batter instead of liquid used in the recipe.

2. Place butter in a 9 x 3-inch (2 L) round cake dish. Microwave on HIGH for 30 seconds or until melted. Stir in brown sugar and cinnamon. Spread mixture evenly to cover the bottom of the pan.

3. Arrange the pineapple slices on top of the sugar mixture and set a cherry in the centre of each pineapple slice.

4. Mix shredded carrot into the gingerbread batter. Pour gingerbread batter into cake pan.

5. Microwave on MEDIUM-HIGH for 7 to 10 minutes.

Your Time: _____

OATMEAL CINNAMON CAKE

Both the cake and its topping are cooked in the microwave.

1½ cup	boiling water	375 mL
1 cup	quick oats	250 mL
½ cup	butter OR margarine	125 mL
1 cup	white flour	250 mL
½ cup	whole wheat flour	250 mL
1½ tsp.	cinnamon	7 mL
1 tsp.	baking soda	5 mL
1 tsp.	salt	5 mL
1 cup	firmly-packed brown sugar	250 mL
¾ cup	white sugar	175 mL
2	eggs beaten	2

1. Pour boiling water over oatmeal. Break butter into chunks and drop over oats. Stir mixture until butter is melted.

2. Combine flours, cinnamon, baking soda and salt. Add to oatmeal mixture. Add the sugars and eggs. Pour mixture into a 9 x 3-inch (2 L) round cake dish. Cover with wax paper and microwave on HIGH for 7 to 9 minutes or until top springs back.

Topping:

¾ cup	brown sugar	175 mL
6 tbsp.	butter OR margarine	90 mL
2 tbsp.	milk	60 mL
1 cup	shredded coconut	250 mL
½ cup	chopped pecans	125 mL

1. Combine in 1½-qt. (1.5 L) casserole dish all the topping ingredients, except coconut and pecans.

2. Microwave on HIGH for 1 to 1½ minutes or until mixture boils.

3. Boil for 1 minute then blend in the coconut and pecans. Mix together and sprinkle over cool cake.

Your Time: _____

HONEY BRAN KUCHEN

A healthy and delicious snack.

¾ cup	whole wheat flour	175 mL
2½ tsp.	baking powder	12 mL
½ tsp.	cinnamon	2 mL
¼ tsp.	nutmeg	1 mL
¼ tsp.	salt	1 mL
1½ cups	bran flakes	375 mL
3 tbsp.	butter	15 mL
½ cup	milk	125 mL
1	egg, well beaten	1
¼ cup	honey	60 mL
½ cup	raisins (optional)	125 mL
2 tbsp.	butter	30 mL
¼ cup	brown sugar, packed	60 mL
½ cup	bran flakes, coarsely crushed	125 mL

1. Sift flour, baking powder and spices together into a large mixing bowl. Stir in 1½ cups (375 mL) bran flakes.

2. Microwave butter for 45 seconds or until melted. Combine butter, milk, egg and honey. Pour into flour mixture. Stir until moistened. Stir in raisins. Pour into a wax paper lined round 9 x 3-inch (2 L) cake dish.

3. Place 2 tbsp. (30 mL) butter in a small mixing bowl. Microwave on HIGH for 30 seconds or until melted. Stir in brown sugar and crushed bran flakes. Sprinkle on top of cake batter.

4. Cover with wax paper and microwave on MEDIUM-HIGH for 6 to 9 minutes, or until toothpick inserted in centre comes out clean — let it stand in the microwave oven for 1 minute before checking.

Your Time: _____

MARIANNE'S CARROT CAKE

Homey perfection.

¾ cup	flour	175 mL
½ cup	white sugar	125 mL
¼ cup	packed brown sugar	60 mL
1 tsp.	baking soda	5 mL
1 tsp.	cinnamon	5 mL
¼ tsp.	ground ginger	1 mL
½ cup	vegetable oil	125 mL
1¼ cup	grated carrots	300 mL
2	eggs	2
¼ cup	chopped walnuts	60 mL
¼ cup	raisins	60 mL

1. Place all ingredients in mixing bowl. Blend at low speed; then beat at medium speed 2 minutes. Spread batter in a wax paper lined 9 x 3-inch (2 L) round cake dish.

2. Cover with wax paper and microwave on MEDIUM-HIGH for 9 to 10 minutes, or until cake top springs back when lightly touched.

3. Let stand on countertop 5 to 10 minutes. Cool and frost with cream cheese frosting recipe below.

Your Time: _____

CREAM CHEESE FROSTING

This frosting is a healthy alternative to sugary sweet icings.

1-8 oz.	pkg. cream cheese	250 g
1 tbsp.	honey	15 mL

1. Place cream cheese in glass mixing bowl. Microwave on DEFROST for 1 minute.

2. Add honey and beat until fluffy. Spread on top of cake.

HINT: If icing is too thick to spread without lifting cake top, thin with 1 or 2 tablespoons melted butter.

SERVING SUGESTION: This tastes great on cookies too. You can use a decorator's bag to pipe faces or words onto cookies.

Your Time: _____

PLATZ

This fruit topped cake is a family favourite. It is just wonderful when served warm with whipped cream or ice cream.

¼ cup	shortening	60 mL
¼ cup	sugar	60 mL
1	egg	1
½ tsp.	salt	2 mL
2 tsp.	baking powder	10 mL
1½ cups	flour	375 mL
½ cup	milk	125 mL
¼ cup	butter	60 mL
½ cup	brown sugar	125 mL
⅓ cup	flour	75 mL
2 cups	fresh sliced fruit, sweetened OR canned fruit OR pie filling	500 mL

1. Cream shortening and sugar. Mix in egg.

2. Combine salt, baking powder and flour. Add alternately with milk, stirring after each addition. Spread in a 9 x 3-inch (2 L) round cake dish.

3. Cut together butter, brown sugar and flour to make crumbs.

4. Spread fruit over cake batter and sprinkle with crumb mixture. Microwave on MEDIUM-HIGH for 7 to 9 minutes or until toothpick inserted in centre comes out clean.

Your Time: _____

BLUEBERRY BUCKLE

The natural flavour of the blueberries is at its best when this is cooked in the microwave. The crumbs give it a nice brown top.

¼ cup	butter OR margarine	60	mL
¾ cup	white sugar	175	mL
1	egg	1	
2 cups	flour	500	mL
2 tsp.	baking powder	10	mL
½ tsp.	salt	2	mL
½ cup	milk	125	mL
2 cups	blueberries OR saskatoons	500	mL
¼ cup	butter	60	mL
½ cup	brown sugar	125	mL
⅓ cup	flour	75	mL
½ tsp.	cinnamon	2	mL

1. Cream ¼ cup (60 mL) butter and white sugar. Beat in egg. Combine flour, baking powder, and salt and add alternately with milk, beating until smooth. Fold in berries. Line a 9 x 3-inch (2 L) cake dish with wax paper. Pour in the batter.

2. Cut together remaining ingredients and sprinkle on top of batter.

3. Cover with wax paper and microwave on MEDIUM-HIGH for 9 to 12 minutes, or until top springs back when lightly touched or edges pull away from sides of dish.

SERVING SUGESTION: This tastes delicious served warm with whipped cream or ice cream.

Your Time: _____

LEMON POUND CAKE

The glaze gives this cake a tart lemon flavour.

4	eggs	4
1 pkg.	(2 layer size) yellow cake mix	
1-3¾ oz.	pkg. instant lemon pudding mix	106 g
¾ cup	water	175 mL
⅓ cup	vegetable oil	75 mL
2 cups	icing sugar	500 mL
⅓ cup	lemon juice	75 mL

1. In a large mixing bowl beat eggs with electric mixer until they are thick and light yellow in colour.

2. Add cake mix, pudding mix, water and vegetable oil. Beat at medium speed for 10 minutes. Pour into a 12-cup (3 L) tube pan.

3. Place cake on a plastic rack or inverted casserole dish in the microwave oven. Cover with wax paper and microwave on MEDIUM for 12 to 14 minutes or until toothpick comes out clean when inserted in centre. Let cake stand 5 minutes before turning out of pan.

4. While cake is baking set a cooling rack over a large plate. Turn cake out on cooling rack. Use a fork to poke cake all over.

5. In a 2-cup (500 mL) glass measure combine icing sugar and lemon juice. Microwave on HIGH for 1 minute or until boiling. Pour glaze over cake. Cool completely before moving cake from rack to serving tray.

Your Time: _____

COOKIES, SQUARES & CANDY

Microwave cookies are truly convenient. Squares and bar cookies are a microwaving specialty. Most recipes can be cooked by microwave in less time than it takes to preheat a conventional oven. No-bake type cookies and squares are easier to prepare in the microwave oven because there is less chance of scorching.

The cool cooking of the microwave oven makes fresh homemade cookies on hot summer days a possibility. Children will also enjoy microwaving cookies or squares and Mom won't need to fear that they will burn themselves. Cookies can also be made ahead and frozen. They can be defrosted in seconds, for fresh baked flavour.

To some, it may seem impractical to microwave individual cookies because only 6 to 10 are cooked at a time. In fact, microwaving saves time and energy even though cookies do require constant attention. A full batch of three dozen cookies can be microwaved in about 10 minutes, the time it takes to preheat a conventional oven, and you need only one cookie sheet.

THE KEY TO SUCCESS WITH COOKIES & SQUARES

The key to success with cookies & squares is to ensure even cooking. Because these foods are high in sugar content they are prone to overcook in some areas while undercooking in others. This problem can be solved by using proper microwave techniques.

The distribution of microwave energy within your oven affects the way cookies bake. If your oven has a turntable, they will cook evenly without being rotated. The test ovens for the recipes in this book had turntables, so no instructions for rotation are given. If some individual cookies or areas on bar cookies cook faster than others, rotate the baking dish twice during the cooking time. If some individual cookies are still cooked before others, remove the cooked cookies by tearing the wax paper. Covering a dish of bar cookies with wax paper during the cooking time will also promote uniform cooking.

Many cookies are microwaved on MEDIUM or MEDIUM-HIGH power to promote even cooking. The temperature of the cookie batter affects the amount of time needed to cook them, but generally they take about 20 seconds per cookie. Most bar cookies are done in 5 to 8 minutes.

INDIVIDUAL COOKIES
TOPPINGS FOR INDIVIDUAL COOKIES

Microwaved cookies do not brown, so for best results use doughs in which browning is not expected, or make changes in the dough before cooking. Dark ingredients like molasses, spices or dark flour can be added to the dough or you can roll dough in nuts or cinnamon-sugar before baking. The cooked cookies can also be frosted or sprinkled with powdered sugar or decorative sprinkles.

UTENSILS FOR INDIVIDUAL COOKIES

Cookies can be cooked in the microwave oven on a variety of dishes. A glass plate or platter such as Versatray by Anchor Hocking will bake cookies well.

Some bacon or meat racks can be flipped over to double as baking sheets. Wax paper is handy for baking cookies. It can be used to line a tray so that when one batch of cookies is done they can be removed to cool and the cookie sheet can be used for the remaining cookies. It can even be used in place of a baking sheet. Wax paper can be set directly on the tray of the oven or on a piece of cardboard cut to size.

Cookies should be arranged in a circle around the outside of the baking sheet. Allow at least 2 inches between each cookie, as they tend to spread a bit more when cooked in the microwave oven.

To remove cookies from a baking sheet or wax paper, allow them to cool slightly but not completely. Then set them on a cooling rack to finish cooling.

HOW TO KNOW WHEN INDIVIDUAL COOKIES ARE DONE

The best way to tell if a cookie is done is to touch it lightly with a finger. If the top springs back, the cookie is done. You can also insert a toothpick into the centre to see if it has set. The colour of the cookie does not indicate doneness because cookies do not brown on the outside. When the microwave oven shuts off, the cookies will look moist on top. This moisture will dry up within a minute or two if the cookies are done. If you are not sure whether or not they are done, let them stand in the microwave oven to see if they begin drying up. If they are not done you can add a few seconds of cooking time.

The cookies will be quite soft when removed from the oven. Allow 3 to 5 minutes before removing them from the baking sheet. Cookies will crisp as they cool.

An overcooked area on a cookie becomes toasted and then scorched. However, this browning will be on the inside and may only be discovered by the smell or when the cookie is broken into pieces.

ADAPTING INDIVIDUAL COOKIE RECIPES

When preparing your favourite cookie recipes for microwave oven cooking, choose a recipe that is similar to the one you want to use from this book or the manual that came with your oven. If the type and quantity of the ingredients are similar, the cooking time will also be similar.

It is important to choose recipes that are compatible with the way microwaves cook. Most microwaved cookies are soft and chewy which is often a desirable quality in cookies. Molded cookies and refrigerator cookies work quite well, as do sugar cookies that don't call for a large amount of butter. Meringue drops get crisper and harder when cooked by microwave energy. Of course, microwaved cookies do not brown, so unless the batter is already coloured or white cookies are desirable, they should be topped with a coating or icing.

To keep cookies from spreading thin and becoming too tender, the dough must be stiffer than for a conventional recipe. As a general rule, most cookie doughs require about 20% more flour for microwave cooking.

Many cookie doughs do not cook evenly; it is possible to have a cookie that is both doughy and scorched. The dry-textured cookie doughs cook fairly evenly. The best way to learn which doughs cook well is to try a few cookies in the microwave, whenever you are preparing a batch. If they work well, you can cook the remaining cookies in the microwave. If not, you can bake the rest in the conventional oven, having wasted very little.

SQUARES

UTENSILS FOR COOKING SQUARES & BAR COOKIES

Bar cookies are best cooked in round dishes; however, they can be cooked in square or rectangular dishes if the corners are shielded with foil during the first two-thirds of cooking time. The baking dish for bar cookies may be greased or ungreased, as desired. The dish should not be floured, since the flour will form a layer on the bottom of the cookies.

Layered squares cook well in a rectangular dish if the crust is baked before the remaining ingredients are layered on top of it.

HOW TO KNOW WHEN SQUARES & BAR COOKIES ARE DONE

Since there is no browning to indicate doneness, check by touching the surface of the squares lightly with a finger. If it springs back, it is cooked. Cake-like bars can also be checked by inserting a toothpick into the centre. If the toothpick comes out clean, the bar is done. Sometimes the surface will remain moist looking, but the bar is set. If this is the case, further cooking may overcook the interior while leaving the moist-looking surface unchanged. It is better to allow them to stand for 3 to 5 minutes after cooking. Some fudgy brownies need as long as a half hour of standing time. During this standing time the moisture should dry up and if the bar cookies are done, they will begin to pull away from the edges of the pan.

Bar cookies do not brown on the outside, but they will overcook on the inside and can even scorch in areas. If bar cookies are hard or tough and dry, they are overcooked. Next time reduce the cooking time.

ADAPTING SQUARES FOR MICROWAVE COOKING

When preparing your own favourite bar cookie recipes in the microwave oven, select as a guide a similar recipe in this chapter or the manual that came with your oven. Then use the same setting and approximately the same amount of time. In general, cook bar cookies on HIGH for approximately one-third of the time required when baked in a conventional oven.

Prepare the batter as you would if you were to cook it conventionally. Don't alter the quantities. Don't attempt to double recipes for bars unless you plan to cook the amounts separately. Large quantities are more likely to overcook in the corners before the center is cooked.

Bar cookies will not brown in the microwave due to the short cooking time. Use dark-colored sugars and spices in the batter to achieve a browned appearance or sprinkle the top of the square with cinnamon and sugar or nuts. Many bar cookies can also be frosted, so the lack of browning is not noticed. If frosting is desired, wait until the bar is completely cooled.

HINTS

- After you have microwave baked brownies, break up a chocolate bar and sprinkle on top of the still hot brownies. Cover with foil and let stand 5 minutes. Remove the foil and spread the frosting.
- For easy storage, slip the dish of bars into a plastic bag.

FUDGE DROPS

These don't last long in our house. They've been a favourite of mine since childhood.

½ cup	butter OR margarine	125 mL
½ cup	milk	125 mL
2 cups	sugar	500 mL
4 tbsp.	cocoa	50 mL
1 cup	flaked coconut	250 mL
2 cups	oatmeal	500 mL
½ cup	chopped nuts	250 mL

1. Place butter, milk and sugar in a glass 4-cup (1 L) measure. Microwave on MEDIUM-HIGH for 3 to 5 minutes.

2. Combine remaining ingredients in large mixing bowl. Add boiled sugar mixture and mix well.

3. Drop by spoonfuls on greased cookie sheet. Chill until firm.

Your Time: _____

IRENE'S BOILED RAISIN COOKIES

An old fashioned favourite sped up by modern microwaves.

1 cup	raisins	250 mL
½ cup	water	125 mL
1 cup	brown sugar	250 mL
½ cup	butter OR margarine	125 mL
3	eggs	3
¼ tsp.	ground cloves	1 mL
1 tsp.	baking soda	5 mL
½ tsp.	cinnamon	2 mL
2 cups	flour	500 mL

1. In a large mixing bowl, microwave raisins and water on HIGH for 2 to 5 minutes, until raisins are plump. Set aside to cool 10 minutes.

2. Mix in remaining ingredients except flour. Blend in flour.

3. Drop in rounded teaspoonsful on a microwave safe baking sheet to form a ring around the outside. Microwave on MEDIUM for 20 to 30 seconds per cookie, or until top springs back when lightly touched.

Your Time: _____

CHOCOLATE COOKIES

A favourite in my classes.

1-9 oz.	one layer cake mix	250	g
⅓ cup	flour	75	mL
¼ cup	butter	50	mL
1	egg	1	
	coconut, chopped nuts OR pecan halves, as desired		

1. In glass measuring cup, microwave butter on HIGH for 45 seconds, or until melted.

2. Combine dry ingredients in mixing bowl. Stir in egg and butter. Blend well.

3. Shape dough into 1-inch (2.5 cm) balls. Top each with pecan half, if desired, or roll in chopped nuts or coconut.

4. Place 8 balls in a circle, equidistantly, on a baking sheet. Microwave on HIGH for 20 seconds per cookie or 2½ minutes for 8. Allow cookies to cool slightly before removing. Repeat with remaining cookies.

Your Time: _____

CARROT COOKIES

I especially enjoy these when topped with lemon flavoured icing.

1 cup	butter OR margarine	250	mL
¾ cup	white sugar	175	mL
1	egg	1	
1 cup	grated carrots	250	mL
2 cups	flour	500	mL
2 tsp.	baking powder	10	mL
¾ cup	shredded coconut	175	mL

1. In a medium mixing bowl, cream together butter and sugar. Beat in egg.

2. Mix in carrots, then flour and baking powder. Blend. Mix in coconut.

3. Drop by rounded teaspoonsful onto a microwave baking sheet to form a ring around the outside of the pan. Microwave on MEDIUM-HIGH for 20 to 30 seconds per cookie, or until top springs back when lightly touched.

Your Time: _____

SOFT GINGER COOKIES

Store dough in fridge or freezer and cut off just enough to bake and eat.

¾ cup	butter OR margarine, softened	175 mL
½ cup	brown sugar	125 mL
1 cup	molasses	250 mL
2	eggs	2
2 tsp.	ginger	10 mL
⅔ cup	cold water	150 mL
1 tbsp.	baking soda	15 mL
½ tsp.	cloves	2 mL
½ tsp.	cinnamon	2 mL
¼ tsp.	salt	1 mL
4½ cups	flour	500 mL

1. In a large mixing bowl cream butter and sugar. Beat in molasses and eggs. Stir in remaining ingredients. Blend in flour, one cup at a time.

2. Roll into soft balls. Place in a ring around the outside of a microwave safe baking sheet. Place 2 cookies in the center. Microwave on MEDIUM-HIGH for 15 to 20 seconds per cookie, or until top springs back when lightly touched.

Your Time: _____

MARIANNE'S SWEETHEART COOKIES

A treat for those who don't need any more sweetness.

1 cup	butter	250	mL
2-3 oz.	pkgs. cream cheese	2 x 125	g
1 cup	brown sugar	250	mL
1 tsp.	vanilla	5	mL
2 cups	whole wheat flour	500	mL
1 tbsp.	baking powder	15	mL
¼ tsp.	salt	1	mL
1 cup	oatmeal	250	mL
½ cup	chopped walnuts	125	mL

1. Cream butter and cheese together; beat in sugar and vanilla.

2. Mix in flour, baking powder, salt, oats and walnuts.

3. Divide into 1-inch (2 cm) balls. To shape hearts, press to flatten slightly. Pinch bottom together to form point. With index finger, press dough from top edge toward point to make indentation in top of heart.

4. Place on a microwave safe baking sheet to form a ring around the outside. Microwave on MEDIUM-HIGH for 15 seconds per cookie, or until top springs back when lightly touched.

5. Decorate with pink icing, if desired, or top with cherry half.

YIELD: 4 dozen cookies.

Your Time: _____

DELECTABLE CARAMEL BARS

So-o-o rich and so-o-o good.

1 cup	flour	250	mL
½ cup	brown sugar	125	mL
½ cup	butter	125	mL
1 cup	butter (do not substitute)	250	mL
1 cup	brown sugar	250	mL
4 tbsp.	corn syrup	50	mL
1-14 oz.	can sweetened condensed milk	300	mL
1-12 oz.	pkg. chocolate chips	350	g

1. Combine flour and brown sugar. Cut in ½ cup (125 mL) butter, as for pastry (I do this in my food processor).

2. Press this mixture into a greased glass 8 x 12-inch (1.5 L) baking dish. Microwave on HIGH for 1½ to 2 minutes.

3. In a 2-qt. (2 L) casserole dish, microwave 1 cup (250 mL) butter on HIGH for 2 minutes or until melted. Stir in brown sugar, corn syrup and condensed milk. Microwave on MEDIUM power for 7 to 9 minutes. Stir twice during cooking time. Pour over base. Chill until set.

4. In a 4-cup (1 L) glass measure, microwave chocolate chips on MEDIUM-LOW for 3 to 4 minutes or until melted. Stir every minute or so to distribute heat evenly. Keep stirring until melted and smooth. Spread over chilled caramel layer.

5. Cut with a sharp knife to mark bars. Chill completely. Cut into bars with a sharp knife dipped in hot water.

Your Time: _____

SWEETENED CONDENSED MILK

Use this recipe to substitute for the 14 oz. can of sweetened condensed milk called for in many of the recipes in this section. It's a lot less expensive!

1½ cups	non-fat dry milk powder	375 mL
½ cup	water	50 mL
⅔ cup	sugar	175 mL
1 tsp.	vanilla	5 mL

1. Combine dry milk and water in a 4-cup (1 L) glass measure, stir until smooth.

2. Stir in remaining ingredients.

3. Microwave on HIGH for 30 seconds to 1½ minutes; just until heated but not boiling. Stir every 30 seconds.

*Yield: 1⅓ cups

Your Time: _____

HIP PADDER BARS

Beware!

1-14 oz.	can sweetened condensed milk	300 mL
2 tbsp.	butter OR margarine	30 mL
1-6 oz.	pkg. chocolate chips	175 g
1 tsp.	vanilla	5 mL
½ cup	butter OR margarine	125 mL
1 cup	brown sugar	250 mL
1	egg	1
1¼ cups	flour	300 mL
½ cup	rolled oats	125 mL
½ cup	chopped walnuts	125 mL

1. Combine condensed milk, 2 tbsp. (30 mL) butter, chocolate chips and vanilla in a 4-cup (1 L) glass measure. Microwave on MEDIUM-HIGH for 2 to 3 minutes. Stir until smooth and well blended. Set aside to cool slightly.

2. Cream ½ cup (125 mL) butter and brown sugar. Beat in egg. Mix in flour, oats and nuts.

3. Spread two-thirds of the flour mixture in a greased glass 8 x 12-inch (1.5 L) baking dish. Spread chocolate mixture over top. Sprinkle remaining flour mixture on top.

4. Microwave on MEDIUM for 6 to 8 minutes.

Your Time: _____

PEANUT BUTTER SQUARES

These are so good, you'll be tempted to eat half before you serve them. Pictured on the cover.

½ cup	butter	125 mL
1 cup	peanut butter	250 mL
1-6 oz.	pkg. butterscotch OR chocolate chips	175 g
1 cup	chopped nuts	250 mL
1 cup	coconut	250 mL
1-10 oz.	pkg. miniature marshmallows	250 g

1. Place butter in 1-qt. (1 L) glass measure and microwave on HIGH for 1 minute or until melted.

2. Stir in peanut butter and butterscotch or chocolate chips. Microwave on HIGH for 1½ minutes. Stir until melted and smooth.

3. In large mixing bowl combine nuts, coconut and marshmallows. Add peanut butter mixture and mix well.

4. Pour into greased 8-inch (20 cm) square pan and chill. Cut into squares when firm.

Your Time: _____

MUNCH BARS

These resemble granola bars.

¼ cup	butter	50 mL
4 cups	miniature marshmallows	1 L
1 cup	rolled oats	250 mL
1 cup	unsweetened coconut	250 mL
1 cup	chopped nuts	250 mL
1½ cups	Rice Krispies cereal	500 mL

1. In a 3-qt (3 L) casserole dish, microwave butter on HIGH for 45 seconds or until melted.

2. Stir in marshmallows. Microwave on HIGH for 3 to 4 minutes. Stir twice during cooking time. Stir well until mixture is smooth and well blended.

3. Stir in remaining ingredients until thoroughly coated with marshmallow mixture.

4. Press into a greased 8 x 12-inch (1.5 L) baking dish. Cool and cut into bars.

Your Time: _____

MATRIMONIAL CAKE

Good and good for you.

Cookie Base:

1½ cups	oatmeal	375 mL
½ cup	flour	125 mL
1 cup	brown sugar	250 mL
½ tsp.	salt	2 mL
¾ cup	butter OR margarine	175 mL

Date Filling:

1 lb.	dates	500 g
2 tbsp.	sugar	25 mL
¾ cup	water	175 mL
2 tbsp.	lemon juice	25 mL

1. Combine cookie base ingredients in a large mixing bowl. Beat at low speed with electric mixer until particles are fine. Set aside 1½ cups (375 mL). Press remaining mixture in a greased glass 8 x 12-inch (1.5 L) baking dish.

2. Microwave on MEDIUM for 6 to 10 minutes, or until just done.

3. Combine filling ingredients in 1-qt. (1 L) casserole dish. Microwave on HIGH for 6 to 9 minutes, or until thick and smooth. Stir every 2 minutes during cooking time.

4. Spread date mixture carefully over cookie base. Sprinkle with reserved cookie base crumbs.

5. Microwave on HIGH for 6 to 8 minutes or until topping is cooked.

Your Time: _____

BROWNIES

A very moist and very chocolatey brownie.

¼ cup	cocoa	60	mL
2-1 oz.	squares unsweetened chocolate OR 4 tbsp. (50 mL) cocoa	28	g
⅓ cup	butter OR margarine	75	mL
1 cup	sugar	250	mL
2	eggs	2	
½ tsp.	vanilla	2	mL
¾ cup	flour	175	mL
½ tsp.	baking powder	2	mL
½ tsp.	salt	2	mL
½ cup	chopped nuts	125	mL

1. Place chocolate and butter in 2½-qt. (2.5 L) glass mixing bowl. Microwave on MEDIUM-HIGH for 1½ to 2 minutes, or until melted. Stir once or twice during melting time.

2. Stir in sugar, eggs and vanilla. Beat well. Combine flour, baking powder and salt. Blend well. Stir in chocolate mixture. Stir in nuts. Spread evenly in greased 9 x 3-inch (2 L) round cake dish.

3. Microwave on HIGH for 6 to 7 minutes, or until top springs back when lightly pressed with a finger. Cool. Ice with Fudge Icing (below). Cut into wedges.

Your Time: _____

FUDGE ICING

2 tbsp.	butter	25	mL
4 tbsp.	cocoa	50	mL
1 cup	icing sugar	250	mL
2 tbsp.	milk	25	mL

1. In a 1-cup (250 mL) glass measure, microwave butter on HIGH for 30 seconds.

2. Combine cocoa and icing sugar in a small mixing bowl. Mix in melted butter and milk. Beat until smooth. Spread on brownies.

Your Time: _____

TOFFEE BARS

These keep well — if your family will let them.

1 cup	butter OR margarine, softened	250	mL
1 cup	brown sugar, firmly packed	250	mL
1	egg yolk	1	
1 tsp.	vanilla	5	mL
2¼ cups	flour	550	mL
1-12 oz.	pkg. semi-sweet chocolate chips	350	g
1 cup	coarsely chopped walnuts	250	mL

1. In a large mixing bowl, beat together, brown sugar, egg yolk and vanilla with electric mixer. Beat until mixture is moist, crumbly and begins to gather around the beater.

2. Stir in flour until blended. Press evenly into a greased pan 8 x 12 inch (1.5 L) baking dish.

3. Microwave on MEDIUM-HIGH for 5 to 7 minutes. Set aside to cool.

4. In a 4-cup (1 L) glass measure, microwave chocolate chips on MEDIUM-LOW for 3 to 4 minutes or until melted. Stir after each minute. Spread melted chips over crust.

5. Sprinkle walnuts over chocolate. With spatula, press nuts down into chocolate. Cool and cut into squares.

Your Time: _____

1. Chocolate Chip Cheesecake, page 214.
2. Applesauce Spice Loaf, page 190.
3. Chocolate Cookies, page 248.
4. Carrot Cookies, page 248.

PUFFED WHEAT SQUARES

A terrific nutritious snack. My kids love them!

¼ cup	butter OR margarine	50 mL
1 cup	brown sugar	250 mL
½ cup	corn syrup	125 mL
½ cup	peanut butter	125 mL
1 tsp.	vanilla	5 mL
8 cups	puffed wheat	2 L

1. In a 4-cup (1 L) glass measure combine butter, sugar, syrup and peanut butter. Microwave on HIGH for 3 to 4 minutes. Stir in vanilla.

2. In a large mixing bowl, combine puffed wheat and syrup. Press into a greased 8 x 12-inch (1.5 L) pan. Cool and cut into squares.

VARIATION: Substitute ¼ cup (125 mL) cocoa for peanut butter.

Your Time: _____

CARAMEL MORSEL BARS

A tantalizing combination of textures and flavours. These were a hit with Marianne's family when she tested the recipe.

1-14 oz.	bag (49) caramels	397 g
3 tbsp.	water	35 mL
5 cups	Rice Krispies cereal	1250 mL
1 cup	peanuts	250 mL
1-6 oz.	pkg. semi-sweet chocolate chips OR butterscotch chips	175 g

1. In a 2-qt. (2 L) casserole dish, microwave caramels and water on MEDIUM for 4 to 5 minutes or until melted and smooth. Stir twice.

2. In a large mixing bowl, combine cereal and peanuts. Pour melted caramels over and mix well. Press into a greased 8 x 12-inch (1.5 L) baking dish.

3. Sprinkle chocolate and butterscotch chips over top. Microwave on HIGH for 1½ to 2 minutes or until chips soften. Spread with spatula to form a frosting. Cool and cut into bars.

Your Time: _____

KAREN'S ALL BRAN BLONDIES

A yummy, healthy snack.

½ cup	butter OR margarine	125 mL
1 cup	brown sugar, firmly packed	250 mL
1	egg	1
1 tsp.	vanilla	5 mL
½ cup	All Bran cereal	125 mL
1 cup	flour	250 mL
¼ tsp.	salt	1 mL
½ tsp.	baking powder	2 mL
¼ tsp.	baking soda	1 mL
½ cup	chopped nuts	125 mL
½ cup	chocolate chips	125 mL

1. In a medium mixing bowl, microwave butter on HIGH for 1 minute, or until melted. Stir in sugar. Let cool slightly.

2. Combine dry ingredients.

3. Mix egg and vanilla into butter mixture. Gradually add dry ingredients, mixing well after each addition.

4. Stir in nuts and chocolate chips. Spread in a greased 9 x 3-inch (2 L) baking dish.

5. Microwave on HIGH for 4 to 6 minutes. Cool and cut into wedges.

Your Time: _____

JOHANNE'S SWEET MARIE BARS

Almost as easy as peeling the wrapper off a chocolate bar.

1 tbsp.	butter	15 mL
½ cup	brown sugar	125 mL
½ cup	corn syrup	125 mL
½ cup	peanut butter	125 mL
2 cups	Rice Krispies	500 mL
1 cup	peanuts	250 mL

1. Place butter, brown sugar and corn syrup in a 4 cup (1 L) glass measure or casserole dish. Microwave on HIGH for 2 minutes, or until boiling. Continue to cook on HIGH for 1 more minute. Stir in peanut butter.

2. Place cereal and peanuts in a large mixing bowl. Stir in peanut butter mixture. Press into a greased, 8-inch square (2 L) baking pan.

3. Frost with Chocolate Icing (below).

Your Time: _____

CHOCOLATE ICING

¾ cup	semi-sweet chocolate chips	175 mL
2 tbsp.	butter	25 mL
1¼ cups	confectioners sugar	300 mL
6 tbsp.	cream	75 mL
1 tsp.	vanilla	5 mL

1. Place chocolate chips and butter in a 1-qt. glass measure and microwave on HIGH for one minute, or until melted.

2. Stir in sugar, cream, and vanilla.

3. Spread over Sweet Marie Bars. (recipe above)

Your Time: _____

Your family may be familiar only with candy that comes in a wrapper because homemade candy takes so much work to prepare but the microwave oven can change all of that. In just a few minutes, you can prepare the most sumptuous candy treats for your family or for gift giving.

Whether you are melting candy-like ingredients such as caramels, marshmallows and chocolate to combine with other ingredients or making old fashioned candy from scratch, the microwave oven can simplify and speed up the process. Chocolate and caramelized mixtures which require careful attention and constant stirring by old-fashioned methods microwave with only occasional stirring.

THE KEY TO SUCCESS WITH CANDY

The key to success with candy in the microwave is to watch it carefully. Sugary substances cook very quickly with microwave energy so it is important that you stir it to check on its stage of hardness. The difference between soft candy and hard candy can sometimes be a matter of seconds. Candy doesn't stick to the bottom of the pan and scorch as it does on the stove but it still can scorch if you cook it too long, so follow the recipe instructions carefully, using the minimum time. Record the correct time with your oven for future reference.

UTENSILS

Candies are usually cooked uncovered to facilitate stirring. Covers are sometimes required to promote uniform cooking, but not often.

Sugary substances like candy get very hot so choose a container that can withstand high temperatures. Oven proof glass is usually best. A dish with a handle is convenient because the heat of the candy makes the dish hot. Keep the pot holders handy, as well.

Some candies require that a sugar mixture boil for several minutes. Be sure to choose a large enough container to allow space for the boiling. Most recipes specify the size of dish required. If you don't have the exact size the recipe suggests, use a larger container. As a general rule, the container should be only one-third full.

Candy thermometers designed for use in the microwave oven are available in some specialty shops. If you make a lot of candy, you may find them to be a worthwhile investment. Conventional candy thermometers cannot be left in the microwave oven during cooking, however, you can set one into the candy to check its temperature when the oven is not operating. The temperature probe that comes with some microwave ovens is not designed for candy making. Its temperature range is not high enough.

HOW TO TELL WHEN CANDY IS DONE

To test the doneness stage of candy, fill a glass with ice cold water. Stir the candy with a spoon and allow some of the syrup to drop off of the spoon and into the ice water. The texture of the candy syrup drop determines its stage:

Thread (230 -234°F) — Syrup spins a 2 inch (4 cm) thread as it is dropped from the spoon.

Soft Ball (234 - 240°F) — Drop can be shaped into a soft ball but flattens when removed from the water.

Firm Ball (244 - 248°F) — Drop forms a firm ball that does not flatten when removed from the water.

Hard Ball (250 - 255°F) — Drop forms a hard but pliable ball.

Soft Crack (270 - 290°F) — Syrup forms hard but not brittle threads as it is dropped from the spoon.

Hard Crack (300 - 310°F) — Syrup separates into hard and brittle threads as it is dropped from the spoon.

PEANUT BRITTLE

Old-fashioned goodness with modern speed.

1 cup	brown sugar	250 mL
½ cup	corn syrup	125 mL
1 cup	peanuts	250 mL
1 tsp.	butter	5 mL
1 tsp.	vanilla	5 mL
1 tsp.	baking soda	5 mL

1. Place sugar and corn syrup in a 4-cup (1 L) glass measure. Microwave on HIGH for 3 to 4 minutes, or until soft ball stage is reached. Stir occasionally during cooking time.

2. Stir in peanuts. Microwave on HIGH for 2 to 3 minutes or until hard ball stage is reached (This is when a drop of candy forms a hard ball when dropped into ice water).

3. Stir in butter and vanilla.

4. Add baking soda and stir gently until mixture is light and foamy. Pour quickly onto a greased cookie sheet and let cool. Break into pieces when cold.

Your Time: _____

CARAMEL APPLES

Just like the ones at the fair!

6	McIntosh OR Red Delicious apples	6
1 cup	chopped peanuts	250 mL
1-14 oz.	bag of caramels	397 g
2 tbsp.	water	25 mL

1. Wash and dry the apples. Insert a stick in the stem end.

2. Place peanuts in a small bowl. Set aside.

3. Place unwrapped caramels and water in a 1-qt (1 L) casserole dish. Microwave on HIGH for 3 to 4 minutes, or until melted, hot and bubbly. Stir after each minute.

4. Dip apples in hot caramel mixture and then roll in chopped peanuts. Let cool on wax paper.

Your Time: _____

BONANZAS

Yummy candy made with nutritious ingredients.

¼ cup	butter	50 mL
1 cup	miniature marshmallows	250 mL
¾ cup	peanut butter	175 mL
1¼ cup	graham cracker crumbs	300 mL
3 tbsp.	cocoa	35 mL
½ cup	chopped nuts	125 mL
1½ cups	shredded coconut OR 1 cup (250 mL) icing sugar	375 mL

1. In a large glass mixing bowl, microwave butter on HIGH for 45 seconds or until melted. Stir in marshmallows and microwave on HIGH for 2½ to 4 minutes or until melted and smooth. Stir twice during cooking time. Stir in peanut butter. Mix until smooth.

2. Combine remaining graham cracker crumbs, cocoa and chopped nuts in a large mixing bowl. Pour marshmallow mixture over and stir until well coated.

3. Form into balls. Roll each ball in coconut or icing sugar. Cool.

Your Time: _____

BUTTERSCOTCH DROPS

These will do a fast disappearing act.

1-12 oz.	pkg. butterscotch chips	350 g
½ cup	peanut butter	125 mL
2 cups	Corn Flakes	500 mL
1 cup	flaked coconut	250 mL

1. Combine butterscotch chips and peanut butter in a large glass mixing bowl. Microwave on HIGH for 2 to 3 minutes or until chips are melted. Stir until smooth.

2. Add cornflakes and coconut. Stir until well coated.

3. Drop by teaspoonsful onto a baking sheet and refrigerate until set.

Your Time: _____

QUICK & EASY CARAMELS

No candy company can match the exquisite taste of these homemade caramels.

1 cup	butter	250 mL
2¼ cups	brown sugar, firmly packed	550 mL
1 tsp.	vanilla	5 mL
⅛ tsp.	salt	.5 mL
1 cup	light corn syrup	250 mL
1-14 oz.	can sweetened condensed milk	300 mL

1. In an 8-cup (2 L) glass measure, microwave butter on MEDIUM for 2 minutes, or until melted.

2. Stir in sugar and salt, then add corn syrup. Mix well. Add sweetened condensed milk, stirring well.

3. Microwave on MEDIUM-HIGH for 15-18 minutes, or until firm ball stage is reached. Check by dropping a few drops off spoon into ice water. If it forms a ball that doesn't immediately flatten when pressed with your finger, it is ready. Stir several times during cooking time.

4. Stir in vanilla. Pour into a greased 8-inch square (2 L) baking dish. Chill until set.

5. When cool, cut into squares using a knife which has been dipped in hot water. Dip pan into a bit of hot water to ease removal of squares. Wrap squares in plastic.

Your Time: _____

MAGIC FUDGE

Almost too simple to be so good!

3-6 oz.	**pkg. semi-sweet chocolate chips**	**175**	**g**
1-14 oz.	**can sweetened condensed milk**	**300**	**mL**
1½ tsp.	**vanilla**	**7**	**mL**
½ cup	**chopped nuts**	**125**	**mL**

1. Place chocolate chips in 2-qt. (2 L) casserole dish. Microwave on HIGH for 2 minutes. Stir until melted and smooth. It may need another 30 seconds to get smooth, but be careful not to overcook it.

2. Stir in sweetened condensed milk and vanilla. Add nuts. Pour mixture into a greased 8-inch square (2 L) baking dish. Chill until firm. Cut into 1-inch squares.

VARIATION: Omit chopped nuts. While soft, mark squares with a knife. Place a pecan half on top of each square.

Your Time: _____

GLAZED PECANS

A sweet and crunchy snack that's so good!

¼ cup	**light corn syrup**	**50**	**mL**
1½ cups	**white sugar**	**375**	**mL**
½ cup	**water**	**125**	**mL**
1 tsp.	**vanilla**	**5**	**mL**
4 cups	**pecan halves**	**1**	**L**

1. In a large glass mixing bowl, microwave syrup, sugar and water on ME-DIUM-HIGH for 8 to 10 minutes, or until it reaches a softball stage (When dropped into ice water it forms a soft ball that can be flattened when pressed with your finger).

2. Add vanilla and pecans. Stir until syrup becomes creamy, thick and rather hard.

3. Spread on waxed paper. Cool. Break into pieces.

Your Time: _____

CHINESE CRUNCHIES

An unusual way to use chow mein noodles.

1 cup	semi-sweet chocolate chips	250 mL
1 cup	butterscotch OR chocolate chips	250 mL
1 cup	chow mein noodles	250 mL
1 cup	unsalted peanuts	250 mL

1. In a medium glass bowl, microwave chocolate and butterscotch chips on MEDIUM-LOW for 4 to 5 minutes, or until melted. Stir every minute or two.

2. Stir in noodles and peanuts. Drop by teaspoonsful onto waxed paper. Cool.

* **Yield:** 19 or 20

Your Time: _____

ALPHA BEETLES

Kids like to make these as well as to eat them.

4-1 oz.	squares semi-sweet chocolate	28	g
3 tbsp.	peanut butter	35	mL
1 cup	*Alphabits* (any other cereal would work)	250	mL

1. In a 4-cup (1 L) glass measure, combine chocolate pieces and peanut butter. Microwave on MEDIUM-HIGH for 1 minute at a time, until melted and smooth. Stir well after each minute of cooking time. This should take 3 to 4 minutes.

2. Mix together cereal and chocolate.

3. Drop by teaspoonsful onto a cookie sheet. Top each with a piece of cereal and cool.

* Yield: about 1 dozen

VARIATION:

WISHING STARS: use *Prostars* cereal instead of *Alphabits*.

Your Time: _____

SAUCES & PRESERVES ▮▮▮▮▮▮

COOKING JAMS & JELLIES IN THE MICROWAVE OVEN

The microwave oven simplifies the preparation of small batches of jam or jelly and keeps both the kitchen and your hands cool. You don't need to stir constantly because there is no danger of scorching. You will find microwave cooking results in a greater yield of jam from same amount of fruit because fruit juices don't evaporate. Best of all, like all microwave cooked fruits and vegetables, jam and relish retain their sparkling fresh flavour and bright colour. Surprise your family with fresh jams and jelly for breakfast. Or store them in pretty jars to give as gifts — they're sure to please anyone on your list.

⚷ THE KEY TO SUCCESS WITH PRESERVES AND SAUCES

The key to success with microwave jams, relishes or sauces is to prepare them in small batches. Small batches are best for even cooking throughout. This is a real advantage for singles or small families. If you have a small garden patch, you can cook up a day's picking right away for maximum flavour, rather than saving several days' pickings to make a big batch.

Although you do not need to stir microwave jams constantly, stirring is important. You should stir very well after adding the pectin, making sure that it is completely dissolved, and again after the addition of the sugar. (Be sure it is completely dissolved or it will sink to the bottom and form a heavy layer.) After this, stirring is needed only once or twice during cooking time.

PREPARATION OF FRUIT OR VEGETABLES

Prepare fruit or vegetables according to the recipe. They can be chopped by hand or with a food processor or grinder. If you like chunks of fruit or vegetables in your preserves, you will find that microwaving is to your advantage as the chunks remain somewhat firm.

To prepare juice from fresh fruit for jelly, microwave it without water until it is very soft and then strain juice through a jelly bag.

UTENSILS

It is important to choose a very large dish when microwaving any food with a high sugar content, such as jam or jelly, because they boil up so high. As a general rule, you should fill the dish only half full.

Be sure to use oven safe (. . . 400°F or 200°C) glass or plastic because the sugar in these foods reaches a very high temperature which could melt some plastics or break fragile glass. I use a 2 qt. (2 L) glass measuring cup. It also simplifies pouring the jam into jars.

267

COVERS ARE NOT NEEDED

Covers are not necessary when cooking sauces, jams and relishes. In fact, they are a nuisance. They interfere with stirring. They may also cause the food to boil over.

DON'T

Don't try to process home canning in the microwave oven. The consistent high temperature that is necessary for proper processing cannot be maintained.

Don't try to melt paraffin wax in the microwave oven. The microwave energy passes through the wax without melting it.

Don't try to sterilize glass jars in the microwave oven because microwave energy passes through them without heating them.

HOW TO KNOW WHEN JAMS & JELLIES ARE DONE

The way to test jams and jellies for doneness in the microwave oven is to dip a metal spoon into the liquid after the cooking time called for in the recipe. If the liquid coats the spoon, it is ready to be poured into jars. You can also watch to see if two large drops of liquid on the edge of the spoon run together to form a single drop. It will be slow to drip because it has started to jell.

ADAPTING JAM, JELLY AND PRESERVES RECIPES

Most recipes need no alteration except that they should be cooked in two batches instead of cooking a large batch all at once. In some recipes that do not call for pectin, it may be necessary to add pectin to ensure jelling because juices do not evaporate as much when cooked in the microwave oven. For best results, find a recipe that is similar to the one you want to prepare in this book or the manual that came with your oven. Follow its instructions regarding quantity, power level and time. Make a note of the correct cooking time on your recipe for future reference.

STORAGE

Jams, jellies and relishes should be poured into sterilized jars. They may be kept in the refrigerator for up to 3 months. If you want to store them at room temperature they should be sealed with two separate layers of paraffin wax or processed in sealers by a hot water bath on top of the stove.

HINTS

- Be sure to use the size container that is recommended in recipes to avoid boilovers.
- You may wish to keep hot pads handy. Sugar mixtures can become quite hot during cooking.
- Stir sauces during cooking, as recommended in the recipes. Stirring will prevent lumping. Less stirring of sauces is required in microwave cooking than in conventional cooking.
- When adding an ingredient such as pectin to a hot mixture, stir it in gradually.

GRAPE JELLY

Assured success, even for a beginner.

1 cup	concord grape juice	250 mL
½ cup	water	125 mL
½ pkg.	pectin (8 tsp.)	40 mL
1¾ cup	sugar	425 mL

1. Combine juice, water and pectin in a glass 8-cup (2 L) measure. Microwave on HIGH for 5 to 6 minutes, or until boiling hard.

2. Stir in sugar. Stir until sugar is completely dissolved. Microwave on MEDIUM for 10 to 12 minutes or until slightly thickened. Stir once or twice during cooking time.

3. Pour into sterilized glass jars and seal with melted paraffin wax or store in refrigerator in a covered container.

VARIATION: 1½ cups (375 mL) crabapple or chokecherry juice instead of grape juice and water.

Your Time: _____

STRAWBERRY JAM

Fresh-picked flavour.

1 qt.	fresh strawberries	1 L
3½ cups	sugar	875 mL
½ pkg.	powdered pectin (8 tsp.)	40 mL

1. Cut open and chop strawberries — should make approximately 2 cups (500 mL) of fruit. Add pectin and mix well.

2. In a 3-qt. (3 L) casserole dish, microwave on HIGH for 5 to 6 minutes or until boiling hard.

3. Stir in sugar. Continue stirring until sugar is completely dissolved.

4. Microwave on MEDIUM for 10 minutes. Stir twice during cooking time.

5. Pour into 3-8 oz. (250 mL) size jars.

VARIATION:
APRICOT JAM

2 lbs.	apricots	1 kg
½ pkg.	powdered pectin (8 tsp.)	40 mL
2½ cups	sugar	625 mL

Same instructions as above.

Your Time: _____

5 FRUIT CONSERVE

A fresh-from-the-orchard blend.

3	peaches	3
3	pears	3
3	red skinned apples	3
½	lemon	½
1	orange	1
5 cups	sugar	1.25 L

1. Peel, core and quarter peaches, pears and apples. Quarter lemon and orange. Process fruit in a food grinder or processor or chop finely.

2. Measure fruit (should be about 5 cups or 1.25 L) and add an equal amount of sugar. Divide mixture in half. You may want to freeze half to make at a later date.

3. In a 3-qt. (3 L) casserole dish, microwave 5 cups (1.25 L) of the fruit-sugar mixture on HIGH for 7 to 9 minutes or until boiling. Stir once or twice during cooking time.

4. Microwave on MEDIUM power for 15 to 20 minutes, or until thickened.

5. Pour into sterilized jars and seal with melted paraffin wax.

Repeat steps 3, 4, and 5 with the other half of the processed fruit, if desired.

Yield: 7 — 8 small jars of jam

Your Time: _____

ZUCCHINI MARMALADE

A delicious way to use up all your extra garden zucchini from Edith Cronfield, one of my students from Limerick, Sask.

3 cups	grated raw zucchini	750	mL
½ cup	water	125	mL
3 cups	sugar	750	mL
1 cup	crushed pineapple	250	mL
¼ cup	lemon juice	50	mL
1-3 oz.	pkg. apricot jelly powder	85	g

1. In a 4-qt. (4 L) casserole dish, combine zucchini and water. Microwave on HIGH for 15 to 20 minutes, or until transparent.

2. Stir in remaining ingredients. Stir well until sugar and jelly powder are completely dissolved. Microwave on MEDIUM for 15 to 20 minutes.

3. Pour into sterilized jars and seal with paraffin wax. Store in the refrigerator or a cool place.

Yield: 5 small jars (250 mL) of jam

Your Time: _____

CITRUS MARMALADE

This sweet marmalade makes a lovely glaze for a cake.

2	oranges	2	
1	lemon	1	
¾ cup	water	175	mL
⅛ tsp.	baking soda	.5	mL
½ pkg.	powdered pectin (8 tsp.)	40	mL
2½ cups	sugar	625	mL

1. Peel and chop the fruit. Finely slice the rind. Set fruit aside.

2. Place rind, water, and baking soda in a 3-qt. (3 L) casserole. Microwave on HIGH for 6 to 8 minutes.

3. Add fruit and Certo. Microwave on HIGH for 6 to 8 minutes.

4. Add sugar; microwave on MEDIUM for 15 to 20 minutes or until it thickens. Stir several times during cooking time.

5. Pour into sterilized jars. Seal with parrafin wax.

Your Time: _____

PAM'S ZUCCHINI RELISH

This relish has a glorious, though not oppressive quantity of spices.

1	medium sized zucchini	1	
1 or 2	onions		
½	green pepper	½	
½	red pepper	½	
2 tbsp.	pickling salt	25	mL
1 cup	water	250	mL
1½ tbsp.	flour	23	mL
½ tsp.	turmeric	2	mL
1½ tsp.	dry mustard	7	mL
¾ cup	vinegar	175	mL
1 cup	sugar	250	mL
½ tsp.	mustard seed	2	mL
½ tsp.	celery seed	2	mL

1. Shred vegetables in a food grinder or food processor. Sprinkle with pickling salt and stand for 1 hour. Pour water over vegetables to rinse them. Drain well.

2. Combine flour, turmeric, mustard and enough vinegar to make a paste. Combine remaining vinegar, sugar, mustard seed and celery seed. Stir into the paste. Microwave on HIGH for 1 minute, or until thickened. Stir once or twice during cooking time.

3. In a 4-qt. (4 L) casserole dish, combine vegetables and thickened vinegar mixture. Microwave on MEDIUM for 8 to 10 minutes. Stir two or three times during cooking time.

4. Pour into sterilized jars. Seal with paraffin wax.

VARIATION:

CUCUMBER RELISH: Make as above using cucumbers instead of zucchini.

Your Time: _____

TOMATO KETCHUP

The best ketchup in the west

12	ripe tomatoes, peeled	12
1¼ cups	white vinegar	300 mL
2	large onions, finely chopped	2
1 cup	sugar	250 mL
1 tsp.	salt	15 mL
½ cup	mixed pickling spices	125 mL
⅓ cup	cornstarch mixed with enough vinegar to make a paste	75 mL

1. In a 4-qt. (4 L) casserole dish, combine tomatoes, vinegar, onions, sugar and salt. Place pickling spices on an 8-inch (22 cm) square of cheesecloth. Form into a pouch and fasten with a rubber band. Place in tomato mixture.

2. Cover and microwave on HIGH for 7 to 9 minutes. Stir once or twice during cooking time.

3. Microwave on MEDIUM for 10 minutes. Remove spice bag.

4. Stir in cornstarch mixture. Microwave on HIGH for 10 minutes, stirring every minute, until mixture thickens.

5. Pour into jars and seal. Store in refrigerator.

BEET RELISH

This relish adds zip to any meal.

1 qt.	cooked beets	1 L
⅓ cup	onion, chopped	75 mL
2	red peppers, chopped	2
2 tsp.	pickling salt	10 mL
¼ cup	prepared horseradish	60 mL
2 cups	vinegar	500 mL
1 cup	sugar	250 mL

1. Shred beets. In a 3-qt. (3 L) casserole dish, combine all ingredients.

2. Microwave on HIGH for 5 minutes. Stir once or twice during cooking time. Reduce power level to MEDIUM and microwave for 5 more minutes.

3. Pour into sterilized jars and seal with parrafin wax.

Your Time: _____

PANCAKE SYRUP

So delicious and so easy, you won't bother buying pancake syrup after you've tried this.

1 cup	white sugar	250	mL
1 cup	brown sugar, packed	250	mL
1 cup	water	250	mL
¼ tsp.	maple extract	1	mL
½ tsp.	vanilla	2	mL

1. In a 4-cup (1 L) glass measure, combine sugars and water. Microwave on HIGH for 3 to 4 minutes or until boiling. Stir once or twice during cooking time to dissolve the sugar. Let stand 2 minutes.

2. Stir in extracts. Serve hot over pancakes or ice cream. Store leftover syrup in a covered container.

Your Time: _____

CHILI SAUCE

The apple in this sauce accentuates its flavour. A tasty addition to burgers or any meat.

6	ripe tomatoes	6	
1	apple	1	
2	stalks celery	2	
1	red pepper	1	
1	green pepper	1	
1 cup	vinegar	250	mL
1 tbsp.	pickling salt	30	mL
½ tsp.	cinnamon	2	mL
¾ cup	brown sugar	175	mL
½ tsp.	allspice	2	mL

1. Peel and chop tomatoes and apple. Chop celery and peppers.

2. Combine all ingredients in a 3-qt. (3 L) casserole dish. Cover and microwave on HIGH for 5 minutes. Stir once or twice.

3. Microwave on LOW for 45 minutes, stirring occasionally.

4. Pour into sterilized jars and seal. Store in refrigerator.

Your Time: _____

HOT FUDGE SAUCE

This sauce is often requested by company.

½ cup	sugar	125 mL
3 tbsp.	cocoa	35 mL
1½ tbsp.	cornstarch	23 mL
	pinch of salt	
½ cup	water	125 mL
2 tbsp.	butter	25 mL
1 tsp.	vanilla	15 mL

1. Combine dry ingredients in a glass 2-cup (500 mL) measure. Stir in water.

2. Microwave on HIGH for 1½-2 minutes. Stir once or twice during cooking time.

3. Stir in butter and vanilla.

SERVING SUGGESTION: Delicious if served on ice cream or layered in parfait glasses with peanuts and ice cream.

Your Time: _____

PEANUT BUTTER SAUCE ROYALE

A hit with peanut butter fans.

½ cup	brown sugar	125 mL
⅓ cup	milk	75 mL
¼ cup	liquid honey	60 mL
1 tbsp.	butter OR margarine	30 mL
⅓ cup	peanut butter	75 mL

1. In a glass mixing bowl, combine sugar, milk, honey and butter. Microwave on MEDIUM-HIGH for 3 to 5 minutes. Stir several times during cooking time.

2. Add peanut butter. Beat with an electric mixer until smooth.

3. Use for sundaes or milkshakes.

SERVING SUGGESTION:

TREAT ROYALE: Layer chocolate ice cream, Peanut Butter Sauce Royale, peanuts and Hot Fudge Sauce in parfait glasses. Garnish with whipped topping and peanuts.

Your Time: _____

CUSTARD SAUCE

Soft, smooth and unbelievably easy!

1½ cups	milk	375 mL
2	egg yolks	2
½ cup	sugar	125 mL
½ tsp.	vanilla	2 mL

1. In a 2-cup (500 mL) glass measure, microwave milk on MEDIUM-HIGH for 2 minutes.

2. Combine egg yolks and sugar in a 4-cup (1 L) glass measure. Gradually add hot milk, stirring with a wire whisk.

3. Microwave on MEDIUM for 4 to 5 minutes or until it reaches boiling point. Stir two or three times during cooking time.

4. Stir in vanilla.

SERVING SUGGESTION: Serve over cake or waffles.

Your Time: _____

FRUITY CUSTARD SAUCE

A delightful blend of colours and flavours that will please your guests.

	Custard Sauce, above	
1 cup	sliced strawberries	250 mL
1	sliced peach	1
1	sliced banana	1
½ tsp.	almond extract	2 mL

1. Prepare Custard Sauce as above. Stir in fruit and almond extract.

SERVING SUGGESTION: This tastes delicious served over white cake or waffles.

Your Time: _____

MISCELLANEOUS HINTS

MICROWAVE MINDERS

- Remember to allow standing time for all foods cooked or defrosted in the microwave. Internal heat finishes the cooking after the oven shuts off.

- Microwave cooking works especially well with foods that have a naturally high moisture content such as vegetables, fruits, fish and poultry. It cooks fatty meat and sugary substances such as jam, sauces and candy very quickly.

- Lift covers from hot foods away from yourself to prevent burns from the steam.

- Keep your microwave oven clean. If you wipe it with a damp cloth immediately after spills or spatters occur, cleanup will be easy. I always give my microwave oven a quick wipe when I am wiping the tables and counter after meals. It is especially important to keep the door and seals around the door clean.

- Place food on a dish or paper towel rather than directly on the glass tray of the microwave oven. It saves wear and tear on the tray (which can be an expensive item to replace).

- If you have an older oven with only one setting, here are a few tips for cooking foods that should be cooked on lower power levels:
    1. Place a measuring cup of water in the oven along with the food you are cooking or set the food in a dish of water. The water attracts microwave energy and slows down the cooking.
    2. Divide cooking time into thirds and microwave food for one third of the time allowing an equal length of standing time after each third of cooking time.
    3. Your oven may have only HIGH and DEFROST. DEFROST can be used for slowcooking or simmering foods.

- COVERINGS — To save on plastic wrap, use a plate to cover foods. Then you can eat off of a warm dinner plate.

- PARAFFIN — This CANNOT be melted in a microwave because it has no moisture in it.

- SHIELDING — When using foil to shield, make sure it does not touch the side or bottom of your oven. A general rule for shielding is to be sure that more food is EXPOSED to the microwave energy than is covered with foil.

- FOOD COOL TOO FAST? Place hot dishes into wicker serving baskets, casserole cozies or wrap with a dish towel.

- If you need to lower your fat intake, microwave cooking can help. Dishes do not need to be greased, no fat needs to be added for cooking.

- To speed up any recipe, even a conventional one, look for things that you can do in the microwave to save time and clean up; like scalding milk, melting chocolate, or softening butter.

KITCHEN HELPS

- ICE CREAM — To soften rock-hard ice cream so you can scoop it, just heat it on LOW for ½ to 1 minute for a pint (500 mL) or 3½ to 4 minutes for a half gallon (2 L).

- LINGERING OVEN ODOURS — To get rid of lingering oven odours; squeeze half a lemon into a 1-cup measure, add the lemon shell and fill with water. Heat on HIGH for 5 minutes and then let stand in oven for 5 more minutes before wiping oven.

- CLEANING YOUR MICROWAVE OVEN — Plain soapy water, vinegar water or baking soda are the only cleaners you need for your microwave oven. If something sticky is hard to remove use baking soda rather than an abrasive cleanser.

- HIGH ALTITUDE ADJUSTMENTS — Those of you who live at high altitudes won't need to make recipe adjustments, when cooking in a microwave, as you do for conventional cooking. When a range of times are given, always use the longest time.

- CHOCOLATE — Chocolate is delicate so be careful not to overheat it. Heat it on MEDIUM-LOW for 2-3 minutes. If it cools before you have a chance to use it; heat it for another few seconds. Chocolate can be melted in its paper wrapper (seam up) and scraped from the wrapper with a rubber spatula.

- SOFTENING BROWN SUGAR — When brown sugar has become hard, you can soften it by putting it in the microwave beside a cup of water. Heat on HIGH for 30 to 60 seconds. Or, place a slice of bread on top of brown sugar and cover.

- DRYING HERBS — Wash 1 cup (250 mL) of fresh herbs thoroughly. Shake off excess water. Arrange on a double layer of paper towel, put a single layer of paper towel on top. Microwave on HIGH for 1 minute at a time until they are thoroughly dry and can be crumbled.

- AVACADOS — You can ripen underripe avacados by microwaving them on HIGH for 1 minute. First pierce the skin. After ripening, let stand for 2 minutes before peeling. Add more time by 30 second intervals, if necessary.

- SOFTEN CREAM CHEESE by microwaving on DEFROST or LOW 1 minute for an 8 oz. (250 g) package.

- SCALD MILK — microwave 1 cup (250 mL) of milk on HIGH uncovered for 1½ to 2 minutes. For 2 cups (500 mL), heat for 2½ to 3 minutes.

- HONEY — Honey can be uncrystalized or clarified by heating 2 cups on HIGH for 1½ to 2 minutes, uncovered. Check every 30 seconds, remove as soon as honey is liquid. Store tightly covered to keep honey soft.

- Toast bread crumbs in the microwave oven. Spread 1 cup (250 mL) over a dinner plate and microwave on HIGH for 3 minutes, stirring after each minute.

BREAKFAST

- Heat water for 1 or 2 cups of tea or coffee in the microwave oven — it's faster than the kettle. 1 cup (250 mL) of water boils in 2 minutes on HIGH and 2 cups (500 mL) boil in 3 to 4 minutes.

- Reheat 4 frozen pancakes or waffles on high for 1½ to 2 minutes.

- HEAT SYRUP — Heat maple syrup by removing the lid from container and microwaving on HIGH for 30 seconds.

- Try heated grapefruit! Heat on HIGH for 30 to 45 seconds.

- You can increase the amount of juice you get by heating each piece of fruit on HIGH for 20 to 35 minutes, before you cut open your lemon, lime, orange, or grapefruit.

- FROZEN JUICE — To defrost juice, remove metal lid. Heat on MEDIUM; stir halfway through defrosting. A 6-oz. (175 mL) can takes about 1½ minutes; a 12-oz. (350 mL) can takes 2½ to 3 minutes; and a 16-oz. (500 mL) can takes about 3½ to 4 minutes.

SNACKS

- TOASTED NUTS — To toast nuts spread about ¼ cup nuts on a glass pie plate. Heat uncovered on HIGH for about 3 minutes or until toasted.

- TOASTED SUNFLOWER SEEDS — Toast on HIGH for 1 minute at a time; stir every minute while toasting.

- SHELL NUTS — An easy way to shell nuts is to pour 1 cup (250 mL) of water over 2 cups (500 mL) of unshelled nuts and heat on HIGH for 4 to 5 minutes.

- POPCORN — Reheat popped, buttered popcorn on HIGH for 15 to 20 seconds per cup.

BABY HELPS

- BABY'S BOTTLE — Your baby's bottle can be warmed in the microwave! Simply heat it on HIGH for 30 to 45 seconds for a FULL 8 oz. (250 mL) bottle. ALWAYS remember to SHAKE the bottle over the sink and CHECK its temperature on your wrist BEFORE FEEDING BABY! A 4 oz. (125 mL) or half full bottle takes only 15 to 30 seconds.

- BABY FOOD — Baby food can be warmed by heating a FULL JAR on HIGH for 25 to 30 seconds. Remove the lid of the jar, before heating. A half full jar takes 15 to 30 seconds. Some manufacturers of baby food warn that the jars are not heat safe. BE VERY CAREFUL THAT THE FOOD IS ONLY WARM, NOT HOT!!

WARMING UP FOODS

- INDIVIDUAL MEALS — For family members who eat at different times, arrange individual servings on dinner plates and cover with plastic wrap. Each plate can be heated as needed.

- Remember that foods around the outside of the plate cook more quickly than those in the centre. When warming a plate of dinner, place slow cooking dense items like meat around the edges and quick heating foods like vegetables and rice in the centre. 1 plate of dinner, covered, heats on MEDIUM for 2 minutes.

- Heat gravy in a glass gravy boat or measuring cup on HIGH for 1 minute per cup.

- Reheat take-out hamburgers in their styrofoam boxes on HIGH for 20 to 40 seconds.

FOOD GARNISHES & SEASONINGS

- Microwaving brings out the natural flavour of food so you can cook without salt; season foods like meat and vegetables lightly with herbs and spices.

- TOAST ALMONDS for vegetables, fish or chicken Amandine: In a glass pie plate microwave 1 tbsp. (15 mL) butter on HIGH for 30 seconds. Stir in ½ cup (125 mL) slivered almonds. Microwave on HIGH 2½ to 3 minutes, until lightly toasted. Stir once or twice.

- TOASTED COCONUT — Spread ½ cup (125 mL) of shredded or flaked coconut in a glass pie plate. Cook on high for 3 to 6 minutes, or until toasted. Stir every 30 seconds.

- GRATED PEEL — For your own dried grated peel, place grated peel of one lemon or orange in a glass bowl. Heat on HIGH for ½ to 1 minute, or until dry. Stir once.

- MELT PRESERVES on HIGH for 5 minutes with the lid removed. Strain the preserves and use as a glaze.

- Warm up sundae toppings in the jar (remove the lid) or a glass measuring cup on HIGH for 1 minute per cup (250 mL).

INDEX

BACON

Aunt Edna's New England Clam
   Chowder 56
Bacon & Tomato Tart 174
Corn Chowder 55
Eggs Benedict 168
Morning B.E.T. Sandwich 171
Tomato Surprise 172

BEEF

Aunt Eva's Cordon Bleu Rolls 81
Barbecue Beef Dip 43
Beef Ragout 60
Beef Stroganoff 79
Beef Sub Napolitana 42
Cabbage Rolls 88
Chinelo's Spaghetti Sauce 86
Meat Balls 85
Meat Loaf 84
Open-Face Reubens 45
Pepper Steak 78
Porcupines 89
Quick Beef Stew 61
Roast Beef Submarine Sandwich . . 42
Smothered Liver 83
Spaghetti Sauce 86
Stuffed Peppers 87
Sweet and Sour Smoked
   Sausages 97
Swiss Steak 80

CAKE

Applesauce Gingerbread 235
Apricot Upside Down Gingerbread 235
Blueberry Buckle 241
Boston Cream Pie 228
Chocolate Layer Cake 229
Chocolate Upside Down Cake 230
Coconut Delight 225
Creamy Christmas Pudding Cake 209
Decadent Chocolate Cake 232
Fancy in a Hurry Chocolate Cake 231
Gelatin Delight Cake 227
Gingerbread 234
Honey Bran Kuchen 238
Lemon Pound Cake 242
Marianne's Carrot Cake 239
Oatmeal Cinnamon Cake 237
Pineapple Upside Down Cake 224
Pineapple Upside Down
   Gingerbread 236
Platz 240
Swiss Almond Mocha Delight 231
Tomato Soup Cake 233

Triple Layer Torte . . . .
White Cake 225

CANDY

Alpha Beetles 266
Bonanzas 262
Butterscotch Drops 263
Caramel Apples 262
Chinese Crunchies 266
Glazed Pecans 265
Johanne's Sweet Marie Bars 259
Magic Fudge 265
Peanut Brittle 262
Quick and Easy Caramels 264

CEREAL

Cream of Wheat Cereal 141
Granola 141
Porridge by the Bowl 141

CHEESE

Amazing Mushroom Quiche 173
Aunt Eva's Cordon Bleu Rolls 81
Bacon & Tomato Tart 174
Baked Eggs Mornay 169
Beef Sub Napolitana 42
Cheesy Creamed Salmon 123
Mini Pizzas 39
Morning B.E.T. Sandwich 171
Nachos 44
Open-Faced Reubens 45
Pam's Nachos 40
Pizza Buns 46
Quiche Lorraine 174
Quick Seafood Scallop 126
Roast Beef Submarine Sandwich 42
Salmon Mornay 124
Sombreros 38
Tomato Surprise 172
Tuna Burgers 43
Tuna Mac 125
Turkey Divan 114
Veal Parmigiana 82

CHEESECAKE

Basic Cheesecake 214
Apricot Cheesecake 214
Black Forest 214
Chocolate Cheesecake 214
Chocolate Chip Cheesecake 214
Marble Cheesecake 214

CHICKEN

Alace's Curried Chicken	104
Barbecue Chicken	104
Chicken A La King	110
Chicken Vegetable Soup	53
Chicken Velvet	108
Country Style Chicken	107
Creamed Chicken and Broccoli	109
Lemon Chicken	106
Moo Goo Gai Pan	111
Oriental Chicken	105
Poultry Dressing	103
Roast Whole Chicken	102
Shake & Bake Chicken	106
Speedy Chicken Salad	112
Stuffed Whole Roast Chicken	102

COFFEECAKES

Caramel Biscuit Ring	195
Crisscross Coffeecake	194
Easy Cinnamon Ring	196
Peach Coffeecake	193

COOKIES

Carrot Cookies	248
Chocolate Cookies	248
Fudge Drops	247
Irene's Boiled Raisin Cookies	247
Soft Ginger Cookies	249
Marianne's Sweetheart Cookies	250

CUSTARD

Baked Custard	216

DESSERT

Apricot Cheesecake	214
Basic Cheesecake	214
Black Forest Cheesecake	214
Chocolate Cheesecake	214
Chocolate Chip Cheesecake	214
French Lemon Dessert	213
Marble Cheesecake	214
Mini Cheesecake	215

EGGS

Amazing Mushroom Quiche	173
Bacon and Tomato Tart	174
Baked Eggs	168
Baked Eggs Mornay	169
Denver Scramble	170
Eggs Benedict	168
Morning B.E.T. Sandwich	171
Plain Omelet	173
Popeye Egg	172
Poached Eggs	167
Quiche Lorraine	174
Scrambled Eggs	170
Speedy Egg Salad	168
Spanish Poached Eggs	167
Tomato Surprise	172

FISH & SEAFOOD

Aunt Edna's New England Clam Chowder	56
Cheesy Creamed Salmon	123
Fish Steaks	121
Freshwater Fillets	120
Jiffy Tuna Casserole	125
Quick Seafood Scallop	126
Pasta and Salmon Medley	139
Salmon Mornay	124
Shrimp Creole	128
Shrimp Stir Fry	127
Skiffle	41
Stuffed Fillet Rolls	121
Stuffed Rainbow Trout	122
Stuffing for Fish	120
Tuna Burgers	43
Tuna Mac	125
Whole Baked Salmon	122

FROSTING

Chocolate Frosting	226
Chocolate Icing	259
Coffee Frosting	226
Cream Cheese Frosting	239
Decadent Chocolate Frosting	233
Fudge Icing	255
Microwave Less Than 7 Minute Frosting	226
Mocha Frosting	226
Peppermint Frosting	226
Seafoam Frosting	226
Tropical Frosting	226

FRUIT

Aunt Edna's Blueberry Oat Muffins	185
Baked Apples	205
Apple Crisp	205
Banana Bread	189
Banana Chocolate Chip Muffins	184
Chunky Applesauce	206
Christmas Pudding	208
Lee's Pear Pie	219
Pam's Fruit Cobbler	206
Peanut Butter & Banana Muffins	186
Platz	240
Pluma Moos	207
Southern Ambrosia	207
Southern Banana Pudding	210
Zucchini Nut Bread	191

GROUND BEEF

Aunt Edna's Porcupines	89
Chili	58
Hamburger Soup	51
Lasagna	140
Meatballs	85
Meatloaf	84
Mom's Cabbage Rolls	88
Pam's Nachos	40
Pizza Buns	46
Porcupines	89
Sloppy Joes	47
Spanish Rice	136
Stuffed Peppers	87
Summer Ground Beef Stew	59

HAM

Aunt Eva's Cordon Bleu Rolls	81
Eggs Benedict	168
Fettucine Papalina	138
Glazed Baked Ham	90
Ham Steak and Pineapple	91
Turkey and Ham Bake	113

JAM & JELLY

Apricot Jam	270
Citrus Marmalade	272
5 Fruit Conserve	271
Grape Jelly	270
Strawberry Jam	270
Zucchini Marmalade	272

LAMB

Marianne's Tangy Lamb Chops	95
Moussaka	94

LIVER

Smothered Liver	83

LOAVES

Applesauce Spice Loaf	190
Aunt Edna's Date Loaf	188
Banana Bread	189
Bubbat	192
Pumpkin Bread Ring	187
Thel's Cornbread	193
Zucchini Nut Bread	191

LUNCHEON MEAT

Meat & Egg Salad Bunwiches	44
Sombreros	38

MUFFINS

Aunt Edna's Blueberry Oat Muffins	185
Banana Chocolate-Chip Muffins	184
Blueberry Muffins	184
Jam Muffins	183
Nancy's Pineapple Muffins	186
Peanut Butter and Banana Muffins	186
Refrigerator Bran Muffins	182
Whole Wheat Muffins	182

PASTA

Fettucine Papalina	138
Lasagna	140
Pasta and Salmon Medley	139

PIE

Boston Cream Pie	228
Crumb Crust	215
Easy Fudge Pie	219
Flapper Pie	210
Lee's Pear Pie	219
Pam's No Roll Pie Crust	216
Pumpkin Pie	218
Raspberry Cream Pie	210
Southern African Milk Tart	217
Southern Pecan Pie	218

PORK

Barbecue Pork Steaks	92
Planned Over Pork & Rice Casserole	137
Pork Chops in Mushroom Sauce	91
Pork Ribs	93
Sweet and Sour Smoked Sausages	97

PUDDINGS

Banana Creme Pudding	210
Butterscotch Pudding	210
Christmas Pudding	208
Chocolate Pudding	211
Coconut Cream Pudding	210
Coffee Pecan Pudding	211
Creamy Pudding	210
Minute Tapioca Pudding	212
Mom's Rice Pudding	212
Packaged Pudding	211
Parfaits	211
Petits Pots De Creme	211
Southern Banana Pudding	210

RELISH

Beet Relish	274
Cucumber Relish	273
Pam's Zucchini Relish	273

RICE

Aunt Sue's Fried Rice 133
Broccoli & Rice Casserole........ 135
Brown Rice..................... 130
Cabbage Rolls.................. 88
Converted Rice 130
Curried Rice.................... 133
Jiffy Spanish Rice 136
Long Grain Rice 130
Mom's Rice Pudding 212
Moo Goo Gai Pan............... 211
Planned Over Pork & Rice
    Casserole 137
Porcupines 89
Spiced Rice and Peas 134
Stuffed Peppers................. 87
Sweet & Sour Smoked Sausage .. 97
Vegetable Rice Pilaf............. 134
Wild Rice 130

ROASTS

Beef........................... 76
Ham........................... 76
Pork........................... 76
Chicken........................ 102

SANDWICHES

Barbecue Beef Dip 43
Beef Sub Napolitana 42
Bun Baskets.................... 41
Meat and Egg Salad Bunwiches .. 44
Open-Face Reubens 45
Pizza Buns..................... 46
Roast Beef Submarine Sandwich 42
Sloppy Joes.................... 47
Tuna Burgers................... 43

SAUCES

Allemande Sauce 160
Baked Custard.................. 216
Bearnaise Sauce................ 161
Cheese Sauce................. 94, 159
Chili Sauce..................... 275
Chinelo's Spaghetti Sauce 86
Creamy Christmas Pudding Sauce 209
Custard Sauce.................. 277
Fruity Custard Sauce 277
Hollandaise Sauce 160
Hot Fudge Sauce 276
Larry's Barbecue Sauce 96
Marianne's Barbecue Sauce...... 96
Mornay Sauce 162
Orange Sauce 209
Pancake Syrup 275
Peanut Butter Sauce Royale 276
Sauce Mousseline.............. 162

Spaghetti Sauce 86
Sweet and Sour Sauce 93
Tomato Ketchup 274
White Sauce.................... 159

SAUSAGE

Mini Pizzas..................... 39
Sweet & Sour Smoked Sausages 97

SNACKS

Mini Pizzas..................... 39
Nachos 44
Pam's Nachos 40
Peppy Nuts..................... 37
Poppycock 38
Skiffle Snack 41
Sombreros 38
Sugar Almonds 37

SOUP

Aunt Edna's New England Clam
    Chowder.................... 56
Beet Borscht 57
Butter Soup 54
Cheddar Cheese Soup 53
Chicken Vegetable Soup......... 53
Corn Chowder 55
Cream of Broccoli Soup.......... 52
Cream of Cauliflower Soup....... 52
Cream of Mushroom Soup 52
French Onion Soup 50
Fresh Tomato Soup for One...... 50
Ham & Cauliflower Chowder...... 52
Hamburger Soup................ 51
Potato Soup 54
Tomato Consomme 51

STEAK

Aunt Eva's Cordon Bleu Rolls 81
Beef Stroganoff................. 79
Pepper Steak................... 78
Swiss Steak.................... 80

STEW

Beef Ragout.................... 60
Chili 58
Country Style Turkey Stew 62
Summer Ground Beef Stew 59
Quick Beef Stew................ 61

SQUARES

Brownies....................... 255
Caramel Morsel Bars 257
Delectable Caramel Bars......... 251
Hip Padder Bars 252

Karen's All Brand Blondies 258
Matrimonial Cake 254
Munch Bars 253
Peanut Butter Squares. 253
Puffed Wheat Squares. 257
Toffee Bars. 256

SWEETENED CONDENSED MILK

Sweetened Condensed Milk 252

TURKEY

Country Turkey Stew 62
Turkey and Ham Bake. 113
Turkey Divan 114

VEAL

Aunt Eva's Cordon Bleu Rolls 81
Veal Parmigiana 82

VEGETABLES

Aunt Eva's Zucchini Creole. 156
Broccoli in Cheese 147
Broccoli and Cauliflower Salad. . . . 147
Brussels Sprouts Medley. 146
Cauliflower & Broccoli Salad. 147
Colorful Vegetable Platter 157
Corn on the Cob 149
Creamed Cabbage 148

Creamed Chicken & Broccoli 109
Crumb Topped Tomatoes 155
Easiest Scalloped Potatoes 154
Green Beans and Bacon. 150
Ham & Scalloped Potatoes. 156
Leah's Green Bean Casserole. . . . 150
Leah's Scalloped Corn. 149
Marshmallow Filled Squash 156
Micro Chips 155
Mom's Harvard Beets. 146
Parsley Buttered Carrots. 151
Peas and Mushrooms 153
Potatoes Au Gratin 154
Pumpkin Bread Ring 187
Pumpkin Pie. 218
Red Cabbage. 148
Salmon Mornay 124
Shrimp Stir Fry 127
Southern Style Greens. 152
Stuffed Mushrooms. 152
Tater Boats. 153
Whole Cauliflower. 151

YEAST BREADS

Cabbage Patch Bread 196
Cheese Croutons 199
Herbed Whole Wheat Croutons . . . 199
Plain Croutons. 199
Proofing Yeast Dough 180
Whole Wheat Bread 198

Share *Master Your Microwave* With Your Friends!

Please send _____ copies of **Master Your Microwave** at $12.95 per copy plus $2.00 postage and handling (total $14.95 per book).

Name: _____

Street _____

City _____

Province/State _____ Postal Code/Zip _____

I am enclosing a cheque/money order for _____.

Please make cheque or money order payable to:
Mainly Microwave
Box 1073
Moose Jaw, Saskatchewan
S6H 4P8

Please allow 4-6 weeks for delivery

- -

Share *Master Your Microwave* With Your Friends!

Please send _____ copies of **Master Your Microwave** at $12.95 per copy plus $2.00 postage and handling (total $14.95 per book).

Name: _____

Street _____

City _____

Province/State _____ Postal Code/Zip _____

I am enclosing a cheque/money order for _____.

Please make cheque or money order payable to:
Mainly Microwave
Box 1073
Moose Jaw, Saskatchewan
S6H 4P8

Please allow 4-6 weeks for delivery